NAVIGATING & AVOIDING AWKWARD CONVERSATIONS

How to speak to anyone about anything

Julie Crenshaw

CONTENTS

Title Page

Copyright

FREE Companion workbook

Prologue   1

Part 1   21

Basic principles   22

Responding without responding   25

The art of keeping your mouth closed   29

No more interrupting   32

The monologuer   34

Helping someone say "no"   39

Helping your children to be polite   43

Exact words matter   47

Giving and receiving compliments   59

When the other person is embarrassed   71

Complainers   80

What if you need to complain?   83

Avoiding embarrassment   85

Meeting new people   86

Demographics   88

Body parts and bathroom breaks   95

The Big 3: Politics, Religion, and Money   101

Politics   102

Religion   117

Money   125

Part 2   139

Dealing with conflict   140

Complainers   142

Gossipers   148

Standing up for others   155

When someone is insulting you   163

How to avoid being a Karen (my apologies to all Karens)   184

How to deal with a Karen   192

Just scan the coupon   195

Inappropriate comments   199

Sexist comments   209

Inappropriate questions/comments   215

Invasive questions/comments   219

Unsolicited advice   221

Disagreeable/rude comments   231

Passive aggressive behaviors   233

Conflicts at work   237

Part 3   261

Illness, Caregiver Burden, and Death   262

Illness   264

Cancer   271

Death   282

Death - Past   285

Death - Present   302

Death - Future   310

Caregiver burden   314

Dementia   322

Final thoughts   341

Epilogue   345

Praise For Author   347

FREE Companion workbook   351

Acknowledgement   353

About The Author   355

                                           357

FREE COMPANION WORKBOOK

The only thing better than learning all the wonderful information in this widely popular book is the perfect journal-style workbook to go with it!

Download the FREE companion workbook here:

https://courses.yourconversationexpert.com/workbook

PROLOGUE

When I was growing up, I usually just said whatever was on my mind. I didn't give a lot of thought to filtering it or phrasing in a way that might be better received. I called it like I saw it. Obviously, that's not the best way to go about things, and I'm sure you don't need me to explain why. It can very often create a lot of drama where there didn't have to be any, and the whole "it's just how I am, deal with it" approach may sound tenacious and sassy, but over the years I've come to realize that it's really just more rude and inconsiderate than anything. You can feel one way on the inside and find a much better way to say things out loud. More flies with honey and all that.

I've worked since I was very young. I babysat and worked in nurseries from the age of 11 and have never stopped. I never had any trouble working with children because I got along with them so well, and their parents were so very excited to have someone else looking after them for a while that there wasn't ever any conflict or problems. I did this until I graduated high school, at which point I relocated to a new area and started working my first big job at a department store. Thus my Jedi training began! Never in my whole entire life have I ever met so many rude people. I've heard it said many times that everyone should have to work a job either waiting tables or working retail at some point in their life to truly appreciate how rude people can be to one another, and I couldn't agree more.

The internal conflict here is that you really want to tell

these people to stick it where the sun don't shine, but you also really really want to pay your bills that month and have enough money left over to eat. So you have to figure out the very particular song and dance of maintaining some dignity in the midst of a lot of snarky comments, and how to turn a potential customer complaint into someone who's willing to open up a credit card with you.

And beyond the skill of learning how to deal with difficult customers, there are a lot of other skills that come up that you wouldn't even dream of until you're dealing with them. I'll never forget the day I was working and had a lady come up to me with this beautiful black dress that she was buying. I was chatting like always and made the comment that it was such a beautiful dress and that I hope she enjoyed the special occasion that she was buying it for. She told me that her husband had died unexpectedly a few days before and she was buying it for his funeral. She was so young. She might've been in her mid-30s and she was shopping by herself trying to find something appropriate for this devastating occasion. I was so shocked that I just set down everything in my hands and asked if I could give her a hug. She said yes and I walked around the counter and squeezed her so tightly. I couldn't help it: I shed a few tears and she did too.

I had felt like such an idiot for saying that I had hoped she would enjoy the occasion, but I couldn't have known. What I learned is that it's not about the words that come out of your mouth, it's about the compassion that you can have for other people in moments like that. This book is full of examples of phrases and things to say, but there's also a lot of lead up in each of the areas that speaks to the mindset piece to approaching different situations. It's not about memorizing exactly what to say, it's about having an approach that is elegant and compassionate and sophisticated, and having some examples to use to build your own vocabulary.

This job also taught me another very valuable set of skills, and that is how to elegantly handle a WIDE variety of conversation topics in a retail setting. As the person on "the other side of the counter," I saw so many different people handling the exact same situation in a wide variety of ways. I saw some people who handled frustration by yelling, others who handled it by negotiating or reasoning, some people who just walked off, and others who simply asked to speak to the manager no matter what (the Karens are real - my apologies to any actual person named Karen who is not "a Karen.").

I also saw how different customer approaches were handled by coworkers with decades of experience (I had the immense pleasure of starting my work in the dress department with a handful of ladies who were all in their 80s), and also by mid level and upper management in the department store. It gave me a very unique perspective on the situation from all sides, and helped me to cultivate a set of skills that I knew would be valuable no matter which side of the register I was on.

I also heard the unfiltered commentary by these individuals regarding the rare (but particularly awful) customers once an ugly situation was resolved and the customer had walked off. Yes, they do talk about you after you leave if you make a scene or are especially rude. They probably even tell everyone in the break room about you if you make a big enough jerk out of yourself. Just FYI. Another motivation to learn how to deal with these situations in a healthier and more respectful way!

Once, I had a group of teenage girls who came in to try on prom dresses. After they left (without purchasing anything), we discovered in horror that they had used the bathroom all over the dresses and had left them piled up in the middle of the dressing room floor. Stunned, we eventually concluded that they were mad that the oldest lady working there had told him there was a limit to how many dresses they could take in at once. The things you see working in retail are truly shocking.

Anothing shocking instance that almost broke my heart concerned a lady who had recently undergone a very invasive stomach surgery. She ended up losing control of her bowels while she was in the fitting room and came out nearly sobbing trying to explain to me what had happened. She was apologizing profusely because there was a stain on the floor and she had attempted to use the trash can in the room to mitigate the situation, so it was a mess as well. She also had ruined her own clothes and didn't have anything clean that she could leave the dressing room with. I had to help ring up a fresh pair of pants for her at the register without her present, which of course I needed to get my manager and security involved in so that I didn't end up looking suspicious myself.

It is important to figure out how to deal with these situations delicately while also maintaining a relationship with the other customers coming in. They may interact with this problem and complain that there is a mess or a smell, unaware of the cause. It is essential to communicate with those customers in a way that smoothes the situation over for the store and helps to maintain dignity for the embarrassed person.

For a cumulative time of about six years across two different department stores, I worked as a certified bra fitter, a position I truly loved. Every woman who has ever worn a bra knows how overwhelming and frustrating it can be to try to find one that fits well and is comfortable. One of the great things about department stores is that they cater to all ages. I would fit anybody from the preteens getting their first bra to the great grandmothers who were only wearing a bra because they felt like they had to, and everything in between. You might be surprised, or not surprised at all, to hear that there are quite a few crazy conversations that come up during those fittings.

I had to learn the art of super nonchalance for the youngest girls. They were ready to fall through the floor with embarrassment that they had been dragged into a department store by their mother or grandmother or well meaning aunt and were having to deal with the life-ending terror of bra shopping. I had some hilarious moments with some much older ladies who had lost all sense of embarrassment or privacy with their bodies, and who had stripped all their clothes off before the fitting room door had even shut. I had to learn how to roll with all sorts of crazy things those ladies would say because if they knew they were shocking you, it would just encourage them to keep going to see how much they could fluster or embarrass you.

I had women who were very stressed out and sometimes in a lot of pain because they had just had breast surgery and needed something that would be appropriate for their recovery. I had mothers who had waited until the ninth month of their pregnancy to realize that they needed a nursing bra. They didn't have the first clue how to find one or what they would really need and were nearly in tears with stress trying to find something. I had conversations with women who had survived breast cancer and needed a new bra after breast removal.

There were women who had gained or lost a lot of weight or had simply had a lot of changes after having children who were very overwhelmed by the prospect of trying to figure out what would fit their newly changed bodies. There were caregivers coming in trying to find a bra for their mother who was homebound and unable to shop for herself. I had women who had been buying the same bra for 50 years and were horrified that the particular make and style of the bra they had always worn was no longer in production.

In each instance, I honestly found it to be an honor to help each of these women find something that would put a smile on their face. I loved being able to serve a need that they had, and hopefully make them feel great in the process. If I could turn bra shopping into something really enjoyable, I felt like I had really won the day. You can imagine all the different conversations that may have come up during these experiences. People expressing all ranges of emotion; fear, worry, pain, frustration, embarrassment. It's really amazing how many different topics came up that I had to learn to navigate through this particular position.

Another topic that I found recurring while working in the department store was how people dealt with the issue of money. I worked in a very large store that had a wide variety of products, from store brand to name brand, costume jewelry to fine jewelry, and everything in between. Dealing with topics such as opening credit cards, using coupons, sale pricing, etc., really opened my eyes to the wide variety of experiences that people have with money, and that the perception of something as being expensive or not is definitely in the eye of the beholder.

I've watched people practically scream at me over a pair of pants priced at $30 and other people who wanted to (and did!) hug me because they were so excited that a purse they loved was on sale for only $400. I was on the receiving end many times of customers handling themselves in a manner that was very elegant and ones who were anything but. I learned a great deal about how to handle conversations around pricing from the customers who were able to navigate those conversations so well, and these are what I will pass on to you later in the book.

I also learned how to anticipate who might be most likely to escalate a situation, and how to best get ahead of the conversation in a way that would keep things as pleasant as possible. I give many tips in that regard later in the book as well. Unfortunately, people can show up as the worst versions of themselves in this setting. As much as I always tried to be as helpful and pleasant as possible, I still found myself on the receiving end of insults, complaints, and rants more often than anyone would prefer. I guess it comes with the territory. People get upset very easily when it comes to money, and I was forced to acquire "a very particular set of skills" (Liam Neeson reference anyone?) with regard to de-escalating hostile situations.

However, if I thought my skills were good working in retail, they were about to become a lot better. There was a period of time in the middle of my college career that the economy took a hit heard 'round the world. Yes, I was fortunate (or not) to have been in the middle of my college years, transitioning from undergrad to grad school during the depression that started in 2008. And it was so *very* depressing. The store that I had worked in for several years was on the verge of closing, and I had to make the hard decision to leave and pursue a different job opportunity to make sure that I didn't miss a paycheck. My new position was definitely not pleasant at all. I had heard of an opportunity working collections for an automobile company. It paid well and had guaranteed hours, two things that were very scarce at that time, so I took it.

Here's a little known fact about me that I think even my closest family and friends might be surprised to hear: I absolutely cannot stand it when people are mad at me, and especially when people raise their voices. I am usually successful in my attempt to appear calm, but I am definitely not calm on the inside. Accepting a call center position where most people answer the phone angry was pretty much the last thing I wanted to do, but sometimes you have to decide to do hard things.

I hated this job; there were no redeeming factors whatsoever. Although the company was very nice to work for and had a fantastic training program with reasonable and supportive managers, the very nature of that industry creates immeasurable stress. I worked the accounts that were considered "early late" which meant 1-30 days past due. Only one payment behind, not yet reported to the credit bureaus, and usually a lot easier to recover and get the account back in good standing.

What I found was that there were generally two approaches to working collections: good cop and bad cop. I saw a pretty decent mix of both from the people I worked with. There was one gentleman who was seriously so unfeeling it blew my mind (picture David from Schitt's Creek working collections). This man would basically tell people "I seriously don't care about your problems, just go find your wallet" with the same kind of David sass. Ok maybe (maybe??) he never said that to anyone verbatim, but he came close enough so many times that I was picking my jaw off the floor on a regular basis. I don't know how many times I hissed at him "you can't SAY that to people!!" but he thought it was hilarious, and I'm pretty sure he did it just as much to get a reaction out of the rest of us as for any other reason.

If we're being honest, I guess he was cut out for the job because he consistently had the highest numbers on the floor every single week. He won all the prizes and bonuses for money recovered and was quickly promoted to a more difficult and better paying department. Even though I saw that his method was effective for getting people to cough up their bank account information, I just had way too much sympathy for a sob story, and I definitely took the approach of trying to help.

To set the scene a little bit, the way that this job worked was that a computer would auto dial out the numbers of all the people who were overdue on their bill. Once the call had connected, it would pop up onto our screen. Let me be clear that it didn't pop up on my computer until the call had connected, which meant that the second something popped up on my screen, I had to start talking right away. So stressful.

There was often a one or two second pause between the person answering the phone and saying "hello" and the call connecting on my end because of the auto dialer. Sometimes that two second pause was enough to send someone into a total tirade. "I said hello! Who is this?! Why are you calling me?! You people are a bunch of jerks. I'm sitting here with my family eating dinner and you feel like it's OK to just call me. I told you people yesterday...!!!"

Also, since it was a collections call, I was required by law to give the disclaimer of who I was and that it was an attempt to collect a debt and that the call might be recorded before I could say anything else at all. THEN I had to verify that the person I was speaking to was an account holder before I could actually discuss the account with them. You can imagine how well that was received when the person was already trying to yell at me from the word go, and instead of being able to answer any of their questions or launch into anything that would help to calm them down, I was further infuriating them by having to get through the formalities before I could actually address the issue at hand. Did I mention I really didn't like this job? Let's not even get started on the situation where I get through all of this and the very irritated person offers to make a payment, but they are not on the account or an authorized user, so I wasn't legally allowed to tell them how much was due on the account (total nightmare). As much as this job stressed me out, I will say that I learned an incredibly valuable skill set that I still use to this day.

What is your natural reaction to getting yelled at? No matter how much we may wish it didn't happen, there is a natural fight or flight response that begins when a situation escalates. In today's world, where we know that the actual threat of harm is usually not present, most people's natural instinct is to argue back when they feel threatened. They will try to reason with the person who is yelling at them. They may ask them to calm down. They might just start yelling back, calling the person names, or otherwise trying to prove that they are right and the other person is wrong. They may feel very justified for acting this way because "the other person started it." Our brains are wired to mirror the other person by raising our voices and posturing similarly. All of these things are understandable, but they only serve to make the situation worse. Thankfully, they can all be mitigated when necessary.

Working in collections, I had more chances than I ever would have cared to have had to practice de-escalating a situation where someone was verbally attacking me. This job was an all day, every day science experiment of "how is the person going to react if I say *this* versus *that*." Once again, I will mention that the training program that we went through before we were ever put on the floor was very thorough. I think they did a really great job of trying to give us the skills we would need to be the most successful in these situations. They spoke to us quite a bit about listening to people, letting them tell their story, approaching issues from a collaborative standpoint whenever possible, and trying to reach a common goal, which is of course for the account to become and remain current. This is the best outcome for both the company and the customer, which makes everybody happy.

Sometimes making everyone happy is a little easier said than done, and there is no replacement for being on a live call. One thing our trainer must have said 100 times during our weeks together was, "the person on the other end of that phone is not going to be able to hear a single thing that you say until they feel like you have heard what THEY are trying to say." We went over so many exercises during the training explaining how word choice, word order, inflection, reflection back to the person of what they have said, etc. are all vital pieces of the communication puzzle.

I seriously wonder if the whole world would be a better place if everyone had to go through that kind of scenario. It has honestly influenced the way that I parent, the way I communicate with my spouse and family, and the way that I communicate with my patients and coworkers. You could even say the foundation for this entire book is based on a similar principle. It's not just what you say, but 1) how you say it, 2) when you say it, and 3) the look on your face when you say it that all play into how well you are or are not received by the person with whom you are trying to communicate.

When I could get to the bottom of why the person was late on their payment, I would find that there was almost always something totally unrelated to their vehicle that was the underlying issue. People are not late on their car payment because they want to be! Being late on your car note has very real consequences. If you're late for long enough, they come and take your car and then what are you going to do? People will ignore every other bill they have, but find a way to scrounge together enough money for their car note if they can, because it is their livelihood. It's how they get to work, how they get to the store. It's how they get to the other people in their lives. So if they are late on their payment, something is going on.

Sometimes they had lost a job or missed a ton of work due to an illness and really didn't have enough money. Sometimes, they were so scattered and stressed by other things going on in their lives that they had just forgotten to make the payment. Often, they didn't understand why it mattered that they were late. I got that one a lot. Maybe they had a spouse or parent just pass away, and they were too busy with those arrangements to pay attention to their bills.

A lot of times, they were under so much stress that getting on the phone with an anonymous stranger and letting loose on them was their way of opening up the pressure valve and letting off some steam. It was a game changer for me when I started looking at it that way. This person is not really yelling at me, they're yelling at life right now and I'm the one hearing it. They are so mad and stressed out and frustrated with their current circumstances, that they just need to yell. They just need to get it all out before they are going to have any kind of emotional bandwidth to have a reasonable conversation with me about what we can do moving forward.

I called people who were divorced and their ex spouse was supposed to be the one responsible for the account in the divorce decree, but it hadn't been refinanced on our end and those people were getting dings on their credit for the bill being late. Sometimes the ex spouse knew that and was refusing to pay the bill just to ruin this person's credit! As I mentioned earlier, I took this job during the depression that started in 2008. I heard so many stories of people in their mid-50s whose companies were closing down and causing them to lose everything. I spoke to people who had been given terminal cancer diagnoses and paying their car note was the last thing on their mind.

It would be easy for a lot of people to assume that if someone is late on their car note, it's because they are lazy or irresponsible, and I've heard people say as much. I know that to be very very untrue. You don't know what people are going through, and assuming things about people doesn't do anything but damage the connection you are trying to make. When a total stranger is yelling at you, it's not about you. There is no way to know what that person is going through, and sometimes they just need to yell. It's like that line in the movie Forrest Gump, "sometimes, there just aren't enough rocks."

Of course, I am not suggesting that you should put up with people being rude or hateful towards you; absolutely not! In fact, we will discuss boundaries later too, as there is a difference between reacting to someone and setting boundaries with them. I personally find it best to use a graduated scale rather than an immediate firm boundary reaction. I start with empathy and only escalate it as the situation requires.

Any form of hostility begets more hostility, so I keep it as an ace in my back pocket for the times when no other solution will do, but I find that the more I can react with softness and kindness, the better the outcome of the situation overall. Helping people preserve their dignity will most often endear them to you, whereas admonishing them will create distance no matter how politely you do it. It's hard to walk with your head up high when you've got your tail tucked between your legs.

One theme that you will find recurring over and over again throughout this book is the one of empathy. If we could all just simply be a bit more understanding with each other, the world would be such a better place. I say it over and over, but I mean it every single time: life is hard. It just is. Life is hard when you're young, and the reasons for the difficulty may continuously change, but they are always there.

It's no fun being a baby who is hungry, tired and miserable with no idea what's going on around you. It's hard to be a toddler and want to be able to do everything for yourself and not have the physical capabilities of doing so. It's difficult to be a young child and be constantly told "no" by everyone around you. It's so stressful to be young, trying to find yourself while fitting in and dealing with all of the ugliness that comes with the social scene around puberty. It's a terrible feeling to have your first crush and get rejected, making you feel as though you aren't good enough. It can be overwhelming to get to the end of high school and feel the constant pressure to decide what you're going to do next.

It's hard when you get out there and have to start paying

bills for the first time without help. It's hard when you're newly married and trying to merge your life with another person and having to learn all of the communication and conflict management skills that go along with it. It's hard to try to juggle school and work and relationships at the same time. It's hard to have children and raise them right and deal with the inevitable guilt that's going to hit you from every angle no matter what.

It's hard when your children get older and don't need you anymore. It's hard when you're going through divorce. It's hard when you've been married to someone for so long that you have to work to find the spark again. It's hard when you get further along in your adult life and realize that maybe some of the decisions that you made when you were younger weren't really the best thing for you. It's hard to deal with work and bosses and custody battles. It's hard to eat healthy and stay fit and meditate and do yoga and every other personal goal you've set for yourself to try to "maximize your potential".

It's hard to work all those years until you make it to retirement. It's hard to retire and figure out what to do with yourself because you're so used to working all the time. It's hard when you get older and you start losing friends and family to old age and sickness. It's hard when you're sick. It's hard when you're well and having to take care of those who are sick. Life. Is. Hard.

Being a pretty positive person, I'm not trying to depress you with all of this, but if we can all just take a step back and realize that every one of us is dealing with something, doesn't it make it a lot easier to have patience with someone when they're not showing up as their best self? It's difficult to be graceful and eloquent when you feel that every mean comment and every snappy person is attacking you personally. When you can step into a more meditative mindset of having patience with those who have run out, having love for those who don't have enough, and for giving comfort to those who need to be comforted, it just makes it so much easier to be kind.

Being a mother, when my young children have a total meltdown on me because I ask them to do something, one of my first thoughts is, "when's the last time they had something to eat?" If they've eaten recently, my next question is, "did they get enough sleep last night?" If that doesn't bring me the answer, I might ask myself, "is there something that might be stressing them out right now?" And if I can't think of anything, I'll ask my husband because he interacts with them during the day more than I do and he might know of something that I don't.

I go through these questions because my boys are sweet wonderful kids and they are usually very well behaved (and no, I'm not just saying that), so when they react so strongly over nothing, it's time to search for the reason behind it. They're not bad kids and they're not really mad at me. Something else is going on, so let me see if I can figure out what that is. It doesn't mean that we don't have a conversation about the appropriate way to express frustration and upset, but I can't have a conversation with them at all if their blood sugar is bottomed out or if they're too tired to focus on or process what I'm saying. I can feed them first, let them get some rest, or address the issue that's really bothering them, and then have a conversation about how they should've reacted instead.

I try my very best to apply this to everyone I meet on a daily basis. If they're infuriated over something that doesn't seem like it should be that upsetting, I try to search through a series of questions. What's going on that this person is snapping at me like this or being so rude? If I can address that issue first, then the person has the emotional bandwidth to deal with me in a way that's more civil.

What I have found to be overwhelmingly true is that if I will simply take a moment to address the fact that they seem stressed, upset or worried, the relief that they get from that is paired with so much gratitude. I've had so many people over the years who have started out yelling or nearly yelling at me end up thanking me for my patience and giving me a big hug. People just want to be heard. They don't want to feel like they're being run over, they don't handle being overwhelmed very well, and it's often easiest to be snappy and rude with a stranger because they feel that there are very few consequences to it.

I am certainly not perfect. I have days when I am upset or overwhelmed and I don't show up as my best self either. On those days, I have to give myself grace and apologize when needed. I try to extend as much of this grace to others as I can when I can, and I hope that it comes back to me in turn.

Five years ago, I started the most recent part of my journey after finishing grad school. I am a physical therapist by trade and transitioned to working in home health after I had been out of school for a year. I work almost exclusively with the elderly population and by the nature of this setting, my patients are usually very sick with a lot of complicated medical problems.

This has brought me face to face with so many difficult topics that have come up again and again. Patients who are dealing with extensive hospitalizations, traumatic fractures from falls, worsening medical problems, and often a new dependence on caregivers when they have always been independent with taking care of their needs. They are often scared, worried, depressed, or frustrated by their circumstances and many times we have to address these concerns before the person can effectively engage in their therapy.

We also have patients with dementia who may be unaware that there is a problem, forgetful that they don't have the physical strength to get up (which means they might try to walk across the room without their walker and fall), or are scared because they can't remember what happened to them. This can cause a lot of stress for them and their loved ones who are trying to care for them, but who might not have a lot of medical knowledge themselves.

Our patients might need to transition to hospice or may be the main caregiver for a spouse who is on hospice. These circumstances can be scary and overwhelming. Many of my patients have lost their spouses or children, recently or in the past. These are hard topics.

How does that relate to you? How are any of those topics useful if you aren't a healthcare worker? You aren't caring for a sick loved one! Well you might be one day. Or, maybe a coworker tells you her mother was just diagnosed with dementia. Perhaps someone you just met blurts out that their dad just went on hospice this week and they aren't handling it well when you innocently ask, "Hi, how are you today?" It might be that a random person in the store tells you about a terrible hospitalization they just had when you ask if you can help grab an item from a high shelf that they can't reach because they are in a wheelchair.

What would you say in those situations? Would those comments make you uncomfortable? Would you be able to say more than a mumbled "oh...I'm sorry." Would you be panicking on the inside wondering how quickly you could get away? Would you cringe later thinking of the reply you gave? Or would you be able to smile warmly, respond appropriately, and leave the situation feeling connected with someone?

We're going to spend some time on medically related topics because they are close to my heart and I think they are incredibly important. Unfortunately, medical problems and death are a part of the experience of life, and we need to be able to navigate these conversations with the same ease that we have when speaking about happier thoughts. Everyone can be polite when ordering off a menu. It takes a bit more to touch on topics that are sad or difficult, and my aim is to help you feel confident and graceful when interacting with all people and on all topics, not just the happy and easy ones.

Who is this book for?

In this book, we address both polite conversation and difficult topics. My sincere hope is that you will find this book to be a blessing in your life in some way. If you are here with me now, you are the type of person who is interested in improving yourself. You want to take things to the next level and be the best and most polished version of yourself possible. It's important to feel like you can handle any conversation and field any difficult comment with ease and grace. Let's make sure your foot never ends up in your mouth ever again. You will be able to connect better with people, whether you are at work, at the store, or at a networking event. I also want you to able to set clear and strong boundaries with others in a way that minimizes conflict.

The inspiration for writing this book came from an amazing community of women who are all focused on upgrading their lives and stepping into the best version of themselves. This community is also built on trying to experience new things, going to different and exciting places, and getting outside of your comfort zone in order to experience all of the richness of the world.

In that vein, an entirely new skill set of conversation strategies and ways of relating to other people might need to be learned. Many of these women are wanting to experience the best places, the most exotic locations, the most exclusive restaurants and clubs. The question of how to speak in a way that conveys elegance and confidence while vibrating on a high frequency with positive energy comes to the fore.

Although this is a skill that I have been cultivating over the last 15 years out of necessity for the different positions I have worked in, it had never occurred to me that this information would be useful to anyone besides myself. Through interacting with this amazing group of women, I came to find that there was an immense need for this kind of candid conversation around so many delicate topics.

How do you speak about the things you're not supposed to talk about (like money)? How are you supposed to learn what to say or how to avoid a conversation topic that you don't *want* to speak about like politics or religion? How do you keep from putting your foot in your mouth when you're around new people? How do you walk into a new place that you may find intimidating and conduct yourself in a way that helps you to feel like you belong there? What do you do when someone else makes a difficult or awkward comment? How do you handle difficult conversations with ease?

As I was trying to think of the best name for this book, I smiled when I thought to myself that it should be named 'Supercalifragilisticexpialidocious' because it's an entire book about what to say when you don't know what to say. I hope Mary Poppins would be proud of the suggestions in this book, and if I ever had the chance to meet Julie Andrews, it would be one of the most amazing things to happen to me in the course of my life. Her poise on and off the screen has long served as an inspiration to me for the kind of person that I want to be, and the way I want to interact with others.

This book is not for everyone, but I hope that if you're reading it you understand that my intention is only to help and uplift. I'm not saying that I am the final authority on every topic mentioned, and I'm aware that not every suggestion in this book is going to work for every person in every situation. There might be cultural differences or personal preferences that might make some of the suggestions less effective.

Full disclaimer, I am a born and raised Georgia Peach. A lot of the approach that I have towards my interactions with other people are firmly rooted in southern charm. That may not work as effectively for you if you don't have the accent to go with it, but you might be surprised! Southern women are known for getting their points across in a way that comes across as sweet, even if they are really meaner than a rattlesnake, bless their hearts.

As with all things in life, take what serves you and leave the rest. Don't force something on yourself that doesn't sit well with you, but push yourself and be willing to try new ways of speaking and interacting. This is not about being fake, about letting others run over you, or trying to be perfect. It's simply about interacting with others in a way that lifts up all parties when possible and creates pleasant conversation. It's about being able to handle any situation with grace and elegance, and having the confidence to walk into any establishment or any conversation and feel like you belong there. It's about being a blessing to others when possible and coming away from any situation knowing you handled it beautifully, or at least the best you could.

PART 1

Don't forget your FREE companion workbook!

https://courses.yourconversationexpert.com/workbook

BASIC PRINCIPLES

We've already covered the biggest principle of this book, which is to be considerate of others and try to give them grace whenever possible. Think about *why* the other person is saying what they are saying. It will give you everything you need in order to know what to say next.

Another earth shattering principle we will visit over and over again is that **you don't have to actually respond to things other people say.** We will cover this in much greater detail shortly, but for now just start to brew this thought in your mind: sometimes the best response is no response. I don't mean to stay silent, but I mean to respond in such a way that you are neither agreeing nor disagreeing. You are acknowledging that something has been said, without actually giving your opinion in return.

Think about the phrase, "well that was a political response." What do people mean when they say that? They mean that words came out of the person's mouth, but there was no content and no conclusion. My apologies to my friends in politics, but it is probably the easiest example to use. I'm sure you have watched a press conference or a debate where the politician is asked a question and they may have a response that lasts several minutes. You might even feel uplifted, encouraged, or inspired by their response, but when you review it later, you realize the person didn't actually answer the question and you still aren't sure where they stand on the topic. Take a page out of their book!

You don't always have to be so forthcoming with your

thoughts and opinions, especially if they are more likely than not to cause a stir. You don't have to agree with what someone says in order to continue having a conversation with them, neither do you have to argue your thoughts. Sometimes you can just let things go (Gasp! The horror!). Sometimes, you can just let someone speak and let that be enough. Sometimes the overarching feeling of goodwill is much more important than being "right." It's called restraint, and we as a society have all but lost the art of it.

The last major theme I want to touch on before we really get started is the concept of boundaries. You might be hearing about boundaries ad nauseum in the self-development space lately. Well, if you are up to your nose in boundary content, allow me to help you get in all the way over your head (I jest, I jest!). All kidding aside, it is unbelievably important. If you find yourself in a position where you feel "run over" by other people in conversation, either because they are interrupting you or because they are pushing the conversation to the point that you are uncomfortable but you can't seem to get them to back off, you are experiencing a problem with boundaries.

If this is a persistent or frustrating problem for you, you might benefit from doing some deeper work on boundaries in general. We will touch on this in several sections throughout the book, and I will identify them as we go along so that I am being crystal clear about the mindset and energy behind certain suggested comments or responses.

I would be very honored if this material helps you to set better boundaries with others during conversation, but this book by itself is not meant to be a book on that topic. There are many great resources out there that dive deeply into this, and it might be to your best benefit to engage a therapist or counselor to help you if establishing boundaries on your own is overwhelming or simply doesn't feel effective.

Time for a very important disclaimer: the intent of this

book is to help you navigate conversation with strangers, acquaintances, work colleagues, patients, professionals, and others such as distant relatives. This book is not meant to address the very important dynamics between the closest and most personal relationships that you have, such as with your parents, partner, or dearest friends. Those relationships require depth, honesty, reciprocity, and conflict management skills. Surely this book can help with the more superficial interactions you have with anyone, but it is not meant to address the complicated nature of ongoing close relationships. This book is not a substitute for counseling, either alone or relationship counseling.

I will come back to this when we cover the topics in the Dealing with Conflict section of the book. There is a difference between setting a topic/conversation boundary with a stranger or acquaintance and addressing ongoing abuse or degrading behavior by someone you have to interact with on a regular basis in your personal life. For now, just keep in mind that you don't have to have conversations that make you uncomfortable, you are not obligated to answer invasive questions, and you are well within your right to refuse to engage in conversations that feel like a trap in any regard.

So there you have it: empathy, restraint, and boundaries. If you can keep these three principles at the heart of your approach to conversation, you can conquer anything. It's time my sweet new friend, let's start conquering conversations!

RESPONDING WITHOUT RESPONDING

Let's dip our toes in the water. We have a lot of ground to cover in this book, and I thought it might be best to start with the basics and work our way up from there. At the very beginning level, we all just want to know how to speak to others on a variety of topics without sounding like an idiot (just being real here!) or putting people off.

We really don't want to rehash the same conversations laying in bed at midnight for the rest of our lives thinking, "WHY did I say that??" or bemoaning the deer-in-headlights look on your face when someone threw a comment out from left field that caught you so off-guard that you couldn't think of the first thing to say.

What if we establish a fall-back plan? What if we come up with a quick emergency checklist of responses to use while you buy yourself a little time to decide how you want to actually respond to something, or if you want to respond at all? Remember that? Yes, we're back to that already. The first question you might want to ask yourself is, "Do I want to engage in this conversation or not?" Think of it like swiping left or right on the conversation. "Yes, sounds like a great/safe topic. Let's go for it!" or, "Nope. This is a trap and there's no way to win and nothing to gain here. Keep it neutral and move on!"

Let me introduce you to the art of being **charming**. What do I mean by that? I mean verbally saying a word or phrase that technically counts as a response to what someone has said without actually saying anything of substance.

Here's the thing: if you literally don't say anything at all, you are creating an awkward silence and bringing attention to yourself. If someone says something to you that is surprising, rude, crazy, controversial, or just plain confusing, saying nothing keeps that person in control of the conversation and puts a negative light on you. They can interpret your silence as being rude, disagreeing, judging them, not paying attention, having no sense of humor, or being offended which can often prod the person into teasing you or taking the conversation in a direction you don't want it to go.

For this to work, you have to be in the energy of someone who is good humored and not bothered. You are not flustered because others don't have the ability to upset your calm. You are amused by this person, but your energy cannot be controlled by theirs, does that make sense? You really have to channel your inner Dolly Parton on this one. I just LOVE her quote, "I'm not offended by all the dumb blonde jokes because I know I'm not dumb...I also know I'm not blonde." Can't you just see her wink and hear her laugh when you read that quote?

It's that kind of amazing self possession that gets the message across. Someone tried to insult her by calling her a dumb blonde and her attitude was "well I guess you can be rude if you want to, but I know what's true and who I am." and she brushed it all off with her beautiful smile and warm laugh.

Here are several examples of **charming** responses that work in tons of different situations. Someone has said something really odd, rude, crazy, or straight up inappropriate. Try an initial response of:

"Goodness! What a thing to say."

"Oh, really?! What about that."

"Is that right?"

"Well that's one way to say it!"

Remember the key is to give these responses in a good-natured way. We're teasing. We're having fun. We're playing up being a bit shocked. Sometimes people just get a huge kick out of saying something wild just to get a response. Don't give them a negative response that they can dig into or that will cause the conversation to take a sharp downward turn. It's a neutral response. We're not agreeing, we're not arguing, we're just being charming. Where you go with it next depends on context. We'll come back to these over and over.

I am a particular fan of the exclamation, "goodness!" because there is something about it that can subtly cue the other person into a feeling that they have said something that may have been a bit too far, inappropriate, or not particularly well received without any actual negativity attached. It can be used in so many ways, but it's a personal favorite of mine because it helps throw up a bit of a caution flag or the beginning of a boundary with someone while still remaining completely positive. I use this one liberally.

The other important neutral set of responses has to do with difficult conversations where you don't know what to say to comfort someone, or conversations where you absolutely don't agree with what the person is saying and you don't want to argue, but you definitely don't want to agree. These comments are focused on acknowledging the complicated nature of things. There are multiple ways to look at something. There are strong feelings about a topic. You know there isn't the slightest chance of changing the person's mind and it's not appropriate to argue the point. These are empathetic comments:

"Life is just hard."

"Sometimes there's just no good answer."

"I hate that you are dealing with something so difficult."

"We're all just trying to do our best. It's not easy."

"People have to do what they think is best, but we don't always agree with it."

"Sometimes people just can't be who they want to be for others."

"I guess there are a lof of different ways to look at it."

"You're doing the best you can. That's all anyone can ask of you."

THE ART OF KEEPING YOUR MOUTH CLOSED

Let's go one layer deeper on the topic of not always having to speak in order to have an effective conversation. We've been conditioned to feel that we have to have the perfect response to everything. We have to be wise, we have to have answers, we have to have the perfect come-back, we have to put rude people in their place, we have to have the last word. We have to educate people (strangers, friends, and family) 24/7 about our opinions on every issue from religion and politics down to the proper way to tie your shoe in order to prevent the world from catching fire and burning to the ground by the end of the day, right? Hold tight while I blow your mind by asking the most bizarre question you've ever heard: **what if that wasn't true?**

How many times have you left a conversation two minutes away from a total melt-down because the conversation escalated from one stupid comment into an entire relationship-destroying argument? How many strangers have caused your blood pressure to go through the roof for an entire day either on social media or in real life because they were an idiot and you weren't going to rest until they knew it? How many times have you spent the rest of a conversation trying to surgically remove your foot from your mouth because you put it in there so tightly that there was no coming back? How many conversations from 5 or 10+ years ago do you STILL replay in your mind from time to time and start cringing all over again at how it went? Has the room ever gone still after you said something because you just didn't think before the words came flying out of your mouth? Let me just be the first to admit that I am guilty on ALL COUNTS.

I am not writing this book because I was born knowing the best thing to say in all situations ever. And even to this day, every once in a while I get caught so off gaurd that I still accidentally stick my foot in my mouth, or I am so appalled at something that someone else says that I rush and respond to it in a less than tactful manner. But by and large, after years and years of working in industries that put me face-to-face with the general population, many times at their absolute worst in regard to stress, attitude, disability, and grief; I have cultivated an approach to interacting with people that honestly makes me very happy. The conversations may not go perfectly, and I may find myself irritated at something someone else has said, but I almost always come away knowing that I handled the situation in the best way possible, and that I came off in the best light possible.

Deep in my heart, I wish we as a society could find our way back to being polite and keeping our thoughts to ourselves more often than not. I know descenters will say that "the truth needs to be said" and "people need to be called out when they are wrong." Again, I ask, **what if that isn't true?** Tell me honestly how many times these attempts at shoving your truth down someone's throat has resulted in you having a new friend? The other person agreeing with you? Swaying anyone to your "side" of things? I bet you wouldn't need both hands to count the times this has happened. I know I wouldn't. But how many times have you chosen to take the high road, refused to take the bait to argue, chosen kindness over force, empathy over righteousness, love over hate, and ended up connecting with someone? I know I have. MANY more times than I can count.

It takes a lot of self-awareness and insight to keep your head on straight in situations where emotions are high, but I absolutely promise that if you can train your mind to zero in on **why** the person is acting the way they are or why they are saying the things they are saying, it will unlock a superpower that you never knew you had. If you can simultaneously come to grips with the FACT that you cannot fundamentally change another person's personality or beliefs, you will be unstoppable.

This entire book is focused on conversation skills that will apply in business, at social events, with acquaintances, and with strangers. I am specifically focused on relationships that are more formal in nature (or should be), but many of the suggestions in this book are not as applicable once you cross the threshold into family and very close personal relationships. In these relationships (especially your partner), a fundamental difference of opinion on an important topic might need to be worked out. A rude comment may need to be addressed head on. A disrespectful nature toward you may need to be dealt with assertively. Please use this book as intended which is to elevate your social skills to the highest level.

NO MORE INTERRUPTING

I am a very talkative and opinionated person by nature. Anyone who grew up with me probably snorted reading that and agreed. An area where I started to find this to be problematic was in the early years of my marriage. I had so much to say, and my husband is a person who thinks before he speaks (gasp!), which means he takes his sweet time before responding. I was so young when we married (19 years old - gasp again!) and sometimes I thought I'd die waiting for him to answer a question I'd asked. I would be too impatient to wait, so I would start speaking again, or I would use his long pauses to insert my thoughts. This was obviously very rude and not well received, but because he is the proverbial "strong, silent type," his reaction would usually be to stop talking all together, which made me feel awful. After this happened a handful of times I finally made a promise to myself: no more interrupting!

I remember so clearly the first time I finally nailed it. We were discussing something (I don't remember what, but it was a more serious topic) and any time he would pause to think I would repeat to myself, "Don't talk. Don't talk. Don't talk. Keep your mouth shut. Let him think. Don't interrupt. Don't talk." It sounds ridiculous, but it's what I had to do! After a few longer pauses without me interjecting, he asked, "are you ok?" and I said, "yes, why?" and he said, "well, you're not saying anything" to which I happily responded, "I'm practicing the art of shutting up!" and gave him a wink. We both laughed and he continued. This happened a few more times over the next several months (which should tell you how chatty I am!), but eventually this became our new normal, and I'm so glad it did because it's so much more respectful.

THE MONOLOGUER

Since we're covering the subject of making a purposeful choice to not speak, and especially not to interrupt, let's look at the opposite extreme for a moment. There are many people out there who monologue, which is a different issue altogether. It can be frustrating to listen to someone speak for 15 minutes without taking a breath, especially when you are trying to have a conversation, which usually takes two people. In these instances, I just smile to myself and think, "I guess I'm going to practice the art of shutting up then," and give up trying to respond or answer their questions, which turn out to all be rhetorical. Why waste my energy trying to get my thoughts in when the person won't be listening anyway?

People who monologue usually have huge anxiety and self esteem issues and often live alone or have abandonment issues that cause them to have a compulsive need to capture someone in conversation. It's dysfunctional behavior, and if you can see it as the symptom of a much larger problem, it's a lot easier to 1. not take it personally and 2. walk away without the guilt of "not letting them finish what they were saying" because they honestly will never be done. It's just a matter of how long you are willing to listen to it. Since we're here, let me address how to deal with a monologuer: listen for as long as you feel you want to and then make up an excuse to walk away. They will NEVER be "done" speaking, so waiting for the end of their commentary is like waiting for your favorite tv show to come back on the air after being cancelled. You might get some false indications that it's coming, but it isn't. Move on.

How do you get away? You have somewhere else to be! You do have to interrupt them, which is going to make every etiquette bone in your body cringe, but it's the only way. The two easiest lead-ins are, "Excuse me for interrupting, but..." and, "Oh! I just remembered..."

"Excuse me for interrupting, but I need to go check on the kids. I haven't heard from them in a while and I need to make sure they're ok."

"Oh! I just remembered that I told so-and-so I'd bring them a plate of something and I haven't done that yet. Excuse me."

"I hate to interrupt you, but I just remembered that I haven't had a chance to speak to so-and-so yet, and I want to make sure and do that before they leave."

If I'm at a patient's house and the person has held me up for an unreasonable amount of time just shooting the breeze after we've technically wrapped up, it's time for polite but firm boundaries.

"I'd love to chat more, but I have several other patients I have to get to today, and I don't want to be late for my appointments. I'll talk to you more next time. Take care!" Exit, stage left.

Here's the thing with a monologuer: it is dysfunctional, and it's also terribly rude. You can have a respectful level of sympathy for their situation (maybe they live alone and rarely get to speak to other people. You know that and you just hate it for them) while maintaining your own boundaries. It is monopolizing your time. They never give you a chance to speak, so you're really not getting to know each other at all, there is no real relationship that's being built through this behavior. They are keeping you hostage from any and all other activity.

Maybe you are at a party full of people you would like to

meet or catch up with, and you can't move on because you are stuck. It could be that you have another engagement that the person is making you late for by refusing to wrap up the conversation. Perhaps the person is playing on your obligation to be "polite" by asking you "just one more question" or telling you "just one more quick story." In these instances, the best thing to do is redirect them to another resource.

"I'd love to answer all of your questions, but I am running late now and I really have to be going. If you will write all your questions down, we can go over them the next time I come by."

"You can call the office with any other questions you have that I wasn't able to get to today."

"I'd love to hear your story, but we'll have to save that one for next time. I really have to be going. Take care. I'll see you in a few weeks/later!"

Keep in mind, the person usually knows what they are doing. It's not that they are ill-intentioned, but many times they just can't help it. It's a compulsive need to monopolize and continue the conversation at all costs. Sometimes they will make a comment about their behavior that twinges your guilt and makes you feel a strong urge to sympathize and sit there for another half hour to see if they can "get it all out of their system" but they can't. You can be kind and firm at the same time. Their comment will often come in some form of, "I know I'm taking up all your time. Just tell me to shut up. I know you don't want to listen to all of this." Repeat after me:

"I am definitely enjoying our conversation. But you are right, I haven't had a chance to speak to many other people tonight and I want to make sure and say hello to everyone. I'm going to free you up to catch up with someone else while I go over and say hello to so-and-so. Maybe we'll get a chance to chat more later. (If it's a stranger I'll end with "take care!" If it's a very close acquaintance or family, I'll give them a hug and say, "I love you. Take care!") and then scamper away before they think of "one more thing" to say.

If it's business you change it to, "I'm definitely enjoying our conversation, but you are right, I have other appointments I have to get to and I want to respect my client's time and not to keep them waiting. We can chat more next time. Take care!"

And lastly: anticipating the monologuer. You have identified someone as a red flag. You can't get around them for whatever reason, but you are very frustrated by the situation. How do you handle it going forward in a way that preserves your sanity while meeting your obligations and refraining from being rude? Keep two things in mind: 1. They are usually nice people who do not have ill intentions. They understand obligations and almost always will be respectful of the fact that you have a time limit if you communicate that there is one. 2. In real life, you can only monologue through speech.

Whenever humanly possible, communicate through text or email. This will be your saving grace. I have called people before to schedule a time to see them and been stuck on the phone for twenty minutes only to send a text message the next time and get a response, "Sounds great. See you then." It will blow your mind to bits and this one tip will be worth every penny you spent on this book. You're welcome.

Secondly, set a time limit for yourself and come into the situation with that timeline. Tell them when you arrive that you have an obligation that will release you at the end of the appointment, dinner, occasion, whatever. It can be anything, and a white lie is your best friend if it has to be. No guilt. Which is worse: "I promised the baby-sitter I woud be home by 9p so she could get home because she has to work in the morning." or "Stop talking. You're driving me nuts." Pick the white lie! It could be a very real obligation, you just need to communicate it. I have definitely come into a situation and when the person says, "Hi, how are you today?" I respond, "I'm having a great day! I am going to have to leave by 3:30p on the dot today though, because I have to pick my kids up from camp by such-and-such time." When the time comes, you wrap up and remind them of your obligation and off you go. Even if they try the "just want to tell you one more thing," you can respond, "oh, I would love to hear it but I really have to leave right now to make sure I get to my kids on time." It works, I promise it does.

If you are a professional and this is a client or patient, sometimes it can help you keep your boundaries around your time very firm by thinking about the other patients who have appointments that day. It isn't fair to them to be kept waiting, and you want your reputation as a professional to reflect that you are punctual and that you value the time of those who took time out of their busy schedules to pay you for your time and service. If necessary, you can employ the use of other staff to come into the room after a certain amount of time and ask you to step outside for whatever reason in order to keep things moving along in a timely manner.

HELPING SOMEONE SAY "NO"

One of the things that can help us to make ourselves and others shine is to minimize the stress of the other person during conversation. It reflects well on us to help that other person feel relaxed and elevated as well. I think that one of the biggest opportunities we have in this area is to help someone else be able to say no to us.

How many times have you agreed to something because you felt that it was too uncomfortable to say no? Maybe you didn't want to hurt the other person's feelings by saying no, or you really wanted to say no but you weren't quite sure how to say no in a way that would be well received?

The times when you might be the most unlikely to say no, even when you really want to, are with someone who you view to be special, important, in charge, etc. You might be the least likely to say no to your manager, the president of your bank or club, or someone who you feel is much wealthier or more mysterious than you are for some reason. When someone is perceived to have authority, real or imagined, it makes it exponentially harder to say no to that person. When we elevate ourselves, I think it is a responsible and kind thing to keep in mind that many people will have a hard time saying no to us.

What can we do to help? We can give that person the excuse they need! We can give them a sample alternative to "yes" that helps them to be the most honest with us about what they do and don't want, and avoid feelings of coercion or manipulation. I personally would much rather someone tell me no to my face than to say yes to me and then tell someone else they felt like they couldn't say no.

I started doing this with my patients about two years ago, and have found that my relationships instantly felt more connected to them as a result. When people feel like they can be honest with you, it helps them to build a better connection.

Here are some examples of an awkward comment "AC" and a replacement comment "R."

AC: "Do you want me to help you with that?"

R: "Do you need some help with that or do you feel like you've got it?"

AC: "Would you like to meet up to discuss this more?"

R: "Would you like to meet up to discuss this more or do you feel like this conversation covered all of the bases for you?"

AC: "Would you like me to schedule the bath aid to come out and see you?"

R: "Do you feel like you need the bath aid to come and help, or do you feel that you all are able to take care of your bathing on your own?"

I think the most elegant people are the ones who keep in mind that not everyone has the same ability to purchase things, and that not everyone likes to spend their money equally. Some people may have money for something, but don't *want* to pay for it. This is perfectly legitimate. I know I have things that I am more than happy to pay extra for, and other things that I feel are a giant waste of money.

Here are some ways to help someone bow out of a charge

that they may not be able to, or may not want to, pay for. Don't overcompensate for this by offering to pay for everything all the time. Sometimes that can actually make the person just as uncomfortable. I know I don't want to feel like the friend that everyone else is always having to pay for because I can't afford to keep up. I would much rather feel like an equal and pay my part just like everyone else. Other times, I simply do not want whatever it is. It has nothing to do with the cost, and someone else offering to pay can be aggravating because it feels like something is being forced on me.

Side note: if you can tell that the person really does want something and you want to offer to pay for it, do NOT ask them if they want you to pay for it. That puts them in a terrible position. Simply tell them that you are going to pay for it, be as discreet as possible, and do not make a big deal out of it. Making a big deal out of it makes it worse for them. I've been that person who couldn't afford bread. I'm telling you this from my own experience. Be generous, but keep it quick, matter of fact, and discreet. Move on quickly.

AC: "Are we doing manicures and pedicures?"

R: "Were you thinking we would do manicures and pedicures today, or do you think we only have time for one?"

AC: "Do you want to (something that's going to add an up charge)?"

R: "Do you want to (do the upcharge) or just pass on that today?"

AC: "Do we all want to order separate appetizers and then have everyone share a little of everything?"

R: "^^comment above^^ or does that sound like too much food/too complicated?"

I don't know if this is as big of a deal in all places, but I live in the south and "not hurting someone's feelings" is of paramount importance in most every situation. I have been using this strategy everywhere with everyone for the last few years and I think it has great results. Keep in mind that if you do use this, you are giving someone an easy out, so if it's something you really are needing or hoping that they will agree to, you may decide not to do this at that moment. For instance, when I need my mom to babysit the kids, I just ask her if she will babysit them. I want her to say yes!

HELPING YOUR CHILDREN TO BE POLITE

Speaking of children, and since we are going over a lot of foundational points right now, let's visit that topic for a minute. As I've already said elsewhere, it's hard for children to navigate successfully in an adult's world. They learn everything by watching and imitating; however, the nuance is often lost on them in the first decade of life. As children develop, they become more and more interested in having conversations with adults and trying out things like humor. Sometimes this can come off poorly and can result in some social faux pas that need to be corrected.

As with adults, I would always suggest assessing the situation for intent. I am never a fan of embarrassing a child. Shame is one of the worst emotions to experience, and to feel shame when you had no ill intent is just awful. I try to address a situation with my children in the following way:

1. Explain why the words they used were inappropriate

2. Give them some examples of what they could have/should have said instead

3. Get a confirmation from them that they understand what I've told them and have them "try again" with the more polite phrase

4. Give a smile and get off the topic

Example 1: Child says "I don't want that food." and it's a bit snippy

Me: "Honey, it comes across as very rude when you say it like that. I worked hard to make this meal for you. You could just say 'no thank you' or 'I'd rather have something else please' instead. Ok? *[childs nods, says ok in agreement]* Can you try that again? *[child says 'no thank you.].* Ok, good job. Who else would like some?"

Example 2: Child responds "I'm going!!" when asked to hurry up and get out the door

Me: "Whoa, bud! That was very disrespectful. I know you're feeling a bit rushed right now, but the appropriate response is 'yes ma'am' or 'I need another minute please.' Got it? [child nods and says ok in agreement] Can you try that again with more respect? [child says 'yes ma'am']. Thank you sir. Ok let's get out of here so we won't be late."

Maybe it's not correction that's needed, but simply good conversation skills. Maybe they are a bit shy, embarrassed, or distracted. Quiet reminders about appropriate behavior go a long way toward growing good habits early.

"Honey, a grown up is speaking to you. You need to look at people in the eyes when they are speaking to you."

"Don't just nod your head. Say "yes" out loud so they can hear you."

"Turn around and look at someone when you are saying 'goodbye' to them."

"So-and-so is leaving. Pause your game, look at them and say 'goodbye' before they go."

"Speak a little louder, honey, so they can hear what you are trying to say."

I have two little boys. They are exactly a year apart, so they are attached at the hip. They get along very well 95% of the time, but they are brothers and it is definitely possible to have too much time together. They know how to push each other's buttons, and will certainly push a topic until someone is throwing punches or crying out of frustration from time to time. If you have children, you are likely very familiar with the sing-song "nuh-uh" that children can throw out over every tiny thing someone else says, especially after a long day.

We use these opportunities to drive home the point from an early age that there is no need to be "right" all the time. It *does not matter* who is right and who is wrong over a tiny detail that isn't important to the story. Just stop. It doesn't matter *exactly* what number of times something was recorded on a video game. We don't have to sit here and nit pick about every tiny detail.

I was beyond proud of my boys the other day when one of them said something that the other didn't agree with (like the number of times they turned a sheep purple on Minecraft or something. Was it 100 or 110 times?). The second one responded "no, that's not right." The first one calmly said "well it doesn't matter anyway" and the second one agreed "yeah, it doesn't matter." I could have fallen over. The important message was "we did this thing that was really hilarious that we both enjoyed" and they were able to blow off the difference of opinion on the exact number of times it happened.

These little conversations add up to big things. It's important for me to really drive this point home to them because today it's video games, but when they grow up it's aggravations at work over numbers of copies or repetitions of instructions. Are they going to act like children and begrudge every tiny detail, or can they zoom out and focus on the issues that matter?

Understanding how to tell the difference between an

important detail and an unimportant one is a life skill. Knowing when to argue and when to let it go is something that many grown adults cannot manage to sort out. This is important for all of us to learn. For those of you with children, I would highly encourage you to promote excellent conversation and communication skills from the youngest age possible. It will pay off in dividends later in life.

EXACT WORDS MATTER

Since we have just discussed helping children learn better speaking skills from an early age, let's spend some time touching on ways that you can graduate your level of speech from being a bit juvenile to sounding more mature and sophisticated.

Has anyone ever told you that you were well spoken? What is it that makes a person seem well spoken to someone else? If you're thinking to yourself that it can't just be about whether or not someone uses crude words, you are right. At the very least, you need to make sure you are using correct grammar all the time without exception. If you use incorrect grammar such as, "she don't like those", or, "where are you at?," you need to start there. Changing everything else in this section without addressing basic grammar mistakes is like trying to put a top-of-the-line roof on a house eaten up with termites. You are defeating the purpose before ever getting started. Your time and energy needs to be spent addressing the holes in the supporting structure first.

If you feel that your grammar needs improvement, I would recommend taking the time to find a resource, perhaps on YouTube, that will help you in this area. This is very important and worth your time to put bad habits on the chopping block and replace them with better ones.

Assuming that your grammar is the best it can be, let's

go another layer deeper. Let's look at word choice. Every word you use has a bit of nuance to it. If I'm describing a room as "beautiful," a slightly different picture will come to your mind than if I describe the same room as being "grand." We will get into some specifics below.

In general, the way you describe situations and other people will be a larger reflection on you than them, and will affect the way your message is received. Your perception of me and the accuracy of my statement may change if I say that the individual I just interacted with was a "jerk" compared to me describing the person as being "very rude." How about if I describe a teenager as "lazy" versus describing the same person as "disorganized and a bit scattered."

I know that I'm a well spoken person because I've been told as much multiple times. I don't say this to pat myself on the back, but rather to explain that this is something I've been complimented on many times in my life. I've never really taken the time to sit down and try to figure out exactly what the difference is in a way that I could use to help someone else. For the sake of this book, I have spent a lot of time trying to come up with a more concrete explanation of why some ways of saying things simply sound better than others.

I am not the language police here. My purpose in this section is to help you take your speech to the highest level possible if you choose. You don't have to, but if you are a person who is striving to try to speak in a more elevated way and you're struggling with how to do that, these tips will be very helpful.

This whole book is really about what words you choose to use. This section points out specific words that might need to be substituted instead of general phrases or ways of phrasing things. Let's review some thoughts for approaching what to say, and then dig down to the specifics of word choice.

1. When you are describing a person, focus your energy on communicating the behavior, not making a generalized comment about the person. An educated person knows that people are multifaceted. Anyone can make a generalized assumption about another person. It takes more thought and analysis to describe exactly what it is about a person or their behavior that you do or do not like.

Saying that someone "is a jerk" conveys a few things, none of which do you any favors. Firstly, it is a general assumption and is an all-encompassing summary of who that person is at their core. It conveys that you feel that the person couldn't have any good reason for acting the way that they did, and that they are like this 100% of the time without exception.

People have a negative knee-jerk reaction to all or nothing statements. They also pull away from those who make sweeping statements about other people because it makes them wonder what might be said about them when they aren't around. If you can be very specific about which trait or behavior is bothersome (or endearing) to you, you come across as being articulate. You convey yourself as a person who thinks before they speak and who analyzes situations and pays attention to detail. Choose your words carefully and you will be viewed as a person who considers what they say before they say it. It's hard to put your finger on, but obvious once it's pointed out.

2. Do your best to avoid the words "always" and "never." As soon as you say that something "always" happens, the initial reaction of the other person is to try to think of an example of a time where that statement was not true. It makes you come across as a person who exaggerates, which is not what you want. If you are trying to convey that there is a problem with something and you say that it "always happens like this," the person you are speaking to automatically discounts a portion of everything you say for the rest of the conversation. If you

are going to exaggerate about one point, you are probably exaggerating everything you say.

You lose credibility immediately when you use one of these words. Again, it's about your level of analysis and attention to detail. You want to be as accurate as possible with the things that you say. It helps others to take you at your word (trust) and to be able to support you and your position. Exaggeration is equivalent to drama, and as soon as you are viewed as someone who is dramatic or causing drama, you are assumed to be part of the problem. Err on the side of under-reporting the frequency of something.

"She's always late," can be changed to, "She's late more often than not and it's very frustrating."

"He never remembers our anniversary," can be changed to, "He has forgotten our anniversary several times, and it always makes me upset."

Even positive exaggeration is still not a good thing because it can come back to haunt you. If you are wanting to help vouch for a friend and you say she "always gets perfect results," then you are now held in a bit of contempt if this person uses your friend's services on your recommendation and has less than stellar results. Now you look like a liar, and this is definitely not what you are striving for. Instead, say only what is true for you.

"Everyone that I have spoken to has been happy with her services." See the difference in this example? You are not promising perfect results every time. This leaves the possibility that there are people out there who have not had a great result, but you personally haven't met any of them. It's more balanced and gets a bit of the liability off your shoulders if this person uses your friend's service and isn't happy with the result.

No one can argue your truth about your experience. This

is the only exception. You can say that YOU have always been pleased with someone's service if it is true for you, but do not extend your comments past your own personal experiences. (I still wouldn't use "never." I would say, "I can't remember a time when." Try to be more accurate and avoid exaggeration.)

"I've been using her for several years and have always been so pleased with the outcome." Maybe add a disclaimer, "but that's just my personal experience".

3. Avoid complaining as much as possible. Complaining in general looks just as bad on you as it does on anyone you are complaining about. What is that old saying? "A dog who has a bone will carry a bone." If you are complaining to me about someone, who are you complaining about me to? It doesn't mean that you are not entitled to your own feelings, but if you are frustrated with someone, try to keep a few rules in mind: a) Be specific about which behavior is bothering you. You are not making an all inclusive statement about that person. You are identifying a specific action or behavior that is upsetting you b) Relay why this is a problem in relation to yourself. Does it make you feel left out? Frustrated? Stressed? The focus should be less about the other person and more about you. You are bringing this situation up to a third party because you need some comfort, support, or advice about your own feelings. You are not simply trying to drag someone else's reputation through the mud.

4. Get rid of deadbeat and frivolous words. I had an English teacher in middle school who made a statement that burned into my brain so strongly that I still think about it to this day. She said that there was no reason in the English language for the word "got." (I think a lot of English teachers have that one word that just eats them alive!) She had us do an assignment where we would use the word "got" in a sentence and then think of a more appropriate or accurate word. Instead of "it got really hot out there," you could say, "it's a lot hotter out there

than it was a few hours ago." Instead of "I got so mad," you can say, "that made me mad." Instead of "that got burned into my brain," you could say, "it was burned into my brain."

Ernest Hemingway, a celebrated American novelist and short-story writer who was awarded the Pulitzer Prize in Fiction (1953) and a Nobel Prize in Literature (1954), is well known for conveying his stories as succinctly as possible. One thing that he felt strongly about was how unnecessary "fluff" words are. Along these lines, words like "very", "super", "totally", and "really" can be left out of the description completely, and it will actually make you sound more well spoken to do so. His thoughts on this concept are interesting to ponder, and you can learn more about his style by researching "iceberg theory" on the internet.

Which one sounds more elegant to you: "this place is totally amazing" vs "this place is amazing." How about "she is so super sweet" vs "she is so sweet" or even "she is a sweetheart." Let's look at "I am really excited about this trip" vs "I'm excited about this trip." Compare "He was very rude" to "He was rude." Say each of these out loud and see if you can feel the difference. It's one of those concepts that are hard to put your finger on, but make a huge difference in how your speech is perceived by others. When in doubt, leave it out!

A word that I try to avoid as much as possible is the word "talk." You might be scratching your head on this one, but hear me out. Say each of these phrases out loud and decide for yourself which one sounds better: "she talks with a thick southern accent." Vs "she speaks with a thick southern accent." What about "I was talking to her about our trip last week" vs "I was telling her about our trip last week." The only time I will use the word "talk" in a sentence is when I'm asking someone the question, "what were you talking about?" I personally have not found a good substitute for the word "talk" in that context that doesn't sound forced and out of place.

Let's touch on that for a moment. You can definitely take this idea way too far and end up sounding a little bit nuts. If you catch yourself feeling as though you should be on a stage because you're speaking Elizabethan English and using words like "thee" and "thou" or phrases like "most pleased" or you're American and using British expressions like "smashing!" instead of "great!", you are taking it too far and it will backfire on you. You don't want to use a word that is so out of place that it causes people to stop and look at you and think, "what did they just say?" You want to sound educated, not eccentric.

The other negative outcome of using unnecessarily flowery words is that it not only makes you seem odd, but it also makes you seem like you are trying too hard. This can be interpreted as you having something to hide, being fake, or overcompensating. In any case, it's not impressive and in the worst case can make you seem less than trustworthy. Why is this person trying so hard? Why can't they just relax and be themselves? Do they think they have to speak this way to impress me? It will actually lower your stance in the other person's eyes.

If saying a word or phrase makes you feel like a teenager, see if there's a different word you can use. Just say NO to sounding dramatic or juvenile.

"Weird" vs odd, unusual, strange or different

"Talk" vs speak or tell

"Always" vs often, usually, frequently

"Never" vs seldom, usually doesn't, rarely

"Jerk" vs rude, inconsiderate, aggravated

"Lazy" vs unmotivated, disorganized, forgetful

"Got" vs had, became, purchased, bought

"Stupid" vs unusual, uneducated, not well thought out, impulsive

"Seriously" vs I agree (if that's what you really mean) or just leave it out all together

The following examples may especially irritate some people for me to bring up. Again, I am not saying that you have to change these things. I am bringing them to your attention so that you can be aware of them and decide for yourself which ones help you to feel more elevated. In the case of the examples below, the reason that the suggested substitutions feel more elevated is because they are more articulate. You are taking the time to say a real word and to avoid slang. It's a very tiny detail that makes it difficult for people to pinpoint exactly why you seem to be so well-spoken, but is definitely noticed.

"What?" or "Huh?" vs Pardon? or Can you repeat that please?

"Yeah" or "Uh-huh" vs Yes

"Nah" or "Uh-uh" vs No

"Thanks" vs Thank you

There used to be a time in the world when people actually paid attention to someone's "diction," which is an assessment of how well a person articulates themselves when they speak. When I first started dating my husband, my grandmother privately mentioned to me that he had very good diction. It was a compliment that made me smile because I had never heard anyone comment on someone's diction before, but I started listening to the way he was speaking and realized she was right. I would encourage you to be aware of this lost art.

Make sure that when you speak, you are not rushing through your words. Be sure to start and end the words completely. Not in such a way that is dramatic, odd, or comes across as obvious that you are putting a lot of emphasis on it. It should seem natural. If you slow your speech down ever so slightly, this will take care of most of the problem all by itself. If you were comparing your speed of speech to the speed of driving in a car, it would be the difference between going 65 mph and 60 mph; just a slightly more relaxed speed.

Now, for the love of everything that is holy: cut out repetitive and filler words and phrases if it takes biting your own tongue to do it. We all know about "umm," but there are TONS of examples of words and phrases that people will say when they are nervous or thinking that immediately lowers the quality of their speech. There is no real purpose to these phrases. They do not add to the quality of the conversation.

Many of these are habitual phrases. It's almost compulsive and very difficult to avoid saying. These phrases are so ingrained in a person's speech pattern that it takes effort to remove them. It is worth *every bit* of effort for you to change these habits. Do not kid yourself, it is irritating for the other person to listen to, even if they say it isn't. The more educated the quality of your company, the more this habit will stick out like a sore thumb and create a negative opinion of you because it is the opposite of being well spoken.

Constantly searching for the words to say or for confirmation that someone understands you conveys the opposite of being calm, confident, and collected. Just assume that they will let you know if they aren't on the same page with you. Allow for silence if you need a second to think of the right word. There is power in silence and confidence in stating your thoughts clearly.

You may need to pay a lot of attention to your speech to catch these problem phrases, or you might be well aware of them. If you have a trusted friend or family member who would be honest with you, tell them you are trying to work on elevating your speech and ask them if there are any words or phrases you say "all the time."

If any of the following come up in your personal audit, make every effort to get rid of them immediately:

"Ummm"

"Hold on" (said in the middle of a sentence because the person is thinking)

"You know what I mean?"

"You know?"

"Does that make sense?"

When someone else is speaking to you, don't constantly say "Yeah. Yeah. Yeah." in agreement. I know you are probably meaning to come across as engaged in the conversation, but it is actually a very distracting and sometimes irritating thing to have someone do to you. I have actually stopped in the middle of a conversation before because I was getting so tired of hearing the person say "right" or "yeah" every three seconds while I was trying to explain something. When you do this, you actually make the person feel very rushed to get to the end of what they are saying. Even though you are meaning to sound supportive, it usually comes across as very rude, dismissive, or too busy responding to listen, so do your best to cut this habit at the root.

It is important to remain engaged in conversation, but a better way to convey your interest is with a warm smile, an occasional nod, and a *light* sprinkling of confirmatory responses: best if varied, and err on the side of less rather than more. Try these instead:

"Yes" (not yeah).

"Sure."

"Of course."

"That makes sense."

"Same."

"Love it."

If you are a person who just *has* to have a rule to live by, try thinking in terms of paragraphs. Instead of saying "yeah" after every single sentence that a person says, try spreading it out to a variation of one of the above responses once every 1-2 paragraphs worth of information. If you are able, try to refrain from any verbal response until the person is finished speaking. Less is more.

Here is a pet peeve of mine. I might be the only person in the world who feels this way, but I doubt it. I cannot stand for people to come up to me and say "guess what?" No, I will not. It feels like conversation baiting and it drives me up the wall. It feels juvenile and frustrates me that I now feel obligated to ask "what?" in order for the conversation to proceed. Just tell me what you want me to know. Don't ask me to guess. It is a completely unnecessary back-and-forth that I wish we could all do away with.

Children may start conversations this way, but adults should not. Instead of "Guess what?" (what?) "I just learned this really interesting thing today…" simply start with, "I learned this really interesting thing today…" Same goes with "you know what?" Instead, dive right in. You've got this! When people start a conversation with, "Guess what?" I usually just give them a smile and a raised eyebrow that conveys my "what" and they typically jump right into the next part of their story.

If you notice a pattern from the preceding suggestions, it is an overarching theme that less is more. Consider this quote by Sophocles, "Much wisdom often goes with fewer words." Whenever possible, aim for less. Less interrupting, less exaggeration, less drama, less chatter, less filler words, and fewer repeated phrases. I definitely don't mean to be silent, certainly not! Just choose your words and your timing more specifically. Trust that fewer words can convey bigger meaning, and be confident enough to enjoy a few moments of silence without feeling the need to rush in with more words.

GIVING AND RECEIVING COMPLIMENTS

We live in a day and age of constant comparison. That may be true for all of history, but it feels more so now, especially in the age of social media. In a world where it seems like no one is ever doing enough, has enough, or is perfect enough, sometimes people can make comments that are difficult to know how to handle.

One particularly difficult comment to respond to is when someone gives you a compliment while simultaneously insulting themselves. Sometimes it may truly be that they are fishing for compliments, but usually it's because they feel self-conscious. They feel that giving you a compliment about something highlights their deficiency in that area.

It can be so difficult to know how to respond to a comment like, "you're so much prettier than I am" or "oh wow, your house is so much nicer than mine."

Let's first make sure we've got this squared away on your end: don't do this. Use every ounce of energy you have inside your body to avoid making this kind of comment to someone. There is no way around the fact that this is awkward. The reason that this comment is so difficult for the receiver is that you are simultaneously giving them a compliment while making them feel bad about whatever it is that you are complimenting.

If you say, "you're so much skinnier than me," the person will very likely have the urge to either insult themselves by saying that they're not really that skinny, or will feel that they've somehow called you fat just by existing. Or, they might feel the need to explain that they used to be bigger than they are now and detail out for you how hard it was for them to get to that size in order to somehow make the situation feel more equal or fair.

If you say, "oh your house is so much nicer than mine," it's the same thing. The person may feel the need to explain how the house isn't really that big, or how they wished they could've had something different that they couldn't afford in order to relate this idea of "not affording" something. They might feel the need to complain about how hard it is to clean, how high the electric bill is, or some other way of tearing themselves down to make you feel better about yourself. I think two examples is enough here. You get the problem. Don't put that sort of guilt and stress on someone else.

OK, but what if somebody does this to you? How do you field this kind of comment? You have to resist the urge to explain or apologize. You do not owe that person an explanation for the things that you have in your life that are good. The comment they are making comes from a place of insecurity within themselves. You don't judge them for their insecurities, but it's also not your job to try to fix them. In these instances, I will remind myself, "I don't accept the negative feelings here because they aren't mine. They belong to the other person."

To be completely honest, I find these to be some of the hardest types of comments to respond to. In some ways it really irks me when people do this because it's creating an uncomfortable situation that is so difficult to get out of gracefully. I don't want to feel obligated to put myself down, but I also don't want to insult the other person. The way I respond will sometimes depend on my mood and how well I know the person. I do tend to lean towards the habit of calling them out for the position they're putting me in by making that kind of comment, or I ignore the insult to themselves all together and pretend like they didn't say it. Here again are some awkward comments "AC" and some suggested responses "R."

AC: "You are so much prettier than I am."

R: "Oh goodness, well that is so sweet of you to give me a compliment, but there's no need to put yourself down!"

AC: "Your house is so much nicer than mine."

R: "Well thank you for your compliment. We are so grateful to have a house that we enjoy so much. I'm sure your house has a lot of love in it. It should be more about the love inside of it than the size of it, right?"

AC: "Your kids are so much better behaved than mine."

R: "Well they sure are great kids. I'm very proud of them, but we definitely work on it. I just love watching them grow up!"

AC: "Oh, your dog is so cute. I wanted one like that but we couldn't afford it."

R: "Well we sure do love our Rosie girl! We are so glad to have her in our lives. She gives the best snuggles!"

Just so we're crystal clear on how the compliment *should* have been given:

"You are so pretty!"

"You have a beautiful house."

"Your children are so well behaved."

"Your dog is adorable."

What about the "I'm insulting myself by comparing myself to you but not technically giving you a compliment out loud" comment? These comments take the cake for worst conversation skills ever. I can't stand it when people make these types of comments because it is nothing more than fishing for compliments, and I don't like fishing.

If this is a stranger, I will respond while internally rolling my eyes all the way into the back of my head and move on with my day. If this is someone that I am friends with or acquaintances with, I will use these comments as gigantic red flags that I need to make immediate distance between myself and this person.

I am incredibly protective of my energy levels, and I am keenly aware of the effect that other peoples' energy and words have on me. I have no intention of spending time with people who are going to be a drain on my energy and positive mindset. Some people are energy and good mood vampires, and there's nothing that can be done about that except to create and maintain distance.

This behavior can be thrown on you unexpectedly, so we need to review how to deal with these comments. You may or may not agree with me that this is the right attitude to have, but I absolutely refuse to compliment people who are fishing. I can't stand feeling like I'm being manipulated by the other person's insecurities or need for attention. Here is an example of these types of comments and how I usually respond to them.

AC: "I'm so much fatter/uglier than you."

R: "You shouldn't speak about yourself that way. You should be more kind to yourself."

They might respond with, "Well I am fat/ugly."

To that I will respond, "Well the most important thing is for you to be healthy/to take good care of yourself, so I would focus on that more than anything."

At this point, I'm going to completely ignore any further attempts on their part to keep on about it, and do my best to change the subject or physically remove myself from the situation. Do not be this person and don't allow yourself to be trapped by this game.

Now, let's focus on YOU! Be honest, can you take a compliment? How do you usually respond when people say something nice to you? Maybe that person says exactly the right thing. Maybe they simply tell you that you look nice, nothing negative to contend with. How do you respond? Do you deny the compliment or start insulting yourself? Do you start listing out all the imperfections you can think of? Do you feel like you compulsively start reciting your faults and insecurities and on the inside you're screaming at yourself to shut up but you just can't?

We've got to address this because it's incredibly important. First let's externalize this a little bit and put yourself in the other person's shoes. Sometimes it helps to imagine someone else you know reacting the way that you react. What if you noticed your dad wearing a brand new shirt and said to him, "dad, that shirt looks so nice on you!" And he responded by saying, "Do you really think so? I put on 5 pounds recently and I feel so bloated right now." I, for one, am cracking myself up thinking about my dad responding that way.

What if you saw your uncle at a wedding looking very

dapper in a suit and tie and you told him he was looking handsome and he responded, "Oh my gosh, I'm so self-conscious compared to these younger guys. I'm thinking about getting Botox." How are you even supposed to respond to that?! Please don't put other people in that position. Repeat after me: "thank you." Full stop. Nothing follows.

Don't elaborate by putting yourself down or explaining all the things you feel like you need to do to improve the situation. Don't respond out of guilt that the person complimenting you may not have something that's as nice as what you have. They are sending love to you by giving you a compliment. Honor that by accepting it with grace and gratitude. If you feel like saying "thank you" is too short of a response, here are some graceful ways you can expand on it.

"You look so nice tonight."

"Thank you so much! I'm really enjoying myself."

"Your house is beautiful."

"Thank you. We feel very blessed to have it."

"Your kids are so well behaved."

"Thank you. I'm proud of them."

"Wow, you have such a nice car."

"Thank you. I'm grateful to have a car that I enjoy so much."

"You did an amazing job with this project."

"Thank you. I worked really hard on it. I'm glad you like it."

"The dinner you cooked is wonderful."

"Thank you. It makes me happy that everyone is enjoying it."

"The donation you gave was very generous."

"Thank you. I am very grateful to have the ability to support such a wonderful cause."

Here's my last thought on accepting compliments. Sometimes getting a compliment shines a light on parts of your life that make you uncomfortable, either because you feel like something is not as good as you want it to be or because you feel a bit of guilt that you have more than someone else does.

At the beginning of this section I mentioned that we live in a world that is so full of comparison and visibility that the aim of perfection is everywhere. Because of this, it feels impossible to have peace sometimes. You know the old saying that "comparison is the thief of joy". When someone is giving you a compliment, use this as an exercise to feel gratitude and peace in your heart for the connection and kindness coming to you from another person.

That person could have chosen to feel jealous of you or to tear you down because of something positive that you have in your life. Instead, they took the opportunity to connect with you and share a compliment with you. They could have been ugly, or they could have kept their positive comment to themselves. They took a chance on being vulnerable with you by saying something nice.

You could choose to say something ugly in return. You could choose to respond in such a way that meets their positive energy with your insecurities and self-doubt. Or, you could choose to meet their expression of connection and love toward you with an expression of love in return. When you think of it this way, it's so much easier to simply say "thank you."

When the compliment goes a bit sideways

What if someone is trying to compliment you, but the words that come out of their mouth are actually insulting? I will never ever forget the first time this happened to me. I went through one of those butterfly moment summers when I was between seventh and eighth grade. My braces came off, my mom bought contacts to replace my glasses, and I was able to go to an actual hair salon for the first time in my life and have my hair styled with some shape and layers.

Once I arrived back at school for my eighth grade year, I was feeling pretty darn good about myself. My teeth were straight and I was braces-free, I was back to two eyes instead of four, and I had learned how to do my make up and hair in a way that at least felt put together. I was also very pleased to find that many of my male classmates had undergone huge growth spurts over the summer, and I was no longer towering over all the boys in school at 5'7"; a height I had achieved at 11 years old.

As a consequence of these beauty enhancing changes, along with my new found confidence in the way I looked, (possibly coupled with the fact that I was visiting the high school regularly to do after school band activities as an eighth grader), I started to finally attract a little bit of male attention for the first time in my life. As much as I had wanted this leading up to this point, I had a bit of an internal struggle going on with the sudden change.

I confided in one of my best guy friends at the time about my concerns. My comment to him was "I don't know how I feel about this. No guy has ever been interested in me until I made all of these changes." His response, bless his heart, was, "well, Julie, nobody knew how pretty you were before!"

He was truly trying to encourage me and give me a compliment. I'm sure you have found yourself in similar situations from time to time. Maybe you've lost a lot of weight and people are noticing. Maybe you've undergone a beauty enhancing treatment and you're getting some positive attention. Maybe your life was generally scattered and disorganized, and now you have a solid direction that you're following, and you are experiencing lots of success.

If you are the person attempting to give someone in this situation a compliment, be sure to refrain from comments that indicate a prior problem. Focus your words only on the good success they are having. Here are some examples of an awkward compliment ("AC") and a replacement compliment ("R").

AC: "Oh wow, you've lost a TON of weight!"

R: "You look wonderful!" (They know they lost weight. You don't have to specify.)

AC: "I'm so glad to see your life finally coming together."

R: "I'm so happy to see all the success you've been having lately. Way to go!"

AC: "I bet you thought you'd never get married."

R: "Good things come to those who wait. I'm so glad you found Mr. Right. You two are perfect for each other."

AC: "I guess third time's the charm, huh?"

R: "I am so happy that you found such a wonderful person. It's been a long road to get here, and I wish you all the happiness in the world."

If someone tells you they have lost a significant amount of weight, refrain from any version of, "Wow, that's a ton!" or, "Man I bet you're glad to be rid of all of that!" Instead, focus on their happiness and health with a comment such as, "Congratulations! You have worked so hard and I bet you feel amazing."

If you are the person having newfound success, be prepared that there might be a lot of well-meaning comments coming your way that might feel a bit insulting. My thoughts when this happens are that we as imperfect people should give grace to those who say imperfect things. I believe that in all circumstances, we should assess the intent of the things that are said and respond to the intent rather than the specific words that might have not come across in the best way.

"You sure do drive a stick shift well for a woman." Yes, this has literally been said to me before. Was it a wee bit sexist of a comment? Yes, it was. Most people would say that I was well within my right to be rude and snappy and possibly give this person a piece of my mind about how women are just as capable as men.

But let's be honest, there are traditionally far fewer women who know how to drive a stick shift than there are men. This person had not experienced knowing many women at all who knew how to drive a straight shift. He was genuinely impressed and was trying to convey this to me. Was it the most graceful thing ever said? No. Was it graceful of me to respond, "Thank you!" and give him a playful wink as he tried to backpedal after realizing what he had said? Absolutely.

He wasn't trying to be condescending and he did not have ill intentions towards me. I really wish that we could all give each other a little bit more breathing room and not be so quick to rain down a holy terror on people for saying something that comes out a little bit sideways.

I'll give you another example. I was at a patient's house one time who lived on this piece of farm property with a long, winding, narrow driveway leading up to the side of the house. The patient's health had declined rapidly and his family was beside themselves with concern for him. When I went in to do the evaluation, his wife and all three sons wanted to be present for the entire process.

When it was time for me to pack up and leave, one of the sons opened the door for me and walked with me outside. He let me know that it was perfectly fine for me to drive the car around the front of the house (through the grass) in order to get back to the driveway facing towards the road because, "I know ladies are uncomfortable backing up cars."

Goodness. Again, was this comment just a little bit sexist? Sure, many people would say that it was, but this sweet man was trying to help make the situation easier for me in case I was stressed. He was offering to let me tear up the front of his yard by driving my car through it just so that I would be comfortable getting back to the main road. Am I really going to be so mean as to return that intended kindness with rudeness?

I thanked him and assured him that I was very comfortable backing down the driveway and that I would turn around in the side yard if he didn't mind. He then offered to get in the car and back it up for me if I wanted him to. What an incredibly sweet and thoughtful person. His mama should have been proud. Again, I assured him that I had a back up camera in the car and then I felt very comfortable navigating the situation. I thanked him for being so thoughtful and told him to have a nice day.

When in doubt, be kind. When someone is trying to be kind to you, be kind to them. If you have ever stuck your foot in your mouth while trying to give someone a compliment, give other people the benefit of the doubt when the things that they say are worded imperfectly.

WHEN THE OTHER PERSON IS EMBARRASSED

Let's look at another way we can be kind to others. There are times when you might come across a person who is feeling embarrassed for one reason or another, which happens frequently in the medical profession. I often see people who are sick and somewhat disabled. Because they cannot care for themselves or their homes the way that they normally would, they tend to apologize to me a lot for the way they look or the fact that their home is messy. There are those times when it seems obvious that the person typically has a home that is a bit less sanitary, and although this is normal for them, they are still embarrassed for me to see it.

First of all, let's make sure to clarify that if the person doesn't look the way they want to look, they have no need to apologize to me about it. They don't owe me anything. I am not entitled to a certain level of cleanliness or tidiness from them or their home. I am a healthcare worker who is there to provide a service to them. I am there to help because they need help, so let's start with that.

Despite the fact that this person does not owe it to me to have their hair perfectly done and to be immaculately dressed, or for every single dish in the sink to be cleaned and put away, they do feel embarrassment about it. When searching for the words to use in this type of situation, we can revisit the idea that I touched on at the beginning of the book about life being hard.

Going through a scary or stressful event, a health problem, or any number of issues can completely drain a person's energy. A person depleted of energy has no reserve to use for cleaning their house. More than that, we never know the internal struggles that a person goes through that can make it so overwhelming for them to keep house.

When it comes to someone's home specifically, I try to keep in mind the idea that a person's external environment is a reflection of their internal world. Maybe I don't understand how a person could live in an environment that is so cluttered you can't move, or so dirty that there is nowhere to sit, but I try to recognize it as a symptom of a much deeper problem.

On the other end of the spectrum, maybe this person has always been the perfect "June Cleaver" wife and they are seeing dust that I don't and small bits of untidiness that I can't recognize. It might be easy to regard this person's embarrassment as unnecessary, but whether it's necessary or not, they feel embarrassed and that is their truth. We need to recognize this and show empathy for them.

If the environment is truly clean and well put together, I will usually make a comment along the lines of, "I think your home looks wonderful. I wish my home looked this nice all the time." This comment is not really about whether this person's home or my home is technically cleaner. It's about the fact that we are all human and we all have times where things don't look picture perfect. I have two little boys, a cat, a dog, and a husband who loves to work outside and under cars. We do our best to keep our home looking as nice as possible, but it is not picture perfect 24/7. I wouldn't want anyone to hold my home to impossible standards, so I would never do that to anyone else.

There are times when the person's house is a little bit of

a disorganized mess. Maybe I can tell that this is normal for them and they are apologizing for the mess, but it's always like this whether they are sick or well. I might have to move piles of papers and boxes just to have somewhere to sit. Telling this person that their home looks wonderful would be an obviously false comment to make. I'm not here to be disingenuous with anyone, and no one appreciates insincerity.

If this person makes a comment apologizing for the state of their home, my response is usually somewhere along the lines of, "well it's just so hard to deal with things like housework when you don't have any energy. I'm not bothered by having to move a few papers. I'm sure you'll get to it when you have time. Don't worry about me."

Or, I might say, "You've been through a lot! No one could expect you to focus on anything except getting better right now. Don't think twice about trying to get up and clean. I'm just fine."

In this situation I am acknowledging that life is hard and that we can't always show up the way we want to. I'm also trying to put the person's mind at ease because a lot of their embarrassment might come from the fact that they feel that I could possibly be inconvenienced by the state of their home, or that I am judging them for not doing a better job of keeping up with the house work.

I usually try to touch on each of the following: 1) acknowledge what they've been through recently that gives them a very legitimate reason why they haven't been able to take care of something (surgery, sickness, caregiving for someone else, etc), 2) acknowledge the feeling they might be having that contributes to them not having the physical or emotional energy left to focus on something like housework (tired, stressed, hurting, etc.), 3) assure them that I am not offended or inconvenienced by the situation (I'm fine, don't worry about me, I'm just here to help, etc.).

Very often, I might deal with a family member who feels embarrassed about the state of their loved one's house. They might be the person who is apologizing for the house, and might be rude or insulting to the patient in the process. I have heard many comments along the lines of, "mom, I can't believe you let the house get like this; it's awful in here."

I'm usually a lot more offended by the person insulting the patient than I am by the home. I do try to recognize that the person making the insulting comment is also feeling embarrassment. They are worried that I am inconvenienced or judging them or their family member for the state of the house. I go through the exact same process I just listed above. I acknowledge that the patient has been through a lot; sympathize with their pain, lack of energy, or stress; and then assure them that I am just fine and that I know they will be able to attend to those things once they are feeling better.

I make sure and address these comments directly to the patient. It is supremely rude to speak about someone who is sitting right next to you without acknowledging them directly. For you, this will probably apply more in the setting of your own family member's house, a friend's house, or a friend's family member's house. It's the same process no matter what. If it's someone who is hosting an event, what they've "been through" is the stress and chaos of planning such a wonderful get together for everyone. You're just happy to be there to visit and enjoy good company.

In a few extreme cases, there really is something going on in the environment that is not sanitary or healthy. There might be a lot of soiled clothes or used briefs in the bathroom that the person cannot clean or deal with because they are too disabled. Perhaps there are several bags of trash leaning up against the back door because the person can't get them out to the bin and doesn't have anyone to help them with that either.

Without drawing too much attention to things such as

smells or messes, I will offer to help. I will offer to put soiled clothes in the laundry, I might clean a few dishes so they will have clean dishes to eat with, I will offer to bind up trash bags in the bathroom and put a fresh bag in the trash can, or I will offer to take the bags of garbage out to the compactor or trash bin. In this instance, the person is embarrassed because they need help and they don't have enough support. If they mention the smell, I will say, "I don't have a great sense of smell anyway. It doesn't bother me at all. I'm happy to help."

It only takes a couple of extra minutes of my time, and it makes a big difference to them. This is more about being a decent human being than anything else. I would hope that if I was in the same situation needing help, someone would be kind enough to offer me the same assistance.

What about smaller comments of embarrassment? Again, the two most common reasons that a person might feel embarrassed is because they are worried that you have been inconvenienced or that you are judging them. If we can recognize which of these is the issue and address it with a friendly, unbothered comment, this will remedy most any situation.

One thing I want you to keep in mind is to never put yourself down in order to lift someone else up. That is unnecessary and not helpful for anyone. We all rise. Here are some examples of comments that stem from embarrassment that someone might make, and the awkward comment "AC" versus the replacement comment "R" I would suggest you use:

"Oh I'm so sorry, I think there's something stuck in my teeth."

AC: "I probably do too."

R: "Your teeth look fine to me. I don't see anything." or "It's just one little spot right there. Yes, it's gone now."

If they make a comment about being embarrassed because something was stuck in their teeth:

AC: "Don't worry it happens to me all the time."

R: "Don't be embarrassed, it can happen to anyone!"

"Don't look at my shirt. It has a stain on it!"

AC: "Oh mine does too. I feel so embarrassed."

R: "I wouldn't have even noticed if you hadn't pointed it out. Don't worry!"

Or if the stain is actually super obvious: "It happens to everyone from time to time. Don't worry about it!"

We are all human. We are all imperfect. We all have things that go wrong, and it is not helpful to the other person when you say something negative about yourself. Instead, help them to acknowledge that to err is human and neither life nor people are perfect. There is no need to apologize for that.

What if the person tries to compare themselves to you in such a way that makes you feel uncomfortable? Maybe you feel that the person is trying to pressure you to put yourself down to stay on equal footing with them, or they are putting you on such a high pedestal that you feel that they are giving you too much credit and not acknowledging your human nature?

Putting yourself down does not lift up the other person. Again, we all rise. It is good to acknowledge that no one is perfect, you included. However, that does not mean that you have to start listing out your sins.

Since no one is perfect, it is extreme for someone to complain or be starstruck by the idea that you are. Different personalities may feel more comfortable addressing this in varying ways, but I tend to take the approach of using a little bit of humor and teasing to gently point this out to the other person.

I do my very best to look put together any time I step out of the house or know that I'm going to have company. I also put a lot of effort into having things in my life be peaceful, which for me includes my things being tidy and my children and pets being well behaved. This doesn't come without effort, but most people don't see that. They only notice the finished product, and sometimes assume that it happened that way by magic.

I don't think it does myself or the other person any good to try to say that something that I have or something about my appearance isn't as nice as it seems. I have tried that approach in the past, and it usually seems to land on deaf ears. It's much more effective to point out that I've put effort into those things. We come across in a more relatable way when we admit that looking nice or having nice things took work. It doesn't feel as satisfactory to the other person for me to say that I have bad hair days too or that I wish I could lose 5 pounds. Here are some examples:

Them: "Please don't look at my hair, it looks awful today."

You: "I think it looks fine. Don't worry about it! I'm just glad to see you."

Them: "Well I wish my hair looked like yours. Your hair is always perfect."

AC: "Oh no, last week I wore a messy bun to the store and ran into my boss. It was so embarrassing!"

R: "That's a very sweet thing for you to say, but I don't know about that. Since the kids are older, I have a lot more time that I can put into taking care of my hair, and that helps a lot."

Them: "Don't you ever have bad hair days?"

You: "Sure I do! I'm just really good at hiding them." (wink, smile, and give a little laugh)

Them: "Your makeup always looks so perfect. I wish I could do mine like that."

AC: "I have to stick with this look because it's the only one I can pull off. I can't do a winged eyeliner to save my life. I always look ridiculous when I try."

R: "Oh that's very sweet of you to say. I found a few girls on YouTube who I love to watch for make up tips. I've changed a few products around lately that I'm really enjoying. I'd be more than happy to share the brands with you or the links to those influencers if you're interested!"

Them: "You always know exactly the right thing to say. I wish I was as well spoken as you are."

AC: "Oh man, sometimes I really mess up. Last week __ happened and I said __ and then I found out __ and I could have died!"

R: "That's a very nice thing to say. I don't know about always, but I do put a lot of effort into the way that I communicate with other people. I'm glad it's noticeable."

Them: "I wish I could eat whatever I wanted to and stay as skinny as you do. It's not fair."

AC: "Yeah right. I'm going to have to spend an hour in the gym every day this week paying for this brownie!"

R: "I wish I could eat whatever I wanted without exercising. Wouldn't that be nice? I do put a lot of effort into keeping up with my healthy eating and exercise plan so that I can have wonderful meals like this on special occasions."

Recap: I am not perfect, but I am not going to let someone else's words cause me to say negative things about myself like how many bad hair days I have, the fact that I can't nail a winged eyeliner, that time last week when I really stuck my foot in my mouth and cringed about it for the rest of the day, or the fact that I really wish I could lose 5 pounds. No. That's not going to make that person feel better and it certainly isn't going to make me feel any better.

This approach is a combination of learning to take a compliment, as mentioned in the previous section, combined with adding a touch of reality and humanity to the situation. I can't think of a time when someone has continued to push back or pout in a conversation where I have responded to these types of comments in this way.

Sometimes you might be in for a real treat where responding in this way prompts the other person to ask you for recommendations of products or resources that you enjoy and can share with them. Everyone wins! Maybe that influencer you want to support gets a new follower, you feel helpful and like you've made a small difference, and your friend feels better prepared to improve something about themselves they might like to work on or learn more about. Isn't that so much nicer than letting the conversation spiral down into a bunch of self hate and complaining about things that aren't perfect?

COMPLAINERS

Oh complainers. Unfortunately, complainers are everywhere, and this is one of the lowest forms of conversation. What happened to that wonderful bit of wisdom that says, "if you don't have anything nice to say, don't say anything at all"?

People can choose this type of communication for so many reasons. It could be a learned habit from being raised by people who complain all the time. It can come from a place of boredom where the person has nothing productive to say, so they start criticizing everything around them. It can come from a place of jealousy and trying to tear down someone or something that is perceived to be better than whatever that person has. In that same vein, it can be a way that a person tries to lift themselves up by comparing their own preferences or standards with something else.

If I complain that the restaurant is dirty, I come across as someone with high standards who is very clean and probably keeps a perfect house. If I complain about the way another person is dressed, maybe I will be perceived as more of something. More righteous in my conservative dress. More fashionable in my beautiful clothes. More knowledgeable in my sense of style. Wealthier to afford nicer things.

The truth is that behaving in this way nearly always comes across as you being snobby, rude, condescending, and without empathy. To make sure we've covered all of our bases, don't be that person. Now the real difficulty is how to handle people who complain. Someone who is used to communicating this way usually does it constantly and loudly. It is a huge social faux pas and something that can take a lot of finesse to handle well.

In my experience, most of the time if someone makes an ugly comment it's either because they are embarrassed about the situation, or they are trying to impress those around them by being snobby. Either way, I usually try to approach these kinds of comments with equal parts compassion and clear communication that I am not planning to indulge in this behavior with them.

The response would have to be based on whether or not the person making the comment was partially responsible for the environment. This might be the case when you visit someone's home and they comment that they are so sorry it's not clean enough. If that is the case, I make an effort to reassure them that I am not offended or upset by the environment through a comment such as, "I think everything looks fine!" or, "The house is well loved. You can't blame it for that!" or, "Well you've got kids living here. No one could be expected to keep everything perfect all the time." I would use the same comments to squash any criticism that someone else might give that would embarrass someone else, such as a patient's daughter criticizing the cleanliness of the home in front of me.

If it's a neutral environment, such as eating out at a restaurant, and someone is making an ugly comment about the restaurant's cleanliness, then I try to redirect the conversation towards 1. If it's that bad, then let's leave or 2. If it's not bad enough to leave, then let's stop complaining about it. How I direct this might also be based on the rest of the party. Is this the only person who seems irritated by this environment, or is everyone looking uncomfortable about staying? If we were to leave, is money part of the problem? If we go somewhere nicer, is everyone in the group going to be able to afford the nicer location or do I need to encourage us all to deal with the current location in order to accommodate the price point needs of the group?

If the general vibe is that the one person complaining is the only one with the problem, I will usually make a much stronger comment such as "I think this place is charming. Why don't we check out the menu and see how it goes? I've heard really good things about the food here." If the energy seems to be that everyone is uncomfortable, I will have no problems taking the lead towards suggesting an alternate option with a comment such as, "You know, I heard really good things about this place, but it's a lot different than what I was expecting. I had also been curious about this other restaurant. Would anyone else be interested in checking that place out instead?"

If we're already sitting down and eating, and I agree that the place is not great, I still don't want to complain. If someone else makes a disgruntled comment, I might also concede, "Well yes, it wasn't exactly what I was expecting. Now we know better for next time. I am enjoying my food though. What does everyone else think about what they've ordered?" In that way I'm acknowledging that the person's comment is legitimate, but I'm also getting off the topic quickly to signal that I don't want to indulge in a neverending list of complaints.

If they engage in this behavior frequently, I will make a point to quit spending time with them. Being around this type of person is draining and pointless. It also signals that the person is fundamentally unhappy with their life or difficult to please, and there is no fertile soil there for a relationship to bloom that will be enriching or helpful to me or anyone else.

WHAT IF YOU NEED TO COMPLAIN?

Surely life isn't all rainbows and sunshine! There is no reason to suffer in silence when there truly is an issue that needs to be addressed. There is a difference between idle complaining and dealing with something that needs attention. The litmus test here is to ask if I am providing for constructive improvement of the problem by bringing this up. Am I addressing my concern with the person who has the ability to fix the situation? Let's look at a few examples:

You are in a public space and have just visited the ladies room. The floor is dirty and they are out of toilet paper.

Complaining: rejoining your party and fussing about how dirty the restroom is and how this place should be doing a better job of staying on top of things.

Constructive: find an attendant or employee and politely and quietly explain that the bathroom needs attention, and exactly which issues you found to be problematic. Thank them and move on; there is no need to say anything to anyone else.

You are outside on a hot day and getting sweaty and uncomfortable.

Complaining: "This day is the worst. I hate this. It's too hot and I feel like I'm dying."

Constructive:" I'm getting overheated out here. I'd like to go inside and see if I can cool off. Would anyone like to join me?"

You've just checked out at a retail store and noticed you were charged twice for an item when you look over your receipt in the car.

Complaining: Getting on social media and declaring that the store you visited has terrible customer service and everyone who works there is an idiot who doesn't know how to ring up a simple transaction.

Constructive: Go back into the store, wait your turn to see the associate you dealt with, show them the receipt and ask if you can get an adjustment for the item charged in error. This will likely require a manager to fix the problem. Be patient and polite.

If the issue escalates, flip to the Dealing with Conflict section. For our purposes here, we'll assume these conversations are easily brought up and fixed.

AVOIDING EMBARRASSMENT

We've spent a lot of time going over different scenarios where other people might be embarrassed or creating an awkward moment. I'd like to spend the rest of this section addressing how to avoid your own potential embarrassment in different situations. We're going to look at how to avoid sticking your foot in your mouth, how to address certain topics that are uncomfortable, and how to converse with people in a way that helps you to feel like someone who "always knows what to say."

MEETING NEW PEOPLE

One of the most common issues that everyone has when socializing is meeting a new person and then having to remember their name. What if someone forgets your name? They might be embarrassed about it!

The flow of addressing this should go something like this:

1. Give a warm smile to assure the person you are not upset or offended and that they should not be worried.

2. Actually assure them that you are not offended and they should not be worried (it's ok, don't worry, it's fine, etc.)

3. Normalize it. Everyone forgets things from time to time.

4. Move on quickly. Pick a different topic and roll right into it. Don't linger on the fact that someone forgot something. Acknowledge, reassure, normalize, and move on!

AC: Anyone who says they can't remember your name in any situation ever

R: "It's __(Julie). Ask me as many times as you need to. I have a hard time remembering people's names too. How are you today?"

What if you can't remember someone's name? Own it! Deal with it immediately and then use a mental trick (associate their name with something else, write it in a note on your phone, etc.) to make sure it doesn't happen again. Asking someone's name a second time is fine. If you have to ask a third time, you are not paying attention and it will leave a negative impression. Something simple like, "oh, forgive me but I need you to tell me your name again" or, "now tell me your name one more time" will be sufficient.

DON'T go on and on about it, explain why you forgot, or become overly apologetic about it. It happens to everyone. Don't make it a bigger deal than that. Smile, acknowledge, act like it's normal, and move on quickly.

DEMOGRAPHICS

Between working over the phone for collections and in home health, I have had more than my fair share of "foot in my mouth" situations that I have had to learn how to avoid the hard way. Some of the examples below are not necessarily things that have happened to me, but they are things that I have heard that have made me cringe nonetheless. Regardless, I hope they never happen to you. If they have, this is going to be an excellent section to help you to avoid these types of awkward conversations in the future.

In gathering information from someone, it is easy to inadvertently touch on a sore spot with that person, or ask the question in such a way that you elicit a response from them that makes you uncomfortable. Instead of giving more lead up to the topic, let's dive right in.

Gender: This is usually only going to be a problem in an over-the-phone situation. However, this happened to me a lot at the beginning of my job working collections. Remember when Taylor Swift dated Taylor Lautner? There are a lot of names out there that are not necessarily gender specific. Perhaps the name is in a language that you are so unfamiliar with that you don't have the knowledge of whether this name would typically be a female or male name. I know over the phone in the south we would typically ask to speak to Mr. Smith or Mrs. Smith. At least, that's how I was raised. Here's the problem:

"Hi. May I speak with Mrs. Smith?"

"Are you looking to speak with Taylor Smith?"

"Yes"

"This is he."

(Oh can I fall through the floor and hang up the phone now?)

The solution is that if there is even the slightest question as to misunderstanding if you are looking for Mr. or Mrs., you ask for the person by their first and last name.

"Hi, may I speak to Taylor Smith?"

"This is he."

Nailed it.

Pronunciation: This was a constant problem working over the phone. A call would flash onto my screen with a person simultaneously asking in a super irritable voice, "Hello? Who is this?"

When you are put in this sort of situation where something is being thrown at you with no chance to prepare, your best bet is to go with either the first or the last name, whichever one you feel more confident you can pronounce correctly. This helps to avoid irritation on that person's part or embarrassment on your part from mispronouncing their name.

It is important to be able to pronounce someone's name correctly. Most people whose names are mispronounced frequently understand that you might need a second chance to say their name. If the situation is very formal, it may or may not be necessary to clarify their first name. In any event, you might need to verify exactly with whom you are speaking, such as when I was working collections and legally obligated to only discuss the account with the account holder. Speaking to a patient's family member who happens to be of the same gender and have the same last name is *not* good enough.

The only graceful way to go about this is to ask them how they pronounce their name. If it's a formal situation, you can ask this as a verification type of question. In other situations, simply ask them how to pronounce it. People would much rather explain to you how to pronounce their name and help you work through it than to listen to you butcher it.

Cringe version: "Can I speak to...blah blah blah (totally butcher their name)

"IT'S...."(correct pronunciation with obvious aggravation)

Solution: "May I speak to Ms. Lolita?"

"This is she."

"Wonderful. Would you please pronounce your last name for me?"

They pronounce it.

"(You repeat it correctly). Thank you so much for helping me with that. I'm calling about..."

Maybe you thought you knew how to pronounce the name, but you said it incorrectly. They correct you. You respond by saying

"(Correct pronunciation). Thank you so much for correcting me. I apologize for mispronouncing your name." Move onto the next item on the agenda.

If you are collecting the person's demographic information for some sort of business related issue (such as intake paperwork or a first meeting where sensitive or protected information is involved), you can really score the gold on this one by simply asking them "Would you please verify your first and last name for me?" They will pronounce it correctly and you never have to butcher it.

Marital status: Oh boy have I really stuck my foot in it with this one working in home health. Part of my evaluation when I enter a person's home requires collecting demographic information including marital status. I originally would ask the person if they were married.

This sounds innocent enough until you have conversations where you ask "Are you married?" and the person responds…"My husband died 6 months ago."

Ouch! I then caught myself backpedaling saying I was so sorry to hear it, and then we would become involved in a conversation about how the person died, how upset they are, and everything that's changed in their life since then. Talk about opening up Pandora's box.

I then thought I had become more clever by changing my question to, "Are you married or widowed?", but had a few responses similar to, "Honey, I've never been married. It's just me. I don't have any kids either. I don't have anyone." Oh boy do I feel like a jerk.

Now, I have finally become smart enough to simply ask, "What is your marital status?" It's a beautifully neutral question with no way to stick your foot in your mouth accidentally. That one has not backfired on me yet and I've been using it for years now.

Family: Along those same lines, I am also supposed to gather information about that person's support system. Do they have someone in the home who can help them if they need it? If not, do they have someone outside the home who can help them?

What I used to ask: "Does anyone live here with you?"

The way they would respond sometimes: "No honey it's just me, I don't have anyone. My husband died last year and my kids don't come around anymore."

Oh dear. How I ask the question now: "Who all lives with you all the time?"

They might tell me that their husband and son live with them. Now I don't even have to ask about their marital status. They just answered it for me!

If I ask who lives with them all the time and they answer "no one," I used to then ask them the follow up question, "do you have any family that comes by and helps you with things?"

I bet you know where this is going at this point: "I don't have any family." or "Yeah right, my kids wouldn't care if I died today. After all I did to raise them, they don't come around anymore. They don't even call me." Dang it.

So now I ask: "Do you have any friends or family who can help you with things such as taking you to doctor's appointments?"

If I already have a strong impression that this person doesn't have much of a support system at all, I might phrase the question: "If you needed to go to a doctor's appointment, how would you get there?"

This lets them tell me everything I need to know about children who help out or friends that can do basic things for them without giving so much of an opportunity to expound on old wounds.

Relationship: My mother used to be a NICU nurse when I was very young. Her job at that time was usually to take the babies who had finally become stabilized to their mothers, and help with some basics such as breast-feeding. A piece of advice she gave me as soon as I said I was going into healthcare was "never assume you know who the mother is!"

Sometimes the mother is the person you thought it would be. Other times it's the person you thought was the baby's grandmother, or the person you assumed was the baby's older sister. She said she would walk into the room and say, "Ok, tell me who's the mama." Same thing with the baby's father. Maybe the mother would say, "can you hand this to my husband?" and she would turn around and say, "all right, which one of you is Dad?"

I use this extensively in my day to day working life. When I come in to see someone for the first time, if the person who answers the door doesn't point and say, "here he is," I will say, "Ok, which one is my patient?"

Maybe there's a person present who seems to be very involved and possibly the patient's spouse, but no one has officially given a title to this person yet. Another thing I have to do in my evaluation is establish an emergency contact person. I might ask who the emergency contact is going to be and this person I've been speaking to says, "I am the emergency contact."

Only one time did I ever make the mistake of saying, "Ok great, and you're her son?" Guess what he answered? "I'm her husband." Can I disappear now please?

Here's how I handle it now: "Ok great. Tell me your relationship to the patient. I don't want to assume anything."

Maybe there's a person who's giving me really odd vibes and I feel like we're riding the line a little bit on giving this person too much information about the patient even though the patient is sitting right there and technically has consented to the information exchange. I might have to say, "I'm sorry, I don't know exactly who you are. Are you a friend or family?" Maybe they try to be coy with me and only say "I'm family." No sister, not happening. I need to know who you are. I'll respond, "Great. Are you a spouse, a sister, a cousin? Tell me what your relationship is."

You may not have a HIPPA related reason to need to be so specific, but if you are legally or ethically obliged to keep this person's information private, and someone seems to be pushing the limits of what is acceptable, it is your job to protect that person's information and make sure you know who you're speaking with before you answer questions. Even if it's not a legally protected situation, you have the right to ask who you are speaking to. You shouldn't be held in the dark and potentially open yourself up to making a comment that will make everyone uncomfortable because no one bothered to give proper introductions.

Race and ethnicity: I think I've given enough examples at this point of how asking a question the wrong way can lead to uncomfortable conversations. Simply ask, "what is your race/ethnicity?"

BODY PARTS AND BATHROOM BREAKS

OK here's the grand daddy topic when choosing your words matters the most. You can take or leave a lot of the suggestions here, but I would strongly encourage you to take this list to heart. The suggested version of the word may not feel the most comfortable to you based on where you live, but do your best to avoid the word on the "don't" list whenever possible. Those words are best avoided everywhere.

Get ready to feel slightly uncomfortable, because I need to be crystal clear about which words are the problem that need to be avoided, so as much as I would rather not, we're going to have to list the words out one by one with some preferred replacements.

I also want to make a small note here that I have to converse with people on this topic on a nearly daily basis because I work in healthcare, and specifically I work in people's homes. It creates an environment where we have to speak about these things in order to make sure that the patient's care is complete and their medical record is not missing any essential information.

If you find yourself struggling with this topic, I would pose this question to you; how would you feel if you were sitting in a room at your doctor's office and after telling the doctor you were having pain "down there" the doctor asked you if your pain was in your vagina and then started giggling because he or she said "vagina"? Would you not be horrified and disgusted? How can this person call themselves a doctor if they can't speak about body parts and body functions without laughing?

Please be an adult here. You should be able to have conversations on all topics without having a fit of giggles. We're going to go over the best words to use in different scenarios so that you can feel equipped to go into these conversations confidently. Don't bring up things that don't need to be discussed, but also don't shy away from what needs to be said or asked when necessary. And for heaven's sake, please do not giggle or get embarrassed over something so much a part of human existence as body parts and body functions. It only makes you look childish.

The conversations I have with people are not uncomfortable because I always use the words on the preferred list below. More often than not, I will have to help prompt the patient with a word that makes them comfortable to use because they are trying to describe something to me and they don't know how to do it in a way that is not embarrassing. So whether I like it or not, I feel like I am becoming an expert on the following:

>Potty vs toilet, but the best word to use is <u>commode</u>

>Pee vs urinate, but if we are referring to the need to use the bathroom, it is the most polite in conversation to simply ask the person if <u>they need to go to the bathroom</u>

>Poop vs <u>bowel movement</u> or <u>BM</u>. If you need to describe the actual BM itself, we refer to it as the "stool." Ex: when you had your last bowel movement, was the stool a normal color or did you see any red or black in it? *We ask this because it can indicate serious health red flags.

>Fart vs <u>having gas</u> or <u>passing gas</u>

>Diarrhea vs <u>upset stomach</u>. Some of my sweet elderly patients will describe this as having "loose bowels." It might not be the most formal description, but it gets the point across in a way that is better than the alternative. The exception here is when you are communicating to your doctor the problem you are having. You want to be specific about exactly which problem you are having so that they can treat it appropriately. No one else needs you to be that specific.

>Crotch vs <u>groin</u>

>Boobs vs <u>breast</u> or <u>chest</u>. Chest is typically going to be the most appropriate term in general conversation. You dropped something on your chest. The ball that your toddler threw hit you in the chest, etc. If the situation is more medical, you might need to use breast such as to describe breast-feeding, a breast exam, or something to do with breast tissue. Maybe you're going for a formal bra fitting and you are telling the fitter that you have more breast tissue on the right versus the left instead of saying, "my right boob is bigger than the left one." See?

>Needing to go to the bathroom: if I am attending to someone (like a small child or a patient), I will usually ask them if they need to go to the bathroom. If I am the one who needs to go, and I am not at home, I will ask if I can use the "<u>ladies room</u>." There are so many words for this particular area of the house. Bathroom, restroom, loo in certain countries. My personal preference for myself is to say "ladies room" or "men's room" in most instances. If you are at certain upscale or five star establishments, you might ask if there's a powder room nearby. I wouldn't use this in someone's home unless they live in a very high end neighborhood, because it can seem like you are trying too hard if you use the phrase "powder room." I don't think this one matters as much as some of the others, but **don't**

say potty. You are not a toddler and you're not speaking to a toddler. "I need to go to the potty" is a big nope here. When I'm at home, I most often say bathroom.

>If you are helping to give care to someone who is sick or otherwise unable to properly care for themselves and they have had an accident where they have gone to the bathroom on themselves and they don't realize it, I never draw attention to it by saying that they've had an "accident." For me, this is about preserving the person's dignity and trying to draw as little negative attention to the situation as possible. I know that it is a sanitation and skin breakdown issue for the person to remain in soiled clothes, so I don't ignore it. I will either say that it looks like they need to get some "<u>dry" clothes/pants</u> or "fresh" clothes/pants.

>Pull-ups or diapers versus <u>briefs</u>. Babies wear the former, adults wear the latter.

If there is a need to directly address the area of a person's penis or vagina, here are the most common scenarios and how to handle them:

>If you are a caregiver of any sort and possibly helping this person to change clothes, change some sort of medical equipment or wound dressing, or get a bath, you might hand them a towel or something to cover themselves. In this scenario I would give them a towel or whatever item and instruct them that they can use it to "<u>put over their lap</u>" or "<u>cover their bottom.</u>" When you refer to someone's "private parts," it does have a connotation of drawing negative attention. It's a very subtle nuance, but you're indicating that this is an area that they should not be showing to people or referring to, and yet here you are having to interact with that part of their body.

I also don't tell them to "cover themselves." Again, I know I'm splitting hairs here, but the point of this book is to pick apart a lot of these subtleties. If you disagree with me, that's perfectly fine. I am simply sharing my thoughts. When you tell a person to "use this towel to cover yourself," it can induce a feeling of shame or embarrassment like they've done something wrong. I prefer to be very specific. This pillow goes under your head. This bandage is for your leg. This towel is to put over your lap.

If you need to refer to the private area of a person's body, saying lap or bottom usually takes care of it. Let's say that for some reason you are having to be more specific. This is not typical, but it might come up if you are helping to care for someone like a child, an elderly family member, or someone who has a disability. It also might come up if you happen to be responding to some sort of injury. You might work in a field where injuries can be more common, such as sports or healthcare, or you might be around when someone slips and falls at a pool party.

If the person is trying to describe an area of pain or possibly a rash or some other first aid issue, you can first ask them where the problem is. Let them name the area. If they are being very vague or embarrassed and only pointing in a general direction, and you need them to be more specific, I try to start with the less sensitive options first. I might first ask someone if the problem is with their upper thigh or their groin. If they say no, then I will ask if it is their penis or their vagina.

Professional people don't avoid the correct names for body parts. It does not make you seem more elegant, educated, or competent to use a slang term in this situation. It actually makes everyone else more uncomfortable that you are going to such lengths to avoid saying the correct word.

You need to be a grown-up, be very matter-of-fact, identify specifically where the problem is so that you can attend to the situation appropriately or pass the accurate information along to the professional who needs to deal with it, and then move on. Speaking of moving on, I think we are ready to do so.

THE BIG 3: POLITICS, RELIGION, AND MONEY

Gird your loins! These are the topics you have likely been told growing up that aren't polite to discuss. Although this may be true, never being taught specifics about exactly why it's not polite to bring these things up or what to do when conversations or situations regarding these topics come up, you might feel as though you are drowning in discomfort when they do. Why should I not bring these things up? How do I respond when other people make comments that make me uncomfortable? How do I navigate these topics in a way that is educated and refined? Most importantly, how do I make sure that I never end up embarrassing myself by saying the wrong thing?

Relax, friend, I've got you covered. Let's get the worst one out of the way first. Don't worry, it's not that bad!

POLITICS

Did seeing the title automatically make you feel like you wanted to be ill? Did you think to yourself, "I've really been liking this girl so far, but this might be where I realize I actually hate her."? Maybe you just rolled your sleeves up to go ahead and start fighting? Perhaps you started pulling up some social media on me so that you could tell the world that I'm actually hateful and terrible?

I'd be willing to bet money that you didn't get excited. "Oh wow, I can't wait to hear her positions on all the latest political drama." Don't worry, I promise you won't know anything more about me in this regard by the end of this section, pinky swear! You can relax now. This entire part of the book is focused on NOT speaking about politics.

I don't know about you, but I grew up being told that it's not polite to talk about religion or politics. As I discuss in the religion section, there are some ways that this rule might need to be bent in order to connect with people and avoid problems; however, I would say that there are absolutely zero exceptions to this rule when it comes to politics. I don't care how well-meaning you are, and it doesn't matter how keenly the other person seems to be into your ideas, please don't take the bait.

The reality is that you could discuss a hundred different political issues with someone and they could agree with you exactly on ninety-nine of those issues. Just when you're starting to feel relaxed, you say something about that 100th issue that completely blows the relationship.

People take their feelings on these topics more seriously than they do religion. You might think that this is an exaggeration, but I assure you, it's not. Most people are understanding of the fact that others may have different religious beliefs than they do. Most people have zero ability to extend the same grace to others when it comes to politics. With religion, you'd be surprised how many people would be willing to agree to disagree. Not so in the political arena.

Working in home health, this dilemma comes up much more often than I would like. Many of my patients are still in the habit of turning the news on at a certain time of the day, or leave it on all day, and will have the news on when I walk into their home. The fact that the news is covering something will prompt that person to ask me how I feel about it. Oh dear.

Not only do I naturally dread having political discussions, in this particular setting I am a professional and my relationship with this person is one of a professional nature. Since I am a healthcare worker, it is imperative that I remain in a neutral position so that my relationship with my patient cannot be negatively affected by this topic.

As we've discussed, most people have zero tolerance for even the smallest variation in beliefs when it comes to politics. I don't want their view of me to be changed for the worse over some small or seemingly innocent comment that I make. And to be clear, I have patients with a wide range of political views who watch every different news station available.

Since many people have zero ability to tolerate differing political views, I have a zero tolerance policy when it comes to having conversations about politics. This is something that takes very firm boundaries at times, and we will discuss how to handle that.

As a reminder, this book is meant to help you maintain

good relationships with others and increase your ability to navigate many different social circles and novel experiences. I am not trying to police this topic, instead I am relaying my experience to you in hopes that you are able to utilize this information in your own life. There may be times when this doesn't feel like it applies, and as I have said elsewhere, take what resonates with you and leave the rest.

Maybe you don't see the problem with discussing politics, and of course that is for each person to decide for themselves. Unfortunately, I have seen many relationships or social experiences where things were going along perfectly until a political discussion was had, at which point people have walked away and resolved to never speak to each other again.

Sadly, I've had to remove myself from relationships where the other person was so insistent about being loudly vocal with their opinions. I found myself so disgusted by that person's point of view that I really couldn't continue to have a relationship with them. The atmosphere around that person became so stressfully charged that I couldn't expose myself to it anymore.

I've heard people make this argument: they say they will "only discuss politics with those who are educated about the topic." This is COMPLETE MALARKY and you are kidding yourself if you think you have somehow found a magic loophole by using this approach. Here's the thing, you are 1000% convinced that your education on the topic is solid, and so is the person who disagrees with you to the point that they would tear you to shreds on a public forum. You can hand two people the exact same stack of papers, research, reports, textbooks, you name it, and those two people can come away with contradictory conclusions. Think about dueling experts in any field; two people with the exact same credentials arguing on the news. Two people with the exact same professional credentials drawing opposite conclusions on the witness stand in a court case. Two experts lobbying for opposite legislation on capital hill. Throw that caveat out the window. It's not helping you at all.

My last point when it comes to whether or not discussing politics is ever ok or worth it is this; how many times in your life have you ever been involved in a political discussion where you have walked away with a differing viewpoint than when you started? How many times have you let yourself engage in a passion filled argument on social media about something only to walk away thinking, "you know, the person on the opposite side of that argument really made some good points."? Never. It hasn't happened.

You are not going to change someone else's thinking and they are not going to sway yours. Your job is to go out and vote on election day. I do stay up-to-date on political happenings. I do have my opinions about most every topic. But you know what they say about opinions! They are like certain parts of your body. Everyone has one, but you should probably keep yours to yourself.

Ok, if you didn't already think it before, I have managed to convince you! You are completely resolved to refrain from discussing politics. This is easier said than done sometimes, right? How do you manage to maintain this resolve?

Let's start by removing temptation whenever possible. One of the worst breeding grounds for political ranting is social media. I made the decision a long time ago that if anyone I followed or was friends with on a social media platform insisted on using that platform to voice their opinions about political issues, I would simply unfollow them. It doesn't mean that I am no longer connected with them or even friends with them on that space, but their posts no longer show up in my newsfeed just begging to disturb my calm.

In a few extreme cases, I have had to block people in order

to protect myself from their belligerent insistence. It's not my preference, but my mental health is more important to me than a loose connection with someone that I don't spend time with much (or any) on a regular basis anyway. If you can't see it, it will not bother you and you will have no reason to contend with your own desire to tell that person what you think about that topic and what you think of them for having a different opinion!

What if you see something that really upsets you and makes you want to post a passion-filled monologue on your favorite platform? Don't. Take a really big breath, put your phone down, and walk away. If you have to remove the social media app from your phone until the urge passes, do it! Take a walk, take a kickboxing class if you have to. Meditate or pray.

Whatever the issue that's making you upset, no matter how near and dear to your heart, ranting about it on social media is not going to change the outcome. Revisit the paragraph above in regard to changing the opinions of others.

Vote if it is an issue that can be voted on. Contact your local and state representatives to make your voice heard by the people who are able to influence the situation, donate to the cause if there is a way to monetarily support the outcome you want to see. Regardless, public displays of distress are not going to do you (or the situation) any favors. Being a millennial and coming up in the age of social media, I have learned this the hard way.

I think that covers the major points with regard to reacting out of passion. In those situations, you are completely in control of whether you do or do not say anything. What if someone is specifically prodding you for your input? This is the situation I find myself in on a regular basis in my profession. I choose to address this with wit and a bit of humor to begin with, and then with boundaries if absolutely necessary.

Let's look at an example. I can't tell you how many times this exact scenario has happened to me. As I enter my patient's home, the news is on, and they ask me what I think of a current situation being covered.

Them: "What do you think of all this?"

Me: "I think I was always taught not to discuss religion or politics." I give a wink and a teasing smile.

Quite often, this is enough to stop the discussion altogether. I have relayed the idea that I'm not keen on giving my thoughts, and the other person receives the message and respects this. Unfortunately, there are times when this response is not enough. This is often the case with men who really like to get into hot debates.

Them: "Oh, does that mean you're a (opposite political party from them)?"

Me: "It means I don't like to talk about politics." Again, maintaining a smile and buoyant attitude. Maybe add a shoulder shrug. (I'm not mad, I'm just not going to talk about it.)

Thankfully, most people who didn't concede after the first statement will relent after this one; although there are times when a certain person (for whatever reason) will not let it go.

Them: "Well it must mean that. If you agreed with me you wouldn't be hesitant to talk about it." (They always think they're so clever.)

Here's where I have to start putting my foot down, because now we are having an issue with boundaries. At this point, this person is becoming hostile and they are ignoring the fact that I have said twice that I don't want to discuss the topic. I will change the tone of my voice to be more assertive. I will not take an angry tone, but I will be crystal clear that they are being inappropriate and I don't appreciate it. I will say as much if necessary.

Me: "Mr/Mrs so-and-so, I am a physical therapist and I am here to help you/your spouse get stronger. I don't feel like it's appropriate for me to discuss politics and I would kindly ask you to stop insisting on it. I feel that it's inappropriate for me to discuss politics with patients, whether we have the same opinion on the topic or not. Can we please move on?"

I have maybe only once had someone try to push more after this type of statement. The one time that it did happen, I basically just gave the person my no-nonsense Mom look (you know the one that says "are you seriously going to keep pushing this?") and stared at them until they conceded. Not only am I not going to discuss politics, I'm not even going to talk about whether or not I will. I am done having this conversation.

I would highly encourage everyone to take such a firm stance in their professional environment. Of course the decision is always up to you, but I don't see a scenario in which it is to your benefit to engage in these conversations.

How do we address this in a social setting? If someone asks for my opinion in this type of environment, I will usually give the same reply that "I was always taught not to discuss religion or politics" with a warm and slightly teasing attitude. If I notice that there is a political discussion that is beginning, I will often excuse myself. I will quietly get up and leave, possibly feigning that there's something I must attend to. Other times, I might busy myself by having a conversation with someone else about a different topic. I will often use this option if I am stuck at a dinner or somewhere that it's not appropriate or reasonable for me to physically remove myself from the situation.

In incredibly rare instances, the situation might escalate, and boundaries have to be set per my example above. Most often, the best option is to politely excuse ourselves and walk away. Whatever you do, don't escalate the situation yourself. Raising your boundaries to meet other people's insistence is only necessary if they refuse to allow the conversation to move in a more appropriate direction.

When others are discussing politics

Now that you are completely resolved to avoid contributing to political conversation, what do you do about others who don't care about your opinions as much as they want to share their own? There is a lot of nuance here and the best answer will of course depend on what you can tolerate. Certain topics may be easier for you to listen to people speak about than others.

Even if I agree with what the other person is saying, I still have no intention of responding in such a way that gives my position on the subject. The reason for this is that by agreeing with them on one topic, I have now crossed the line of "giving my opinion" and I have destroyed my position that "I don't discuss politics" when something comes up in conversation that I don't want to discuss. Another reason is that agreeing with someone on one small point will open up one or both of you to start down the road of other political topics. You may find out very quickly that the first point you agreed with was the only topic you seem to feel the same way about as this other person. Now you are in over your head trying to figure out how to get off the topic before an argument begins.

Sometimes I don't necessarily agree with the person's feelings on a topic, but the topic itself doesn't really bother me a lot and I find it easier to just roll my eyes on the inside and smile on the outside. Other times, people's opinions can make me see red and make my head want to pop.

Sometimes it's really not about whether I agree with what's

being said as much as the fact that the topic of politics makes me very exhausted, and I may just not have any emotional bandwidth to listen to it at that moment.

Here are a series of responses that you can use to refrain from being rude, acknowledge the person who is speaking, and simultaneously keep your opinions off the table. I use these frequently at work. Maybe the patient or family member isn't asking me my opinion, instead they are simply offering their own. I don't necessarily want to hear it, but I would rather stay neutral than attempt to ask them to stop discussing it. I will usually look for any and every opportunity to change the topic whenever possible.

"Oh really?"

"That's an interesting thought."

"I hear you."

"Is that right?"

"It's definitely a complicated topic."

"I understand; there are a lot of things to consider here."

Smiling and nodding works wonders! I've had a few instances where I've been to a patient's house, and after several visits a new friend or family member will be there. I've had someone tell this new person that I agree with them on a certain topic and I am very surprised to hear it because I absolutely don't agree! Apparently the fact that I simply refrained from arguing with them about it gave them the confirmation they needed to assume how I felt.

Dissenters of my approach might say that I am being fake or dishonest by not letting someone know when I don't agree with them. I wholeheartedly disagree with this conclusion. Refer back to my comment about heated debates and ruined relationships.

How I feel about a topic is inconsequential to my ability to have an enjoyable interaction with someone. I am not going to put my mental health and emotional calm on the line in order to voice an opinion that will be unwelcome, and will create distance between myself and another person. My aim throughout my day, and in life in general, is to connect with people. I choose to share love and joy, to uplift and encourage, to bring healing and peace. None of those goals can be met by bringing negativity and controversy into the situation. You have the option to choose something different for yourself if that feels like the right course for you.

There are times when I approach a group of people only to realize too late that they are engaged in a fairly political discussion. I will make an excuse to immediately leave most of the time. I might say that I forgot something like a purse or a drink and excuse myself to go retrieve this item and simply never return to the conversation. If I have caught someone's attention, I might tell them that I wanted to give a quick little 'hi' and that I wanted to make sure and catch up with them before they left, and then I make my exit.

If I'm stuck without one of these convenient excuses, I might jokingly point out that the conversation seems too heated for me and that I need to excuse myself to somewhere that is a bit more calm. "I'll leave you all to solve the world's problems" with a wink and a smile of course.

Now, my husband is someone who enjoys discussing politics. He is truly curious to hear what other people have to say about things and remains unbothered when people have conflicting opinions to his, unless of course, it's me. We definitely had a few differences of opinion on politics when we were first married and it drove him crazy. He enjoys keeping up with varying media outlets to see how the stories compare and contrast. There are various influencers that he follows to hear their opinions, and he can often be caught discussing politics at various functions with friends and family.

I had to put down a very firm boundary nearly a year ago because he insisted on carrying on with various political topics everywhere we went. Since this was directed toward me, it meant that I had to listen to it and did not have the option to remove myself from the conversation. This one was tougher to deal with because of course it is my husband and it's a lot harder to stay neutral with your partner. It's also impossible to walk away when the person is speaking to you directly. This can create a conflict between the two of you when he wants to discuss something and you don't.

Do you know that old phrase about picking your battles? Well, I finally had to engage in this one. I'll spare you the details, but the punchline is that I gently but firmly insisted that if he absolutely had to talk about politics, that we could go visit my parents so that he could discuss his opinions with my dad, or he could call one of his friends and have a conversation with them, but it was no longer a topic I was willing to tolerate.

He wasn't happy about this. I love him to death and he prefers to talk to me about his varying thoughts and opinions, but I couldn't take it anymore. It's not that I disagreed with him. I agreed with him on 99% of everything he had to say, but the topics themselves were incredibly distressing to me. No matter what, and in every situation and relationship, you have to make your mental health your own top priority. No one knows where your limits are except you and it is YOUR responsibility to communicate and reinforce your boundaries.

Now, if he has something he's dying to tell me, he will ask me if he can share an update with me. I might ask him to clarify the topic before I answer. My answers might be 1) sure go ahead 2) I can only handle the highlights today. Can you keep it short? Or 3) Can you ask me again a little later? I really don't have the emotional capacity to hear anything political right now. Being the wonderful and amazing husband that he is, he respects my answer no matter what.

In some extreme cases where I am locked into a situation, most likely a meal of some sort, where the discussion is getting heated and people are starting to escalate the energy, I will make an attempt to shut the conversation down. I might announce, "This seems to be getting a little too exciting for me. Do we think we could move on to a conversation that's a little less heated?". I might even have to say, "It seems like everyone's getting a little tense right now. I propose we change topics."

Again, I have had to learn this the hard way. Absolutely nothing can come of something like this except hurt feelings and damaged relationships. I would rather choose to be the person looked at as a jerk for shutting down a conversation then having someone despise me for my comments about their political views. Sometimes my announcement that I would love for the conversation to stop and the topic to change irritates people, but I am always met with a few looks of gratitude from those who also wanted the conversation to stop but didn't feel like they could say anything.

When you think you're not talking about politics, but you are

This is the last section that I have to address in order to have covered the topic fully. We need to be very clear about what constitutes "talking about politics." The obvious political conversations are who you are voting for, which party you identify with, how you feel about big-name topics that are always being debated in the political arena, etc., but what else?

Sometimes there might be an idea that for your entire life up until this week, everyone agrees with. Let's say that everyone has always agreed that the tooth fairy is a harmless idea and that there's nothing inherently wrong with telling your small children that she exists. As of the date of the publishing of this book, I have never been made aware of any controversy related to the tooth fairy. Should such controversy arise after the publishing of this book, please understand that I am not referring to this instance specifically.

Let's say that something crazy happens in the news related to the tooth fairy. Maybe someone goes on a serial killing rage dressed up as the tooth fairy. Maybe a child winds up severely harming themselves by accident because they jumped out their window trying to catch her in the act or something.

Suddenly, people have very strong, *different* opinions about the tooth fairy. There are groups of people who are trying to get all books about the tooth fairy taken off the shelves. There are other groups who are trying to have parents fined for telling their children about the tooth fairy, and the list goes on and on. In this context, the tooth fairy has become a political topic. It is now controversial as to whether or not it is responsible parenting to tell your children that there is such a thing as the tooth fairy. Until this blows over, or possibly forever more, you must now keep your opinions to yourself about this topic. If you don't, you open yourself up to others thinking you are either an extremist or neglectful/apathetic, depending on which position you choose. C'est la vie.

Here's the litmus test: if one news station is going to take one stance on a topic and the other news station is going to likely take a differing stance on the topic, it is now controversial and you would do best to leave your opinions at the door.

If your sentence is going to start with, "I don't want to be political, but…", refrain from making your comment.

If you can't refrain from referring to a person's politics before you give a compliment about them, then keep your opinion to yourself. I saw something the other day where a person had posted a picture of a woman who is involved in the political arena. The reason the person posted the picture was to say how nice they thought this woman looked in the dress she was wearing.

There were some who couldn't help themselves and commented, "I don't like her politics, but I like the way she dresses." Please stop doing this! Either find the kindness within yourself to simply say, "I think that dress looks really nice on her," or don't say anything at all. By saying, "I don't agree with her politics," you have now spread your political opinion all over the room. No one wants to hear it. Keep it to yourself.

If we want to get down to it, the person who posted that picture really shouldn't have. By posting a picture of a controversial political person, no matter what reason you give for it, you are provoking a political discussion. The person who posted the picture did contribute to the problem here, which is something to keep in mind for yourself going forward.

What if you are having a discussion and it becomes political after a comment you have made that you didn't realize would be controversial? Perhaps you said something that you never thought could be polarizing, but now you find yourself defending whatever it was that you said. Zip it up quickly with an apology (own the fact that you started it) and a statement about wanting to avoid a problem. The floor is now hot lava. Get away from it so you don't get burned! Here are a few ways to diffuse the situation:

"You know, I'm so sorry. I didn't realize that comment was going to start a problem. I really don't want to keep discussing it because I don't want anyone to have hurt feelings. Why don't we change the subject?"

"I think this conversation is going in a direction I wasn't intending. I feel like there is a fundamental difference of opinion here and we should probably move on to another topic. I didn't mean to upset anyone with the comment that I made, and I apologize for that."

Even if you are the one that made the comment that started a problem, if you can recognize it and become the peacekeeper instead, it will redeem a lot in the other person's eyes. You are valuing respect and congenial interactions over "being right" and that will go a long way. You are also providing for the other person to step away from also needing to "be right," and modeling a more mature approach, which they will appreciate.

Well my darlings, I think that covers it all. We survived! Now that we're done talking about how we're not going to talk about politics, let's move on to something else! Anyone else needing a glass of wine right now?

RELIGION

If you grew up in a traditional family, you were probably told not to speak about religion or politics. We've already covered politics. We need to cover religion, although I honestly don't feel like there's too much that needs to be said here.

The thing that most people do tend to concede is that this is something very personal. Many religions will have teachings on the topic that each person has to decide for themselves what they will believe. You can't believe something for someone else, and that person has to decide in their heart what is true for them.

Even within the same religion, each individual group of people may collectively agree on a slightly varying set of ideas within the same belief structure, take baptism for example. Most Christians would agree that baptism is an essential ritual for the Christian faith; however, there is a large split between whether baptism should occur when the child is a newborn baby or whether they should make that choice as an adult and elect their own baptism.

Each group tends to feel very strongly that their way is the right way, but they can usually concede that it's not hurting anything for the other group of people to do it a different way. Even if it's a begrudging "well that's their problem if they want to do it wrong" sort of idea, you will rarely see people getting into a yelling match over the age of a person at their baptism. This is what I meant in the previous section about people having more flexibility with accepting varying beliefs when it comes to religion versus politics.

I think that the biggest faux pas made in this area would be having an open discussion about things that are "right" or "wrong." When we start to get into the specifics of what is considered to be acceptable or not with regard to dogma, the conversation can become very uncomfortable. There are obviously certain topics that are hot button issues between different beliefs. Those are the things that can become problems very quickly.

I don't feel that it's necessary or helpful for me to list these topics out specifically, as I'm sure you know what they are. If you need to do a quick check within yourself to decide if a certain topic is one that is acceptable or not, I would always err on the side of not. Unless it's a universal truth that should be accepted in all religions *and* those of agnostic faith, it's probably better left unsaid. Keep those conversations private in your religious space or your home. I would encourage you to avoid getting into lengthy discussions on these topics or making off the cuff comments to people that you don't know very well, as it is a recipe for disaster.

Similar to the reasoning behind why it's so important to keep your political beliefs to yourself, making grand religious statements ("they're going to hell because...") in mixed company never lifts you up in the other person's eyes. They *may* agree with you, but more often than not there's something about what you've said that they don't completely agree with. Or, they may agree with you but feel that you declaring your opinion out loud was inconsiderate and in bad taste.

They may completely disagree with you and now you have lowered your status in their eyes. They might be very concerned about what you are comfortable saying to someone else when they are standing next to you. For that reason, they may feel an urge to keep their distance from you. They don't want to be associated with your strong opinions and they no longer trust you to be discrete and considerate in mixed company.

I do acknowledge that there are many religions that teach that you must "go out into the world and make disciples", and that sharing your beliefs with other people is not only a good thing to do, but highly encouraged. I am not here to conflict with your spiritual teacher or teachings, but I am going to put my foot down and insist that it is not polite conversation and is usually very unwelcome. You must decide for yourself how you're going to handle this if it is a conflict for you. I am simply delivering the message.

We've established that delving into the specifics of religious topics and beliefs is generally not a good idea. What about other things like identifying your beliefs, asking others about their beliefs, or inviting people to certain religious events? I am not telling you to be ashamed of what you believe or to hide who you are. I am simply stating that it is not other people's business what you believe and it is not really your business what they believe.

I find it very offensive when people have the audacity to simply look at me and ask me what I believe. It happens quite a bit in my profession. A patient will look at me and say something like, "You're a Christian aren't you?" which is wildly inappropriate. What I believe is my business; it is personal to me, and I consider it to be private. I most certainly don't wish to discuss this with strangers, and it is never appropriate to discuss in a professional relationship like a healthcare provider and their patient.

I know that there are going to be many who disagree with me on this point. There are lots of people who believe that it is not only appropriate but highly appreciated when a healthcare provider will pray with them, etc. While I'm not here to tell you how to run your life, I would be remiss if I did not address this.

While you may have all sorts of patients who want to pray with you and appreciate you praying with them (who feel very touched by this exchange), how many people have you made very uncomfortable by allowing this discussion into the professional relationship? How many people now feel that they can't be as open with you or as trusting of you because their beliefs don't match yours and they are worried that if they express a difference of opinion you will somehow provide a lower quality of care to them? It is something worth very serious consideration.

This is a discussion that was brought up for me during grad school. What do you do if a patient asks you to pray with them? There were a wide variety of answers in the classroom and some very strong opinions in every direction possible. I thought that the teacher had the most appropriate answer. She said that if a patient wanted to pray with you, that you should tell them that you were more than happy to bow your head in prayer while they said the prayer.

We don't want to ostracize someone by refusing to participate in something that means so much to them; however, we do not need to put ourselves in the position of saying a prayer or speaking on religious topics because all it takes is one wrong word from you or one idea that is slightly different from theirs, and it can put a bad twist on the situation. Now they feel uncomfortable with you because of something that you said.

It is not your place to be in a religious position with your patients or clients. It is your job to be professional with them and to support them in whatever way that they need. By agreeing to bow your head in prayer, but insisting that they be the one to say the words, you are simultaneously supporting them while maintaining your professional stance. This is a personal decision that only you can make. Take what serves you from these thoughts, and leave what doesn't resonate.

What if the person who is asking you to participate with them in prayer follows a completely different religion than you? Again, questions of religion are very personal in nature. You must do what feels right to you. If a person has asked you to join them in a prayer, they are asking for connection and support. Possibly they are trying to extend love and support to you because of something difficult you are going through. It might be that they are the ones in need of love and support and they are asking you to bear witness to their needs.

I believe that we as people need to show love and support to each other as often as we can. If someone feels moved to connect with me through prayer, I don't mind at all. I don't have to believe in the same higher power that they do to believe that we are all connected by love, and the power of love between two people is something to be cherished and appreciated.

I have had people of different beliefs than mine tell me that they have said a prayer for me or that they were going to say a prayer for me, and I genuinely with all my heart have appreciated that. What a beautiful act of love for that person to take time out of their day to think of me and to beseech their higher power on my behalf in order to ask for goodness to come my way. How could I ever want to discourage that or be dismissive of it? Why would I ever turn it down? Just as I would never want someone to be dismissive of my attempt to encourage them or encourage healing or beauty to come into their lives, I would never do that to someone else.

What if someone invites you to a religious event because they don't realize that you have differing beliefs from them? Again, I always appreciate the intent behind this offering of connection and love. I don't want to highlight the difference in beliefs because that could create distance or embarrassment.

Please do not respond with, "No thanks. I'm not (their religion)." I will often just reply with some variation of, "I appreciate the invitation. That is so sweet of you to think of me. I don't think it's going to work out this time, but I hope that you enjoy the event."

Sometimes this comment might be followed by the person asking me if I am of the same particular faith as they are, because they are now wondering if that's why I turned down the invitation. There is no need for anyone to ever apologize for their beliefs, or the differences between their beliefs and someone else's. I usually respond to this question very cheerfully with some variation of, "No, I'm not, but I appreciate your invitation. I'm glad you thought of me," because I *am* glad they thought of me. It's an invitation for connection and an expression of love, and I always feel touched by that.

There are times when people might feel a little embarrassed or uncomfortable by the fact that there is a difference of beliefs between you. They may feel embarrassed that they have invited you not realizing the difference was there. Or maybe they're just not sure how to respond to the fact that you have admitted that you feel differently than they do. The very best way to handle this is with a warm smile and a positive attitude. I'm not concerned by our different beliefs and they shouldn't be either. If you are relaxed, they will be relaxed.

What if you are invited to a religious event, such as a baptism or christening or a wedding at a church or synagogue, and you would really like to go but you aren't sure how to participate? You don't know what to wear, you don't know what you're supposed to say, you don't know where to sit, when to stand, and you are feeling very nervous about embarrassing yourself or the person who has invited you. Simply share your concerns with your host. If they have invited you, they are responsible for making sure that you can participate without feeling uncomfortable, embarrassed, or lost.

I have been to many religious functions and ceremonies that were novel experiences for me. I went through a lot of exploration in my teen years while traveling to all sorts of different and new religious places. I wanted to experience new things and decide what felt the most right for me. I usually went with a friend, but not always.

Here's the long and short of it: just ask! Whoever brought you or invited you is surely glad that you are there. They want to share this very important part of their lives with you, and they want you to have a positive experience. They want you to be as comfortable as possible, so just be really open and honest with them. Tell them, "I've never been to a ceremony like this before and I have no idea what I'm supposed to do. Can you help clue me in so that I don't embarrass myself?"

I have never had anyone decline to help me in this situation. On the contrary, I have been overwhelmed with gratitude and connection by people who have been so very willing to help me. I have had people point out places on the wall that told me what the order of the ceremony would be. I've had people pick up books off of benches and flip the pages for me and hand me the song book or the scripture book opened to the correct page and pointed to exactly where I needed to look on the page.

When I studied abroad in Paris my first year of college, I desperately wanted to attend mass at the Notre Dame de Paris cathedral even though I am not Catholic. It was a religious experience that I wanted to have for myself. You can note the added complication that I was traveling alone to this service and didn't speak the language. I chose to sit in a pew midway between the front and back of the sanctuary area. Someone sitting next to me noticed that I seemed a little lost and was able to help keep me on track through the entire ceremony, even though they didn't speak English, I didn't speak French, and the ceremony was mostly conducted in Latin (which was entirely new to me).

It was a beautiful and amazing experience that I will never forget. I was so touched by the sweet woman who was so willing to extend love to me as best she could in the way that she could, despite the language barrier. People are just wonderful if you are kind, open, and honest when you need help. Yes, of course it can make you nervous to step into a religious space where you are unfamiliar, but if you are coming into that space with an open heart and good intentions, you have no reason to feel embarrassed or uncomfortable.

Please don't ever turn down an invitation to something that you want to participate in because you're not sure how to dress or how to act; instead, ask for help! I feel very confident you will get all of the assistance you need and more.

MONEY

We've made it to the last "taboo" topic, money! This is such a tricky subject. There are so many situations in which the topic of money might come up. We can break this category into two subsections: 1) you asking about other people's money vs other people asking about your money and 2) you dealing with your own money.

Specifics about income and spending habits

This category is pretty black and white. When it comes to other people's money, it's none of your business. Sorry, not sorry, right? Let's elaborate. WHY is it considered so rude to ask other people about their situation with money? There are several reasons.

If the situation is not good, it can be very embarrassing for that person to end up admitting to you that they are having a hard time paying their bills, paying for an unexpected repair in their house, or managing their monthly expenses. You might unknowingly be putting that person in a very uncomfortable position by asking them a question that causes them to disclose this kind of information to you.

Now, if they are openly coming to you for help because they are in a financial crisis and they don't know what to do, of course you should help to connect them with resources that might be of assistance. Perhaps you can help point them in the direction of government aid or sit with them while they make a stressful phone call to a utility resource (light bill, water bill, etc.) to ask for an extension or a payment plan. It might be that you can help look up potential resources online and write down a few phone numbers for them to call. It is possible that you know of a community resource or charitable organization that is designed to help with their exact situation.

I need to assess whether or not my patients have adequate resources for things such as medication, food, transportation to doctor's appointments, etc., as part of my work in home health. I will often pose the question this way, "Do you have all the resources you need to meet your monthly bill obligations or do you need our social worker to come and see you to do an assessment for community assistance?" This allows them to tell me 1) yes, they have what they need or 2) no, they need help from someone who is qualified to connect them with other resources. I ask the question in such a way that bypasses the need for them to go into detail about their circumstances.

I might need to clarify, "is there anything specific that you want me to make sure to tell the social worker that you need help with such as paying for food or medications?" I need to ask that question so that the social worker will have some resources ready prior to entering the home instead of going in with no idea what kind of assistance the person needs. By phrasing my question this way, I am not asking them how much money they make, where their funds are coming from, how much their rent is, etc. Those specifics are not my business. The social worker will need to acquire those details because it is her job and she cannot connect them with the appropriate resources without that information, but it is not *my* business.

What if we are dealing with the other end of the scale? What about a person who seems to be well off? Why would they care about a few harmless questions or comments here or there? The fact is that you never truly know what a person's whole financial picture is and **it's not your business**. You might think your family member or friend who is a physician is doing very well, and maybe they are. They may also be buried in half a million dollars worth of student loan debt, coupled with the astronomical cost of malpractice insurance (especially in the US where suing people is a favorite pastime of absolutely everyone for every reason under the sun). Maybe they're feeling tighter in the wallet than they would like and they really don't want to discuss it.

It's definitely possible that they were fortunate enough to have their parents or the military pay for their entire schooling experience (or they've put an enormous effort into paying their loans off early) and they are happily living the good life. Good for them! **This is still not your business.** Have you ever had a fight with your spouse or significant other because you were furious over how much money they spent on something (guns, playing golf, tools, etc.), while completely ignoring the fact that you spent nearly that much or more on clothes or your own hobby the previous month?

Everyone has things that they feel are completely worth spending money on and things that they think are a complete waste of resources. This is different for each person, and those who do have extra money coming in will often indulge in things that others may perceive as "wasteful." Don't ask them how much they spend every month on bourbon, how much their boat set them back, how much their stock dividends pay out each quarter, or how they're able to afford xyz. They might be able to justify one thing because they've cut back somewhere else. Or, they're simply doing really well and enjoying themselves. No matter what, **it's not your business**.

The single only exception to this rule is if you are wanting to attempt to buy or pay for the same thing that they have and you are trying to get an idea of how much it will set you back. Even then, this is only appropriate to discuss with a close, personal friend. A discussion of this nature is off the table when it comes to strangers or someone you don't know very well.

You must be up front with the person at the beginning of the conversation about why you are bringing up the topic, or they will probably be sitting there the whole time thinking, "ugh, where are they going with this?" Maybe you would say, "I've been thinking about getting a boat for a while and I found one that I'm really interested in. It's got (description) and they're asking (whatever price). Does that sound like a good deal to you? Is that reasonable?"

This is a much better approach than asking, "How much did you pay for your boat?" or even, "I'm thinking about getting a boat. How much did you pay for yours?". The person wants to know that you aren't only fishing for information. If you are serious and can back up your inquiry with some previous research that you have done, people will be much more willing to be open with you.

It's possible that they realized after the fact that they overpaid and they're irritated about it. On the other hand, someone might have practically given them their boat to get out from under the maintenance, insurance, and fuel costs, and the deal they found really isn't helpful to you. If their boat is four times larger than the one you are considering, how much they paid for theirs has no bearing on your purchase. What you really need to know is what to expect when attempting this purchase and what is considered a reasonable asking price. This person could be a good resource, but how much they paid for theirs really doesn't matter. See the difference?

If someone is so rude as to start getting really nosey about how much you paid for something, put it back on them.

"Oh, are you interested in getting one of these as well? Let me see what you're looking at."

"I purchased it from (store or website). I don't know if there are any still available or not, but you can look."

"You know, I really can't remember how much I paid. I'm sure you can look it up and get an idea of how much they are if you're thinking of purchasing one."

"I don't know how much it cost. It was a gift."

A lot of times, people would rather that you did not ask how much they paid for something because they don't want the "look" of you being shocked by the number. They don't want to hear your commentary about how you would never spend so much on that item or hobby, or about how your significant other would "kill you" for buying the same thing. They also don't want to hear the uncomfortable comparison of you admitting that you wish you could afford the same thing, but you can't. How are they supposed to respond to that? "Sorry"? If someone makes such a comment to you, bypass every explanation and other thought and respond:

"Well, I am very grateful to be able to enjoy it."

The end. It's not your problem if they are shocked, appalled, jealous, or forlorn. You didn't ask their permission to spend your own money, and you definitely don't owe anyone an explanation or an apology for the decisions you make about spending what's yours. Besides, you didn't start this conversation, they did.

Let's quickly touch on the "must be nice" comments. They are usually either petty, rising out of jealousy, or forlorn. Either way, these comments are not appropriate. They don't take into consideration the place they are putting you in to feel as if you have to explain yourself or explain how something isn't as great as it seems. When someone makes a comment to you in the realm of, "it must be nice...", your answer is always simply, "it is", with a smile (as usual). If you want to be less succinct, you can add a comment about being grateful to have whatever it is. Gratitude is gracious. Apologies are unacceptable. You don't owe anyone an apology for your happiness.

The last set of reasons why it is inappropriate to ask someone about money (in particular income), wills, inheritance, etc., is twofold; this person may feel uncomfortable letting you know how much money they have or make because it highlights the difference between what they have and what "most people" have. They don't want to feel guilty and they certainly don't want to be made to feel like they need to apologize for not struggling.

Very few people inherit wealth, and many who do inherit wind up squandering it because of poor money management skills. If someone is doing well financially, it is usually because they have struggled and sacrificed to get there, or because they have been careful stewards of the blessing that was given to them by their loved ones. They have put in a massive amount of effort to secure their finances and they both 1) know the struggle personally and don't want to make you feel shamed by being where they once were and/or 2) don't want to be made to feel guilty about what they have or why they have it.

They also don't want to feel like a bank for all their family and friends. If it is commonly known that you are worth a lot of money or have a lot of money, it makes you a prime target for theft, being hacked, or being asked for a loan or a gift of money at every turn. This is emotionally exhausting and very unwelcome. People who do have money prefer to keep the specifics unknown for their own peace of mind and to encourage healthy, balanced relationships in their lives.

What if someone is bold/inappropriate enough to ask you about your specific income, inheritance, settlement, etc? This might either feel like you are not making enough, you feel fairly neutral (your income is adequate or comfortable, but you wish it could be better), or you feel pretty good about yourself. Here are some appropriate responses to the question of, "how much money do you make?"

"Things are a bit tighter than I would like right now, but we're working on it. We'll get there!"

(Please note that you do NOT have to indicate to someone that you aren't making "enough" money. However, this might be the best response when speaking to someone who knows that you are struggling. There's no sense in pretending like you aren't, but it's still none of their business exactly what you're situation is.)

"I'm pretty happy with where I am right now, but I'm always staying open for the next opportunity. You never know what's out there."

"I'm pleased with my income. I'm also very grateful to be able to be paid well for something I enjoy so much." Then you change the topic to how you enjoy your job, or more specifics about the work you do.

You can also just respond with a one word answer: "enough."

Let's say you've got that one pushy person who can't take a hint and tries to push again, "ok but seriously, how much money do you make?" Now it's time to put down a boundary. Sing it with me, **it's not this person's business** how much money you make. You can assertively respond:

"I don't feel comfortable discussing my finances. I feel that it's a private issue and I'd appreciate it if we could move on to another topic."

Last boundary layer: this person now feels that they've been called out and might be embarrassed that you didn't fold. They may make a comment about you being "touchy" or "too good to talk about it" or "making a big deal out of nothing." We're back to the Mommy Stare; is this person seriously going to act this childish? Why do they feel so entitled to this information? The most powerful thing you can say at this point is nothing. They will eventually give up and move on, and you will feel like a total boss for standing your ground without losing your head. Good job!

Them: "How much did you get in the will/inheritance/settlement?"

You: "Enough."

It doesn't matter if it was nearly nothing or an overwhelming amount. It was enough, and that's all you need to say about it. If it was an inheritance, you could say that your family member had been generous and you were grateful to them. If it was a family member who had nothing to leave behind, "they did the best they could." or, "It was modest, but it covered their final expenses and that was a huge blessing to us."

Exchanging money and paying for goods and services

When we went to a cocktail party at our club recently, we met another couple and we really hit it off. At one point the husband leaned over and jokingly said "just so you know, the golf lessons aren't free!" Apparently he had racked up $1000 worth of golf lessons the month before and was a bit sticker shocked when he got his statement. That really inspired me to address how to ask about cost without getting embarrassed.

The thing is, as we are upgrading and stepping into situations that are novel to us or are outside of our comfort zone, the question of money comes up. How do you deal with it? How do you ask about money when we're not supposed to talk about it? How are you supposed to find out how much something costs without feeling like a "poor person"? After all, wealthy people don't care about the cost of things, right? If you were truly wealthy, cost would be no object, right?

Absolutely not! The fact that you have the money to pay for

something, doesn't mean that you don't want to know where your money is going. It also doesn't mean that you aren't interested in finding a good deal on something, nor does it mean that you like to get a surprise at the end of the night or month loaded with unexpected charges. There are times when you might only be interested enough in something if it's included in the price, but not be interested in it enough to pay extra for it. You are simply trying to make an informed decision, and that's all!

Let's look at a few ways to handle questions about money. It is all about how you ask, not the fact that you are asking, just remember that. There are a few words that you want to avoid as much as possible because they create an awkward feeling around a conversation, and can potentially make the entire interaction uncomfortable. Those words are "free" and "cheap." Here are some awkward comments "AC" and some replacement comments "R"

AC: "Wow, that's so cheap!"

R: "Wow, what a great price. Thank you so much."

AC: "I'm looking for a wine that's cheaper than that."

R: "I'm looking for one that's more conservatively priced."

AC: "That's a lot cheaper than what I was looking for."

R: "I was looking for something a bit higher end."

AC: "Take one, they're free!"

R: Take one, they're complementary.

How much is that ?

AC: "It's free."

R: "It's included in the cost."

Another easy rule of thumb to keep in mind is to always assume that everything has a charge. You're just trying to find out what the charge is. If the charge happens to be zero, the person will gladly tell you that. But it saves them from the awkward response of having to tell you that something is not free. "Oh, are these free?" "Umm..no they're not."

This section also emphasizes the importance of word choice. Sometimes it's just about choosing a slightly different word that can make all the difference in how you are received, how well-spoken you seem, and how comfortable you feel in a new environment.

AC: "How much is it?"

R: "What is the charge for that service?"

Waitress asks if you would like avocado on the side.

AC: "Does that cost extra?"

R: "Is it included in the price or is there an up-charge? (*notice my use of the OR!*)

You find an item you like in a store, but the price tag is gone.

AC: "How much is this?"

R: "I'm interested in this item but I don't see the tag anywhere. Can I get a price check?"

The price of the item makes you want to fall over.

AC: "Oh my god, that's so expensive, no thank you."

R: "Ok, thank you so much!" (quietly return the item to where you found it)

or

"Thank you. I'll keep that in mind. I think I'll pass on it for today. Can I leave the item with you?" (Let them put it back where it goes.)

A salesperson asks you if you would like to put the item on hold. (Having worked retail for six years, please do not put the item on hold if you are not planning to come back and get it. It's better to put the item back into circulation right away so someone else can purchase it, rather than to inconvenience the staff and the establishment by having an item set aside that you have no intention of purchasing.)

AC: "No. There's no way I can afford that."

R: "No thank you. I'd rather keep looking around to see what else I can find."

Sales person tells you about a 15% off coupon that is being offered that doesn't put the slightest dent in how out of your price range the item is.

AC: "It's still too expensive even with the discount."

R: "Thank you for letting me know. I'll keep that in mind."

Let's say that you are in a store where there are no prices listed on anything and you're not sure what to do. Usually it's best for a sales associate to approach you and ask if you're seeing anything you like. You can also take a few items to the counter if that's appropriate in that store. Otherwise, get the attention of the sales associate at the counter and bring her over to the items you are considering.

Please have it narrowed down to only a handful of items, perhaps five at the very most. Three is better unless you are planning to buy more than one. Please don't monopolize the salesperson's time for the next hour simply because you got their attention before you were ready or knew what you thought of the items.

AC: "How much are these?"

R: "These three purses are all so beautiful. Can you let me know the price on each of them?"

You ring up at the register and the person asks if you want to donate to the fundraiser the store is running, and you don't want to.

AC: Any comment that is rude, snippy, or overexplaining every donation you've ever made in your life, or how you just donated to such-and-such last week, etc. The person doesn't care. It's their job to ask you if you want to donate, and you look like a crazy person for making a bigger deal out of it than that.

R: "Not today, thank you."

You are in a restaurant and looking at a menu that has no prices on it.

AC: "I don't see any prices. How much is all this stuff?"

R: "I've never been to this restaurant before. You'll have to explain to me how the menu works." Most of the time that's all you need to say and the server will explain everything to you. If they happen to look at you a bit confused because they're not sure what you're asking you could add, "Is each item priced separately or do you pick an entrée and a few sides? Every restaurant does these things differently." (Warm smile included of course)

There are times when you receive your bill and something has been charged incorrectly. First, you are not obligated to pay for something you didn't consume! Second, please don't assume that the person charged it incorrectly on purpose. I'm sure none of the wonderful people reading this book would be so rude, but I have been horrified in the past hearing some of the accusations that people throw out in a restaurant about a server trying to "steal their money" or some other ridiculous claim.

AC: "Hey this is wrong."

R: "Excuse me, would you mind taking a look at this? We were charged for ___, but we did not order it."

or

"This charge should've been for a children's buffet, but we were charged for an adult." (This exact scenario happened to me recently.)

What if you have paid for a service but feel very unsatisfied with the quality of the experience or product? I debated about whether I should put this scenario in the section about complaining versus constructive feedback, but I ultimately decided it was a bit too soon in that section, and more relevant to money matters. This one is a bit tricky because it is more subjective than the others. You didn't "feel" that the experience or product was worth the price you paid.

In order for this to be handled best, you need to make it more objective and you really need to think about *why exactly* you are unsatisfied. I will also say that you should keep in mind that "you get what you pay for". You can't pay a rock bottom price for something and expect a five star experience; it is unrealistic. However, if you are paying for a five star experience and receive a bare bones product, you are well within your right to speak to someone about a price adjustment.

When paying premium pricing for a product or experience, you are also paying for a certain standard of cleanliness, service, dependability, etc. Let's say you stay at a five star hotel and your room has an odd smell, the sheets have a stain on them, you had the hardest time getting someone at the concierge desk to answer the phone, the bathrooms in the lobby are dirty, and the pool hasn't been serviced lately. You have a very specific list of multiple items that are well below the typical standard for that hotel (and the price you paid to avoid these negative experiences); at this point you are well within your right to address them.

Always remain calm and polite, ask to speak with the manager "regarding some concerns with my stay" and explain to the manager in a pleasant but matter-of-fact way *exactly* what your concerns are and what you would like them to do about it. Do you want to change rooms? Do you want a discount or refund for a portion of your bill? Is it the first day and you just want them to take care of the issues by the morning so the rest of your stay will be as you expected? The key is to remain polite, calm, and respectful. The situation should be handled appropriately from there. If not, we will refer to what to do when a situation like this deteriorates and how to avoid "being a Karen" in the next section of the book, Dealing with Conflict.

PART 2

Don't forget your FREE companion workbook!

https://courses.yourconversationexpert.com/workbook

DEALING WITH CONFLICT

Up to this point, we have focused on polite conversation, including how to be well spoken, and how to navigate the three big topics of conversation that we are most commonly advised to avoid. There have been a few mentions here and there of how to deal with a situation when it becomes a bit escalated or touchy, but we have not yet addressed the difficulty of managing outright aggressive, negative, or ill-meaning people.

As nice as it would be if everyone was well spoken, courteous, empathetic, and reasonably minded, life unfortunately does not work that way. Even the most polished of people can have low days or days where they don't show up as the best version of themselves. As nice as it is to be nice, we do need to develop a strong set of skills for dealing with conflict, because conflict will arise from time to time.

I would make a small note that if you find that conflict is arising frequently for you, you may want to step back and examine whether or not you are provoking this and causing the problem. You may need to consider whether you are spending your time with people who do not respect you or your boundaries, and it may be important to rethink some of your relationships. These scenarios are better left for other books and resources. I simply mentioned them here to make sure all the bases have been covered. It's not healthy to blame yourself for everything that goes wrong around you, but a healthy reflection of "am I the problem here?" is a great step to take. The best people can recognize when their approach is ineffective and take steps to change it. Perhaps you're reading this book because you are trying to take those steps. If that is the case, I applaud you!

In order to successfully navigate the issues in this section, you are going to have to call on your mindset and boundaries to get the outcome you desire. Being able to deal with aggressive, rude, or overbearing people requires keeping the right mindset and having very firm boundaries about what you consider to be appropriate and acceptable behavior.

A final disclaimer: I would like to reiterate that this book is geared towards relationships that are not intimate in nature. This book is intended to help with your communication skills at work, when out and about, with acquaintances, with meeting new people, etc. If you find yourself regularly dealing with the issues in this section from someone who is a close friend or family member, it is possible that using some of the techniques that I discuss can help to improve the situation; however, I would strongly recommend that you seek further guidance from a counselor or other professional resource in this instance. Untangling and navigating issues with a partner, parent, sibling, or very close friend are beyond the scope of this book.

COMPLAINERS

Let's ease into this topic by starting out with a discussion about complainers. Of course everyone is entitled to have negative feelings occasionally. Nobody is going to be cheerful and upbeat 100% of the time, but some people only know how to communicate by complaining which is incredibly draining and irritating to the listener.

We've all been there, whether it is a friend, family member, or a coworker. There will always be someone in our lives that we can dread being around because we know it's going to be a constant string of negative comments. What to do?

Mindset: You cannot change a complainer. You cannot reason them into happiness. There is no way to convince them that whatever they are complaining about is not that bad. They are complaining because they want to, and no amount of logic or reason is going to change the fact that they *want* to complain. There are many reasons why a person constantly defaults to complaining as their only method of communication.

Perhaps they are bored. People who don't have anything productive to say can always find something to complain about. This person may have absolutely nothing going on in their lives worth sharing, so they spend their time gossiping and relating drama because it keeps things interesting for them.

It is possible they are seeking attention. Many times complainers have been conditioned throughout their lives that the only time someone (like a parent) would ever pay attention to them was when they were complaining about something. This person may have been raised to believe that people only want to listen to what they have to say when it's coming through in the form of a complaint. It is impossible to change conditioning that has been reinforced since childhood with logic and reason in the break room at work.

They may be completely miserable because they hate their lives; maybe things didn't turn out the way they wanted. They can't stand the situation they're in and they have no idea how to get out of it. This can or will surface in the form of constant criticism of everything and everyone around them. They are so highly critical because of their own dissatisfaction with themselves and their lives. Again, not something you're going to be able to fix by "helping them see that it's not that bad."

There can be other contributing factors, but you get the idea. A person who complains all the time has something going on within themselves that has nothing to do with you and cannot be fixed by you. You are not going to be able to lift that person's spirits for more than a few minutes. You are not going to be able to convince them that things are better than they think they are, because this would require a complete mindset overhaul on their part. Neither are you are not going to help yourself or them by indulging them in their complaining; therefore do not let yourself get swept into it.

If you are the person who is complaining all the time, I would highly encourage you to seek out a qualified counselor or professional that can help you get to the bottom of way you behave in this way. It's going to require a lot of deep digging and reconditioning, but you will feel so free and peaceful on the other side.

Boundaries: If you are the person on the receiving end of constant complaining, the issue here is setting a boundary of zero to minimal tolerance. Now, if someone is having an actual problem and you feel the need to try to give some feedback or help, feel free to try; however, my general rule is that if the person is not responding to my attempts to help, I will abandon that aim almost immediately. This doesn't mean that I expect people to take my advice all the time, but if I make an attempt to help that person and their response is one of digging in their heels that, "the situation can't be helped, it's just that the other person blah blah blah," I shut my emotions down immediately. The second I get the impression that the person only wants to complain, I'm done.

To be clear, I am not referring to isolated incidences where the person has had something truly go wrong. Maybe they have just experienced being screamed at by someone, and they are sharing it with me because it has stressed them out and they need validation that the other person's treatment of them was unnecessary. In that case, it isn't complaining, it's sharing something that happened to them.

I'm referring to the person who is continuously saying, "This place is so dirty. This food smells bad. That waiter has a weird look on his face. Look at the scratch on my purse that the cat made. I can't believe my hairstylist increased her prices by five dollars. What a selfish person. Can you believe that so-and-so said such and such to me the other day? She's the worst." See the difference? I'm referring to the people who have nothing to say except negative things. There's not really a point to what they're telling you. They're just being negative.

If you give them an inch they will take a mile. If you indulge their complaining even a little, they will latch onto you as someone that they can go to when they want to chatter off every thought in their mind for the next hour. Depending on the person and the situation, I will take one of two approaches.

If this is a person that is completely optional for me to be around, I will usually take the approach of ignoring them. The second they start complaining, I emotionally shut down and make myself busy with something to make it very obvious that I'm not listening. I keep my responses very limited to mostly, "mmm hmm," or a faint smile if I feel obligated to be cordial. If I'm unable to leave the situation (such as sitting beside them at a meeting), I try to make it very obvious that I am super bored (or really into the meeting) and not listening. They will usually become irritated or possibly a little confused at my reaction and move on to someone who will indulge them, and thank goodness for that!

I would MUCH rather be considered a stick in the mud, rude, aloof, whatever definition fits, than be stuck listening to so much negativity for the rest of my life. I don't mind this person not liking me one bit. As a matter of fact, it does me a huge favor if they don't like me. Beware, you might then become the focus of their next round of complaining. That person will likely enjoy complaining about how rude you are to the next person they can corner. Please see this behavior for what it is and let it go. If the other person is going to indulge them, they are also a drama seeker and not someone you want to be around. The people who are worth your time and energy will also recognize this person for who they truly are and would rather be with you than them anyway. Your vibe will attract your tribe.

A note on this; don't complain about the complainer. It puts you in the exact same box as them and does you no favors. You complaining about how much other people complain is totally pointless and counterproductive. Even if someone makes a comment about someone else being a complainer and you totally agree with them, you can keep it very short with a response like, "Well, I don't disagree," while smiling and moving on to the next subject. You both get it. You both agree about it. There is no need to stoop to that level and elaborate on it.

Whenever possible, I will simply walk away. If I walk into

the break room at work and there's that person who only ever complains about things, I will grab the coffee or whatever I came in for, smile at everyone and walk right back out the door. If you are not in the room, they can't corner you. If I am chatting with a group of people and the complainer walks up and starts complaining, I will turn around and walk off. No need to bring any attention to it, but no obligation to indulge that person either.

If this is a person who you want or need to spend time with, ignoring them is not going to be the best approach. You're going to end up causing a bigger problem, especially if this is a family member or a supervisor and you are coming across as rude and uncaring. In this instance, the best approach is either distraction or focus.

I generally make a very large effort to not interrupt people, but similar to the monologuer we spoke about at the very beginning of the book, the person who is complaining doesn't really have a point to what they're saying. They are not really going to get offended if you suddenly change the subject because they're not emotionally invested in what they're talking about. They simply don't have anything else to say most of the time. If you can change the subject, they will be just as happy to chat about that.

The way you do this is by reacting as though a sudden thought has come to you that you've just remembered and can't wait to share. You show your excitement about the story that you have and launch right into it. It could be a funny video you saw the other day, an adorable puppy you met last week, something funny your child did this morning, a hilarious story on the news about a duck befriending a deer, etc. Maybe something pops up on your phone and you share it. Anything will work. Just change the subject.

Usually, this strategy will be successful. Every once in a while, the person is so stuck on their mode of complaining that they can't let it go, and as soon as you are done distracting them they launch right back into it. Here's the thing though, the boundary that you are laying down is an unwillingness to indulge the complaining because simply put, it's irritating and also stressful and emotionally draining to listen to other people complain all the time. You have a right to protect your personal energy and mental health by refusing to allow yourself to be surrounded by negativity.

If the person tries to go right back to complaining, I might go back-and-forth once or twice on interrupting them and changing the subject again. If they are persistent, I will either make up an excuse to walk away or rarely, I might point out the problem in a bit of a joking way with a comment such as "wow, isn't there anything nice going on you want to talk about?", but be careful as this can be taken the wrong way and go downhill quickly. You're going to have to be the judge of when, if ever, you might feel that this comment would be appropriate. Sometimes simply calling the person out will be enough to subdue them and stop the behavior. You might decide it's worth ruffling their feathers and making them mad if it will get the point across that you aren't enjoying this type of conversation. In the future, they will be more aware of the topics they bring up around you. Use with caution.

GOSSIPERS

The reasons why a person will gossip are the same reasons why a person complains. They are bored, they are unhappy with their own lives, they were positively reinforced with this behavior growing up, etc. The difference here is that complaining is usually harmless, but gossiping is often malicious.

Mindset: Beyond keeping in mind the dysfunctional reasons behind why a person would gossip, it is also important to remember some things when a person is trying to gossip about someone to you.

The first thing to keep in mind is that what a person is saying about another person is not necessarily true. No matter the source they heard it from, no matter if they say they witnessed it with their own eyes. If they are spreading rumors about someone else, their intent is malicious and therefore suspicious.

There are two sides to every story, and without knowing all the details,we are unable to draw a conclusion. And here's the real rub, you're never going to know all the details. This person has one version of the story, just as the person who is the subject of their gossiping does. As with most things, the truth is probably somewhere in the middle. Unless the situation directly impacts you, and it might not *really* impact you even if you initially think it does, it is still likely none of your business. Oh yes, we're back to that again! It's amazing how many things in this world are simply none of our business.

Oh she stole so-and-so's husband? Maybe she did, maybe

she didn't. Maybe there is a whole truckload full of information you don't know about the situation. Maybe she's a homewrecker, maybe the home was already wrecked. Maybe this, maybe that. It's not my husband, and it is most certainly not my business.

Oh she did this or that when she was younger? First, it might not even be true. Secondly, even if it is true, who am I to judge someone else's decisions or actions when I don't know the full story? Did I somehow get harmed by one of those actions? No, so it's not my business.

Oh he's a gigantic liar and can't be trusted? Maybe. Maybe not. Maybe the person telling me the story is the liar. Maybe the person lied about one thing for a reason deeply personal to him and it's not my business whether he decided to divulge the truth or not. Did he lie to me and cause me to make a decision against my best interest by trusting him? If not, it's not my business. I might be a little bit more cautious and do some more fact checking because of this information, but usually people who are pathological liars have a lot of psychological issues going on that creates this compulsory problem. I don't want to be around people like that, nor do I wish to indulge them. This person is wasting my time and again, this is not my business!

She's had this surgery or that procedure done? Good for her! She did something for herself that she felt improved her appearance and her self-esteem, well more power to her. Someone else's negative opinion of her decision is not my business.

He's really into this weird thing over here? Who cares! Is that weird thing he's into affecting my daily life? How in the world could it? Perhaps I won't go to those parties with him or maybe I won't invite myself over to whatever it is. He didn't ask my opinion anyway. As my husband would say, "I don't care if that's what you want to do, but don't get mad at me when I turn down the invitation to join you".

Boundaries: Again, the boundary issue here is not allowing yourself to be surrounded by negativity. It's not good for our mindset or energy. Another negative side effect is that entertaining someone by listening to them speak in this way implies that you are also prone to this behavior and will tarnish your reputation. Remember as a child being told to be careful who your friends were because you would be assumed to be guilty of the things they got in trouble for? It's the same principle here; by listening or giving minimal feedback, you are complicit in the gossiping by not actively doing something to put a stop to it.

When it comes to this behavior, simply ignoring the person while they gossip is not going to be as good of an approach as it is with the person who is complaining. There is an implication of condoning the gossip if you are not speaking out against it. Anyone who overhears this can imply that instead of, "she was gossiping to so-and-so about something", that, "they were gossiping about so-and-so" and by default you are part of "they."

Let's look at some comments that you can make to help cut off a gossiper from continuing with their juicy news:

"You know, I wasn't there so I can't say for sure what happened and I think it would be best to not make assumptions."

"I really hope that's not true, but I wasn't there so I think it's best if I mind my own business."

"If that happened, it's a shame, but I would rather not talk about it since the person is not here to give their side of the story."

"We never really know all the details of how things happen. There might be more to this than we are aware of. I'd rather not get myself mixed up in it."

"Of course I don't condone sleeping with someone who is married, but I don't know the full story and I don't feel comfortable talking about people behind their backs."

"You know, I've heard from other sources that there was a completely different set of circumstances around that. I think that none of us here really knows what happened and we should probably let the people who are involved handle it."

"I think there's a lot more to the situation than what I know about it, and I would rather keep my nose out of other people's business. I know I wouldn't want people sharing my business with others who it didn't concern."

"I know people aren't perfect, but I like to give others the benefit of the doubt wherever I can. I'd rather hope that they had the best of intentions and leave it at that."

In each of these sets of remarks, I am clarifying that I am absolutely not comfortable continuing with the conversation. If necessary, I will clarify that I don't condone the accused behavior, while also phrasing it in such a way that I am not assuming that the information is true. I usually try to point out that there is missing information to help cue the other person that they might want to back off about their certainty with the "facts" they are presenting.

Very rarely do I get pushed back on this. To be honest, it usually is a bit shaming to the person who is gossiping that I am responding to them in this way. I have made it clear that I feel like they are gossiping and that I'm uncomfortable with it. People don't usually insist on continuing after these types of comments. The response is usually somewhere along the lines of, "Well I guess you're right. We can talk about something else," and the conversation moves on. Sometimes I will get a person who is honestly curious about my response and may ask something along the lines of, "so you don't believe that any of that's true?," and I respond with something like:

"I don't know whether it's true or not, but I know that I don't feel comfortable talking about it, and I would rather give people the benefit of the doubt when I don't actually know what happened. I would rather leave the situation up to the people involved in it and not give my opinion on something that I don't have all the facts about."

That's usually enough to stop it. I'm really repeating what I said in the first place. I'm not elaborating on what I do or don't think. I'm being very clear that there's a boundary around my willingness to participate in something I perceive as gossip.

What if the person is gossiping about someone who they feel has wronged them in some way? What if their husband left them for another woman and they are complaining about this other woman? This situation does affect the person who is gossiping, but it does not directly affect me, and what that "other woman" does is not my business.

In this type of situation, I try not to encourage the person to divulge a lot to me, but I also am not wanting to be heartless about the very real stress and hurt that they are feeling. We might need to go back to some of the "non-comment comments" that I referred to at the beginning of the book.

"Oh goodness."

"Oh dear. That's not good."

"Well that's definitely a lot."

I absolutely WILL NOT make comments that hype the person up and encourage them to go on and on about it. You will not catch me saying things like, "He did not!" "What a hussy!" "Girl I would slap her upside the head!" No, no, no. Now if this is your very best friend in the whole world, that is a different subject entirely. We all need that friend who will go there with us over a glass of wine in our living room and call our ex all the mean names.

I'm talking about maybe one of your favorite friends at work and you both are on the clock in the break room. Or any time there is a third person standing there. A third pair of ears comes with a third mouth and that mouth will run off and repeat everything the ears heard to the last person you want to know about it.

With the exception of your very best friend in the privacy of somewhere no one will hear you, your best bet in this situation is to express condolences to them for the hardship they have been through while continuing to remain neutral about the third person who is not there to defend themselves.

This is the time to revisit that conversation you and I had at the beginning of the book about life being hard. Life is hard for everyone. It's hard for me, it's hard for you, it's hard for the person who is hurting, it's hard for the person who wronged the person who is speaking to you, and it's hard for everyone caught in the middle of the situation.

People are humans and humans don't always make great decisions. Hurt people hurt people. I try really hard to maintain the stance that I may not understand why someone did what they did, and I might not agree with their decision, but I still don't know all the facts. I don't know everything that went into why that person made the decisions that they did.

And as a last resort, when I'm really feeling compelled to chime in because the situation is so extreme, I remind myself that speaking ill of that person does not improve the situation at all. Dragging out everything that person did into the open is not undoing the hurt, it's not going to put the broken glass back together, it's not going to help anyone for it to be talked about. Even if what that person did was awful, what good does it do for me to talk badly about them? What positive outcome could be had from calling them names and bringing up their mistakes or listing out all their sins? Nothing. It changes nothing. It only mixes me up in somebody else's drama and brings down my reputation as someone who indulges in people speaking badly about other people.

So I try to focus on what does matter. "Are there kids involved in the situation? How are they handling all of this distress and change?" "I'm so sorry you've gone through so much stress, do you have a counselor that you're able to speak to about these things?" "I'm so sorry she does those things to you when you're around her. Have you made moves to remove yourself from the situation so that you are no longer around her anymore?"

Let's not focus on the actions of the past that can't be changed. Let's focus on making sure the people we care about are supported and cared for and safe. Let's brainstorm action steps we can take to improve the situation for ourselves and those we care for, such as children who may be involved. A lot of times if someone is trashing another person to you, it's because the person who is speaking is stressed out and overwhelmed. Let's focus on that instead of the third person. You and I can't control what that third person chooses to do, but we can come up with an action plan to keep the stress about it minimized.

STANDING UP
FOR OTHERS

What if the situation becomes more pressing than simply ignoring gossip or changing the subject? What if someone is being bullied, put down, or overwhelmed by another person? Let me be abundantly clear that I would never encourage you to put yourself in an unsafe situation. I do not condone you taking an action that could bring harm to you by putting yourself in the middle of something you cannot control.

Do not attempt to resolve a violent situation by stepping into it. Alert the proper authorities. Call the police. Call 911. Let the people who are professionals in this situation do their job. Unless you have a badge or a license showing that you are the person who is supposed to step into a violent or potentially violent situation, you have no business attempting to do so. You are only more likely to make the situation worse and cause harm to yourself.

Whew! Glad to know you've got common sense and you are planning to use it when it comes to these situations. I am not referring to extreme situations. I'm referring to general nit picky, rude, or condescending types of comments.

Yes, there is the option of not saying anything. Simply ignore the comment and pretend like it wasn't said in the first place. You ALWAYS have the option of not saying anything with every topic in this section of the book. I, however, can't. I cannot tolerate rude behavior, nor stand by and watch when someone is being embarrassed by someone else.

Our focus is on what to say when you *want* to say something but you aren't sure the best way to navigate the situation. I will tell you in these scenarios how I usually handle it, because I nearly always say something, and very rarely end up in any kind of escalated altercation because of it. On the rare instance when that does happen, it still feels worth it to me because at least there is a chance that the person will think twice before doing something like that again. If they can be called out once, it can happen again, and it might make the idea of making those comments seem less appealing. And maybe, the person who was on the receiving end of the mean comment might feel more justified in standing up for themselves next time.

Mindset: The person who is being mean, rude, or condescending in this situation has a problem that you are not going to be able to fix with a single comment. People who are this negative and hurtful have layers and layers of issues that they don't deal with, and the negativity is spilling over from there. Remember that comment above, "hurt people hurt people"? This is it on full display.

This person is likely so unhappy with themselves or their own lives that they are lashing out at those around them. There is no real purpose to their hurtful comments except to open the pressure valve on their own frustrations, overwhelm, dissatisfaction with life, and/or to display their lack of maturity. I have actually had to deal with on a grand scale working in home health. It never fails to shock me to see the way people speak to their family members. There may be a wide range of reasons, and we will get further into issues specific to caregiver burden later in the book, but let's examine the most negative situations here.

There is no point in trying to argue the validity of the negative comment that has been made. If a person is frustrated and makes a mean comment and you take the approach of trying to prove that person wrong, you are feeding the monster. Don't give them carte blanche to list every single thing this person has ever done that has frustrated them or every time they've been in a similarly frustrating situation. They now have a foothold to dig in and prove that they are right because you have posed the problem as one of "right and wrong."

Boundaries: Instead, focus on the real issue, which is that it's not ok to be rude to someone else. The boundary here is setting the standard that you will not tolerate or condone ill treatment of other people while you are present. You will not allow yourself to feel complicit in a demeaning behavior or let a situation around you be controlled by the angriest/loudest person in the room. You are also helping to give an example of setting boundaries for the person who is being demeaned. Your actions will give them the confidence or the words to handle a similar situation differently in the future.

An older patient may drop something while trying to bring it to me and her daughter says with irritation, "Geez mom, you're so clumsy. What's wrong with you? Why can't you hold onto things?". Well good grief, perhaps the mom is clumsy, or maybe she drops things all the time because of weakness, arthritis, or coordination deficits. On the other hand, this could be the first time she's ever dropped anything. It doesn't matter if the comment is technically right or wrong. Is there any good reason to be so disrespectful?

Whatever the reason the daughter in this scenario has for making the comment, it's not going to be helped if my response is one of equal aggravation. If I respond, "That's a rude thing to say. What's wrong with you? Why would you speak that way to your own mother?," I am as much a part of the problem as anyone else. Now I've opened a whole Pandora's box of giving the daughter free reign to list out everything this mother has ever done to aggravate her, and I'm going to get it line by line or all smashed together in a fit.

No matter what, my rude comment has now put us on equal footing. We are both being rude or condescending. She to her mother, and me to her. This option will never end well. This also immediately places the other person in defensive mode by calling them out so directly, and they will certainly not back down. Now you have challenged them to prove they are right or justify themselves, but you have not left any room for them to correct their behavior or apologize.

Instead of being snippy, I will keep my tone even, my volume soft, (and even a bit lower than usual,) and make a kind comment directed at the mother. We're going back to the "life is hard and none of us are perfect" approach. When the daughter makes a comment about the mother being so clumsy, I might respond by smiling at the mother and saying, "Don't worry. I drop things all the time! Nothing was broken. Everything is just fine." No one is perfect. We all make mistakes (including the daughter). No damage done. No need to be upset. You are sending this message to both of them, but addressing the comment to the mother.

Another example is when an elderly wife is caring for her husband and he asks her to bring him something, but she brings the wrong item. He says, "Danggit, can't you get anything right? I didn't ask for that, I asked for (whatever other item)!" Whew! Hold on while I smooth my feathers because they are definitely ruffled. Ugh.

As much as I might want to get on my soapbox about how he's perfectly capable of getting up and getting whatever it is himself, and she's working herself to the bone trying to keep up with his demands, and would it kill him to get his own dang whatever-it-was, I will refrain. However, I will not let the comment pass unnoticed. I might smile at her and say, "It's so hard to keep up with everything when you're doing so much. You take great care of him and I'm sure he really appreciates it," and then I might give him a serious Mom Look that says 'aren't you going to say thank you to your wonderful wife?'

I had a patient one time who I had started to dread to see because of how rude and dismissive he was toward his wife. This woman did everything for him. She cooked, cleaned, kept the house, ran all the errands by herself, and even paid the bills because he couldn't anymore. She bathed him every single day, shaved him, combed his hair, ect. She took excellent care of him, but he only grunted and commanded her to do things continually. "Martha, get me a glass of water." "Martha, get my comb." "Martha, move that chair." "Martha, cut on the lights for her so she can see. She can't work like this." (referring to me)

It was all I could take just to listen to it. This woman darted around without a word doing anything and everything he said to do. One time she made a comment about making something for dinner and I said it sounded like it would be a wonderful meal and he said, "Probably not. She's not a very good cook.", and I thought my head was going to explode. She looked like she wanted to disappear, which broke my heart.

I looked at him and said jokingly, "Oh no! Is that you volunteering to start cooking around here?" "No, no! I sure can't cook." he said. I kept pushing the idea, "Well with everything she does around here all day, every day I'm sure she'd be more than happy to have you cook for her! She could put her feet up and rest and let you do everything. That would be a real treat for her. Why don't we work on that in therapy today? How about we go into the kitchen and figure out what you're going to cook for dinner tonight?" (I gave her a big wink. She thought it was hilarious and she ventured in on the joke too: "Oh sweetie, that would be so nice! I'd love for you to cook for me.")

He was definitely flustered at this point. "Oh no, no. Not me. I can't boil water." I went for it. "Well then you better start being a lot sweeter to her if you want her to keep cooking for you. I don't like cooking and I sure wouldn't spend so much time in the kitchen for you, if you were going to tell people I wasn't any good at it!" "Oh, she's not a bad cook. I was only saying that to tease her." I had to give one more little push because his original tone had been anything but teasing. "Well you better be careful with that teasing, she's likely to get upset and take it personally. I know you wouldn't want to hurt her feelings. She takes such good care of you and works around the clock to do everything for you. You better not give her the impression she's not appreciated. That might really make her upset." He finally conceded, "Oh I know she does. She takes good care of me. I'm sorry honey. I didn't mean anything by it."

Whew. I can't fix their marriage, and I'd probably never convince her to really push back on his attitude if I spent a year coaching her about it, but for one sweet beautiful moment we at least had a little fun, she was able to laugh and crack a smile when she had been on the verge of tears, and she got an "I'm sorry" out of him. It might be the biggest win she'd had in a decade. I also made it pretty clear to him that, at least while I was around, he needed to keep that whip cracking in check. Most importantly, I acknowledged her efforts, and validated her hard work and any frustrations she might have been feeling about how unappreciated she was. That was the bigger point. I was pushing the issue for her.

Perhaps we have a female patient who I am explaining the exercises to, and I make a comment to the husband about doing some certain thing with her. She might dismissively say, "Oh he doesn't know how to do that." as if he was an idiot or incompetent. I then look at the husband (who is clearly embarrassed or irritated by this comment) and smile and remark, "Well I certainly don't know how to do everything. I'll explain how to do it. I'm sure we can get it figured out." I wouldn't want anyone to hold me to the standard of being perfect or all-knowing, and I definitely don't expect that of others, and neither should anyone else.

I've had countless children walk into their elderly parents' house and say something along the lines of "Mom, it looks awful in here. I can't believe you've let it get like this!" and that poor mom look so ashamed. I usually respond by looking right at the mom and smiling kindly and remarking, "Well it's hard enough to take care of yourself when you've been feeling so bad, much less take care of anything else. The house will survive until you can get your strength back. I think it's just fine." Let's all remember for a second everything your mother has been through, and where *exactly* have you been anyway if you didn't know this house looked like this?

When I worked retail, there were a few occasions where I was helping a woman with finding an item of clothing or answering a question about something and the guy (I won't call him a man) she was with would make a horrible comment to the tune of, "It doesn't matter if they have it in your size. It's not going to fit you/look good on you anyway." Murder is wrong, right? For some awful reason, I don't have the power to make people disappear or the ability to convince people in abusive relationships to leave their abusers, but I can at least make an attempt to show the insulted person some kindness.

I would look straight at her and say, "Well you won't know until you try it. I try on things all the time that I think will look great and then they don't. If this one doesn't work we can look at a different one." If I could, I would find an excuse to have her come with me to the fitting room so I could have her try on something I 'thought she would like.' It was really an excuse to get her away from this awful person for a few minutes so she could cry privately or collect herself. If he tried to follow I would give a cheerful, "Now, now, you know I can't let men in the ladies fitting room! You'll have to wait here."

I would never tear down her boyfriend because she already knew the truth. She didn't need me to point it out. I wouldn't attempt to convince her to leave him. She already knows that too. I would tell her that it hurt my heart to see her insulted like that and ask if I could give her a hug (I'm a hugger, if you couldn't tell). I would squeeze her really hard and say something like, "Don't let other people make you feel bad about yourself, ok?" and then give her some space. You can't fight other people's demons for them.

The pattern across all these scenarios is this:

1) Address your follow up comments to the person being insulted. The insulting party has said something to make this person feel "less than." You can help to lift them back up by addressing them directly. Make sure you are using eye contact.

2) Smile. Whoever insulted them might have been being rude, but you intend nothing but kindness. Reassure them with your smile and energy that there is nothing to insult as far as you can see.

3) Make a comment that effectively neutralizes the insult. You aren't arguing with the rude comment ("she's not clumsy" "the house isn't messy" "I'm sure she's a good cook" "she's not overweight"), you are helping to give a voice to that person by pointing out that no one is perfect and you are not bothered. There's nothing to be upset or embarrassed about. Everything is fine.

When the person sees that you have no intention of entertaining the rude comments (boundaries!), they will usually stop. You didn't argue with or insult them, so they have no need to become hostile or defensive towards you. They also recognize that if you are trying to provide a feeling of positivity, understanding, and empathy, they are going to look like the bad guy if they continue making negative comments. They would usually rather preserve their own reputation than continue trying to drag down someone else's. Checkmate.

WHEN SOMEONE IS INSULTING YOU

It's one thing when you are listening to someone being insulted by a third party. It feels like a *completely* different issue when you are the target of rude comments. When someone around you is being mistreated it can be irritating, even upsetting, but it doesn't have the same fight or flight response as what occurs when you are the one on the receiving end. Let's spend a little time going over some very necessary skills to help you deal with these overwhelming situations.

It takes a lot of self awareness and self control to maintain your composure when someone is inciting a cascade of adrenaline to course through your veins. It can be helpful to remind yourself "I'm not actually in danger here. This person might be yelling/aggressive, but they are not actually going to hurt me. I'm not in physical danger." That may feel a bit extreme, but when someone starts yelling or being aggressive, your body will start reacting as though you *are* in physical danger, and reminding yourself that you are not can help you to gather your thoughts.

When someone starts yelling at you, your heart rate will speed up, your thoughts will start to race, your hands might even start to shake. It's a normal reaction, and it can be modified. Reminding yourself that you are not actually in physical danger will help organize your thoughts. Take a really deep breath, hold it at the top for 2-3 seconds, and let it out slowly. Take a few purposefully slow and steady breaths to calm yourself down. You can even place your hands together to steady them. Give your hand or forearm a little squeeze with your other hand. The deep pressure is calming to the nervous system.

It is natural to start fidgeting (tapping your fingers, shaking your foot, bouncing your knee, etc.) because of all the nervous energy. The best remedy? Do the opposite! Instead of tapping your fingers, use them to slowly stroke the backside of your hand or the side of your leg back and forth. The slow back and forth movement will steady the nervous system (it will help calm you down) and you can focus your attention on following the movement instead of jumping all over the place. Alternatively, tell yourself to be as still as a statue and refuse to indulge the urge to move. The fidgeting will actually increase the internal response you are trying to calm, and will also cue the other person that they are flustering you, which will make them feel even more bold.

Research has shown that the human brain is wired in such a way that people use a lot of mirroring behavior when interacting with others. If someone we are speaking to tilts their head to the left, we unconsciously might tilt our heads in a mirrored fashion. If someone leans in when speaking to us, we often feel the urge to lean in towards them as well. If someone's voice becomes louder, we will raise ours to match without even realizing it. And when we lower our voices and slow the pace of our speech, the people listening will mirror this by lowering their voices and also become more calm and attentive. Use this knowledge to your advantage!

This is honestly the Secret Sauce to dealing with every single one of these scenarios here. If your tone, pitch, pace, and volume all start to escalate, the situation is completely hopeless. You have lost control of yourself and therefore the entire situation. It is only through calm inner strength that you will be able to navigate these spaces. You MUST remain the eye in the center of the storm. Everything around you can be whirling chaos, but you must be calm and centered. If you cannot manage this, you must remove yourself as quickly and gracefully from the situation as possible.

This is why I spend so much time and energy explaining the mindset you need to successfully navigate these situations. If you can keep in mind the real reason (that has nothing to do with you) that a person is acting in a negative way, you can remain calm. You aren't taking it personally, therefore you can maintain an emotional distance between yourself and the situation that will help you to keep your wits about you and help you make good decisions with your words and actions. You are choosing to act with reason, instead of reacting from passionate emotions.

Remember what I mentioned about mirroring behaviors? You will feel a strong urge to speak quickly, to interrupt the person, and to raise your voice because they are doing that to you. The cure? Do the opposite! Make a very purposeful effort to speak a little bit more softly and slowly than you usually would. When you feel the urge to interrupt the person, use it as an internal cue and an opportunity to breathe deeply and slowly instead. Let them get all their words out while you focus on breathing.

The goal is to try to calm yourself down back to a normal/neutral disposition. You might be able to achieve it, you might not, but do the best you can and accept it as your best effort. Have you ever tried to run in the shallow end of a swimming pool? Not swimming, but a silly effort at "speed walking" through the water? Think about moving through water when you move your body during these situations. No matter how much effort you put into moving quickly, the resistance of the water simply won't allow it. And the faster you try to move, the more resistance is built up in the water and the harder it actually is to get to the other side.

You will successfully get to the other side of the pool by taking slower but longer (more purposeful) steps. You will be moving more slowly than if you were on dry land, but much more efficiently than when you are flailing. Your movements during an overwhelming situation should be similar. Slower than "on dry land" (a usual situation where you are not stressed), and very mindful and purposeful. The adrenaline in your system will make you want to zigzag around like a squirrel trying to decide how to get out of the way of a moving car. Instead, move as though you are in water.

You should have the time to think, "I'm placing my hand on the computer mouse. Now I'm moving it back to the keyboard. I'm picking this pencil up off the floor. I'm reaching for the phone to pick it up." etc. Place things down very carefully. People drop things when they are stressed because the fight or flight reaction in their bodies is throwing off their coordination and sense of timing, and then the clumsiness flusters them even more. Force your hands to place things down carefully on the table or desk in front of you. Take the extra second to straighten it after you've placed it.

These small actions will help you to calm yourself down and will also cue the other person that you are calm and collected (even if you are not). The mirroring will now be working in your favor. They will lower their voice if your voice is soft. They will slow their pace if your pace is slower. They will slow down if you slow down. This may not happen immediately. Sometimes it might work like that, but it will likely require persistent calm on your part before they can also calm down to match your energy, but stick with it.

And here's my ace in my back pocket; take a brief moment of silence. This is not an ugly silence. This isn't me glowering at them or giving them an evil look. This isn't the deep breath you take right before you start yelling, in fact it is the opposite. This is like yogic breathing. Think of it as an energetic reset for both of us. A chance for the both of you to connect to yourselves and the situation before taking another step.

If you have ever practiced yoga, you might be familiar with the pattern of breathing that is frequently paired with movements. It enhances relaxation and connection with your body. It helps to facilitate the "flow" of movement that promotes so much peace and balance in your body and energy. You will often be instructed to take "a big breath in" and then move through the next motion "as you exhale." This is exactly the approach I mean. You take a big centering breath in and then respond to the person on the exhale.

Sometimes my pause might be a bit more pointed. I will often use silence to give the other person a chance to collect themselves. Sometimes if they have just said something especially rude to me, I might give them that Mom Look where I will freeze and raise an eyebrow with a very controlled expression that conveys the thought, "Did you hear what you just said? Are you sure that's what you wanted to say?" I have used this a number of times working retail. It can work over the phone too, but it's most effective in person.

Mindset: The person who is yelling or out of control is not in their right mind. This might be a temporary moment of insanity. Maybe their dog had been run over the night before and they are on the brink of a meltdown already, and the card machine at your work being out of order was the last straw before they totally lost it. Maybe they are a person riddled with emotional issues that they refuse to deal with, and they are like this to everyone they meet. It is possible that they have 25 things to get done in the next 3 hours and they are so stressed out and overwhelmed that they can't function properly.

Whatever it is, 99.9% of the time it has absolutely nothing to do with you. I am NOT saying that it is ok for them to be rude and impatient and treat you poorly. I am only trying to help you get into the right mindset to deal with it so that you can have the best outcome possible. I don't allow people to treat me poorly, but I have to start by getting into the right headspace, and that means trying to understand the situation for what it is and what it isn't.

As I suggested when it comes to dealing with someone insulting another person, when someone is insulting you it is the most effective course of action to focus on the behavior that is unacceptable rather than trying to parry their complaints point for point. If some calls you a jerk, there's no point in you retorting, "I am not a jerk! I'm a very nice person! I even got a customer service award last month and they don't give those to jerks!" We're not on the playground. You can do better than that.

Are you a jerk? Well I hope not. If you are, you should probably do something about that. Most likely you are not a jerk, so let's not focus on trying to prove it either way. The problem with that is that you can't win. You can't prove to someone that you are not a jerk, so let's move on. How about we focus on the fact that it's not nice (or mature) to call someone a jerk?

There are a million ways to approach these problems incorrectly. These situations are very delicate because the person is already super hyped up. When someone is very upset, they are in the middle of their own fight or flight response. Try to keep that in mind. Their hearts and thoughts are racing. They are probably shaking. Their ability to reason is diminished, and they will have to put effort into calming themselves down before they can effectively communicate with you.

I had to deal with this constantly when I worked in collections. People would answer the phone yelling, cussing and carrying on. They didn't know me. They'd never met me. They couldn't tell you a single fact about me. They were yelling at me, but they weren't yelling at ME. They were yelling because they were frustrated and overwhelmed, and I was an easy target for their anger.

Boundaries: It is not ok for someone to overwhelm you with their words or actions. It is not ok for someone to be rude, condescending, or abusive with their approach, no matter how bad their day has been or how much stress they have been under. We're going to go over several ways to help de-escalate a situation, but I want to explain a sticking point for me. I have had countless times when a person has apologized to me at the end of my interaction with them because of their behavior. I WILL NEVER respond to their apology by saying "it's ok."

Let me be very clear: it is NOT ok for them to have acted the way that they did. The reason behind the actions may have come to light. Maybe it was stress or overwhelm or a misunderstanding. Maybe we got to the bottom of it, but they lost control of themselves and mistreated me with their behavior and that is not ok. If someone says, "I'm sorry I yelled at you" or, "I'm sorry I was so rude to you" or whatever, I never ever respond by saying, "it's ok." I will always respond by saying, "thank you." They apologized and I thanked them for their apology. If I want to be extra graceful about it and am feeling amicable towards them at this point, I might add something like, "Thank you. I'm glad we were able to get to the other side of it and find a good solution for you. I hope you have a great rest of your day."

For my own sake, for the next person's sake, and in case they feel the urge to act that way towards someone else in the future, I will not let them off the hook by saying that yelling at me or calling me names was ok. It wasn't. I do truly appreciate their apology, and I have no intentions of holding a grudge or shaming them, so I accept their apology with a thank you and well wishes for a better end to their day. I would strongly urge you to consider this for yourself. This is yet another example of how exact word choices matter and make a difference.

Right out of high school, there was a night at the department store when I was working until closing time. My department was very large and extended around a corner out of sight of the registers. It was so late at night and so close to closing that I was folding clothes and straightening my department, unaware that any customers were in my section. All of a sudden this lady appears out of nowhere and with as much sass as she could muster, snarls at me and shouts, "ARE YOU COMING UP HERE TO CHECK ME OUT OR WHAT??"

Whew. Breathe. Instead of hurling a belt buckle at her head and telling her I wouldn't check her out if I was starving and she was trying to buy me food, I simply froze and stared at her really hard for about 3 solid seconds with my mouth tight and my eyebrow raised. Did you hear what you just said? Did you hear how unbelievably rude you just were to me? I made myself breathe and let that insanely ass-y comment hang in the air like a bad smell. Only for a few short seconds. Just long enough to let the comment process in her own ears. It worked. She visibly shifted in front of me from intense anger and impatience to a calmer and more reserved demeanor.

I spoke very calmly and more slowly than usual (trying to control my own anger). I tried to keep my tone mildly friendly but notably controlled. You cannot sound like a child and be in control of that kind of situation. This is not the time to kill them with kindness. I finally said, "I did not know that anyone still needed to check out. I was straightening the department since we are closing down. I can check you out now if you come with me to the register."

During the checkout process I moved with control. Not like a sloth. Not being slow to be petty, but deliberate calm movements. I refused to show this lady that she had upset me or that I was going to rush around in a tizzy simply because she was feeling impatient. She made a few attempts to chit chat with me while I rang up her purchases as though we had been shooting the breeze all night. I was not rude. I did not want to make the situation worse by acting angry, petty, sarcastic, etc. I was a good person and a hard working employee and I had been treated very poorly for no good reason. I was understandably reserved and careful.

My energy conveyed to her that she had made a mistake. It was the energy of someone who refuses to say, "it's ok" when someone apologizes for wronging you. It's not ok. And what's more, there had been no apology. She was attempting to pretend like she had not been unbelievably rude. She was attempting to make it seem that she had been nice to me this whole time and that we were now going to have a slumber-party-sweet check out process, and we weren't.

Let's talk a bit more about the person who is off the deep end with their frustration and is flat out yelling at you. What do you do? I will tell you what doesn't work first. Trying to become bigger and louder and attempting to overpower that person back does **not** work. At least it never has for me. If someone is yelling at you and you try to 1) talk over them or 2) yell at them to stop yelling or 3) become hyper aggressive and say snappy harsh things like, "don't talk to me like that," the situation will only escalate.

This person is already in the midst of an adrenaline cascade. If you start yelling back at them, it will only dump more of that adrenaline into their system and cause them to take it up to the next level. Fighting fire with fire here is not going to work. You have to douse the fire with water, and the water is your calm disposition.

It is not ok for that person to be so aggressive and rude, but trying to explain that somehow rarely gets the point across (surprise). Here's what I usually do. I usually give the person a minute or two to get whatever it is off their chest. I let them say all the words that they want to say and blow off the steam of their stress.

Interrupting a person while they are in the middle of a rant typically makes the whole thing worse and can easily kickstart them into one of those, "and that's another thing!..." sort of issues. While they are yelling, I am practicing my deep breathing, finding my center of calm, gathering my thoughts, and trying to figure out the root cause of their upset.

I am listening to what they are saying, but I am not taking it personally and I am not listening with the intent of trying to pick apart their argument. As I've already said, trying to argue their points with them is not a successful approach to dealing with these situations most of the time.

I am trying to assess the root issue. Are they frustrated because something didn't go the way they planned? Are they overwhelmed because something has gone wrong and they think there's no way to fix it? Are they feeling insulted by something that happened? Does what they're saying make any sense?

A lot of times if what they're saying doesn't seem to be making any sense, it's because they're really angry about something unrelated to what they are saying. Maybe their wife walked out on them that morning and they're mad at all women right now and the fact that you gave them the wrong amount of change with their order means that you're trying to steal all their money because you're an unfaithful man hater.

Letting them yell actually gives you some much needed time to figure out how to best approach the situation. Funny enough, sometimes the people who refuse to keep yelling are the ones that are the hardest to deal with because you have no idea why they're upset which means you have no idea how to fix it. You have to play detective a lot more pointedly with those people and it can actually take longer to resolve the problem. Not that I want people to yell at me; of course not! I only mean it can be a lot easier to figure out the real issue when they're handing me everything I need on a silver platter by saying it all out loud.

Many times the person will yell until they run out of things to say. The fact that you have not interrupted them actually allows them to get to the end of their thoughts. When you interrupt them, a lot of times they will start over at the beginning. By sitting calmly with a neutral face and posture and simply letting them express their distress, they will often calm themselves down.

This situation is similar to how a toddler will often yell and scream and flop on the floor and roll around and sob. Eventually they get up and walk off because they got it out of their system, they are rebalanced, and they feel better. When people are yelling at me, I try to create emotional distance between them and myself by regarding them as throwing a temper tantrum. They need to emotionally flop around on the floor for a second and pound their fists, and then when they've collected themselves we can attempt to be adults again.

Once they have yelled it all out and taken a breath, there will usually be a bit of a pause where they are waiting to see how you are going to react to everything they have just done. Make no mistake, they are primed and ready to roll up their sleeves and go right into round two with you if you use this pause in a way that makes them feel further threatened. They know they were acting like an ass. They are well aware of it, and they are well aware of the fact that you could then yell back at them, be very aggressive or hostile, make comments about their behavior, etc. They are now preparing to defend themselves against the ugly behavior they just displayed.

The balance you have to strike here is tricky and delicate. The person is being very aggressive and I don't want either of you to have the impression that they are in control of you because they are not. They are 100% in the wrong, but your reaction to them will determine what happens from there and if you could possibly also be regarded as equally part of the problem.

If your words and actions could be viewed as "egging them on" or "making it worse," then you're not going to be able to come out on top. At the same time, if you don't draw a boundary line with the situation, then it can spiral out of control if they feel like they have you pinned in a corner and they have free reign to chew you up and spit you out.

Let me throw this out there, you're not going to be able to win with everybody. You're not going to be able to get every situation to result in a pleasant ending. Some people are going to yell at you until they've said everything they want to say and then they're going to walk off. Absolutely not acceptable behavior, but in that instance what allows you to "win" is refusing to lose your cool or stoop to their level. If you can remain calm, then they come out looking like an idiot. Sometimes that's the only win you're going to get.

The people around you are watching the situation. They know that the other person is out of line. They wouldn't want that person speaking that way to them. The way you react is what will form their opinion about you. Did you fall right into it? If you start yelling back, you're just as bad as that other person is and you two deserve each other for all anybody else cares.

Did you crumple into a ball and burst into tears? Yikes. She really doesn't know how to stand up for herself? Careful around her, she's as fragile as glass. Or did you handle the situation like a boss? Were you rubber and that person was glue and everything they said bounced off of you and stuck onto them?...Ok, that phrase doesn't work very well when you're trying to refer to it in the second person, but you get it.

Have you ever seen a big dog and a puppy interacting where the puppy is barking its head off and jumping around the big dog, biting it on its ear, rolling underneath its feet and going nuts trying to get its attention while the big dog is standing there like, "would you please stop"? You've got to be the big dog here. That little yipper can't actually hurt you. They might be aggravating, but they're not a real threat. Enough theory, here are some examples:

Them: "YELL, YELL, YELL, I'M SO MAD. YOUR COMPANY SUCKS. YOU PEOPLE ARE ALL IDIOTS. I WANT A REFUND!!!"

You (calm, neutral, quiet, friendly): "Ok, I understand. You want a refund. I can make that happen for you. Do you have your receipt?"

Them: "NO I DON'T HAVE A RECEIPT! I THOUGHT THIS ITEM WAS GOING TO WORK. I DIDN'T REALIZE EVERYTHING IN HERE IS GARBAGE. I LOST THE RECEIPT."

You (calm, neutral, quiet, friendly): "Ok, I understand. You don't have a receipt. That's ok. Let's see what we can do for you. I can either give you the refund on a store card or I can return the item to the card you used to purchase the item if you have it with you. Do you know which card you used to make the purchase?"

Them: "NO I DON'T KNOW WHICH CARD I USED. CAN'T YOU LOOK THAT UP?"

[At this point, I am getting tired of listening to the loud yelling. I am trying to help them, but they are not calming down. I know that they are feeling super anxious at the idea that they are not going to get the refund they wanted. If I can assure them that they will definitely get the refund, it will likely help them to quit yelling.]

You (calm, neutral, quiet, friendly): "Don't worry. I know you are feeling stressed about this refund. We will definitely be able to get this done for you, but I have to follow our protocol to process it. If you can be patient and give me a few minutes, we'll have it finished and you can be on your way. Does that sound ok?"

Them: "Ok. Thank you."

Assure them you understand what they want by repeating it out loud, "I understand you want a refund." Assure them that you intend to grant their request, "I can help you with that." If that doesn't seem to be enough to help them calm down, name their fear, "I know you are feeling stressed about receiving this refund." Assure them again, "we will definitely be able to take care of it for you." Remind them that you are human, "I have to follow our process to get you what you need," and only then make your request "please be patient."

Let's look at a scenario where you made a mistake (it happens to everyone).

Them: "YOU CHARGED ME TWICE FOR THIS SWEATER AND I ONLY PURCHASED ONE OF THEM. THIS IS RIDICULOUS. DON'T YOU KNOW HOW TO DO YOUR JOB? I'VE GOT PLACES TO BE RIGHT NOW. I DON'T HAVE TIME FOR THIS."

You (calmly): "Oh no! I'm very sorry. I didn't mean to ring that up twice. I know how inconvenient it is to have to come back in here to get it fixed. I apologize. If you can give me the receipt, I can get this straightened out for you right away so that you can move on with your day."

Them: "WELL HOW LONG IS IT GOING TO TAKE FOR ME TO GET MY MONEY BACK? THIS IS INCREDIBLY INCONVENIENT FOR ME."

You (calmly): "I know it's inconvenient and very stressful to have more money taken out of your account than you intended. The refund will be processed immediately, but it might take up to 48 hours for it to appear in your bank account. I know that's not ideal. I really do apologize."

Them: "Ugh. Well fine, just fix it I guess."

In this example I made a mistake. This mistake is inconvenient and stressful for the customer. I truly feel bad that I caused a problem and I want them to know that I'm not blowing it off or acting like it's no big deal. It was obviously a big deal to them and it was my fault. Be quick to apologize when you mess up. People will respect it when you own your mistakes instead of trying to justify them or acting like they don't matter. People also want their feelings acknowledged as justified when they have been wronged.

Note that in the last example, my impression was that the person's main source of stress was the extra time it took from their day to fix this. They said, "I don't have time for this," so my response was to assure them that I would be speedy, "I can get this fixed right away." However, in their second statement, I get the impression that the extra charge itself was causing a problem. Usually when someone is excessively upset about a small extra charge or needing a refund, it's because their bank account balance is low and they are feeling it. That extra $10 on their bill might send them into an overdraft. They might have an automated bill coming out of their account tomorrow that will bounce if the refund isn't present by that time.

Understand that what might feel small and insignificant for you might be huge and overwhelming to someone else. You don't know what other people are dealing with in their lives, and when they present themselves as this upset, there could be a very legitimate reason behind it that you don't know. Maybe their boss is a time tyrant and they only had enough time to run into your store on their lunch hour and grab a shirt they needed for an after work event and squeal back into the work parking lot before clocking back in. Having to deal with this unexpected charge has now made them late and possibly caused a huge problem between them and their manager. You don't know. If you have made a mistake, it's on you to apologize and do what you can to rectify the situation, not on them to "get over it."

How to handle a situation that seems confusing:

As I've mentioned before, one of my responsibilities in home health is to assess my patients for any other services they may need or other disciplines we might need to provide for them (nursing, social worker, occupational therapist, etc.). Sometimes I will have a conversation that takes an unexpected turn when I have to relay that a service the patient or family is expecting won't be available, or at least not as frequently as they had expected.

Them: "So mom will have someone coming out 7 days a week to give her a bath, right?"

Me: "No ma'am. Our bath aide comes out either once or twice a week for our patients, depending on their need."

Them: "Wait what?! We were told you all were going to send someone out here 7 days a week to bathe her!"

Me: "I apologize that you were told that. That was a miscommunication. Our services are not designed to accommodate someone coming out that frequently for a bath. The most we are able to send the bath aide is twice a week."

Them: "THIS IS RIDICULOUS! THEY TOLD US YOU WERE GOING TO COME OUT EVERY DAY! THAT'S WHY WE SAID WE WANTED YOUR COMPANY! WHAT'S THE POINT IN EVEN HAVING YOU COME OUT AT ALL IF YOU CAN'T COME ANY MORE OFTEN THAN THAT?!"

[Whoa. This is a very excessive reaction to this information. This is an immediate red flag to me that something else is going on that needs to be addressed. This person is obviously very stressed and we need to find out why.]

Me (calmly): "Ok, hold on. Let's talk this out and see what we can do for you. I want to help you and make sure you have all the support you need. Tell me what your major concerns are right now with regard to getting your mom's needs met. Let's come up with a game plan for you."

There could be a million reasons why this person had it in their head that their mom needed the bath aide to come out 7 days a week. Maybe the daughter works constantly and doesn't feel like she's ever going to have time to give her mom a bath. Maybe someone at the hospital made a comment about how important it was for mom to stay really clean and dry to prevent skin breakdown or infection, and she's feeling overwhelmed at the idea that she might do something wrong. Maybe she's got back trouble and she's worried she can't give her mom a bath without hurting herself. Maybe she's willing but has never done anything like that before and feels overwhelmed at the prospect of trying. Maybe her mom has always kept herself neat as a pin and she wants to help her stick to her normal routine as much as possible. Maybe her mom has memory trouble and she's worried about her being home alone during the day and she wants people coming into the home frequently to make sure mom is ok and hasn't fallen.

You will never find out what the real problem is by simply arguing, "well we can't send someone out more than twice a week so get over it." There are lots of ways to get this person's needs and fears addressed, but first we have to know what the real fear is. I have a solution to every one of the problems listed above, but until I can find out which of them is the cause of the stress, what I know doesn't matter.

After we find out the problem and come up with a game plan, always reiterate the plan and ask, "does that sound like a good plan to you? Is there anything else we've left out?" In this situation, I like to go one step further and really assure the person that we are there for them. They are very overwhelmed by their situation (much more about this in the Caregiver section later in the book), and by assuring them ,"We are here for you. We are here to support you. We've got you. Don't worry," and following up with a big hug (I'm a hugger!) you will help them to feel calm and secure. As a bonus, it will make you feel amazing to be able to provide so much support and care to them.

There will be times where you have to address a person's behavior straight on. You have attempted to solve the issue. You are actively working on a solution for them, but they are so wound up that they won't stop yelling or calm down no matter what. Do not start with these comments, because if said at the beginning they will only make the person more upset. However, if you have spent some time with the person and you have maintained an even demeanor, and nothing you say is helping them to really calm down, here are some things you can try:

"I understand that you are mad. I would be upset too, but I need you to lower your voice. I'm trying to help you but it's overwhelming to me that you are being so loud."

"I know that you are feeling overwhelmed about this situation. I am doing my very best to help you and I'm working very hard to get this fixed, but I really need you to take a few breaths and calm down. If you can calm down, it will help me to think so I can get this fixed faster for you."

In each of these statements, you are doing multiple things. You are 1) identifying their feelings (mad, overwhelmed), 2) acknowledging that their feelings are justified if you feel that they are (I would be upset too), 3) reminding them that you are a person (I'm trying to help you, I'm working hard to get this fixed) 4) giving them a specific request (lower your voice, calm down) and 5) explaining how it would be to their benefit to calm down (I won't be so overwhelmed, I can get this fixed faster because I will be able to think more clearly).

Unless you are a person who enjoys conflict, avoid these types of comments at all costs:

"You are overreacting."

"This isn't that big of a deal. Calm down."

"You're making this harder on me."

"You are being unreasonable."

"If you would calm down, I could fix this faster."

What about the person who has gone full scale "off the deep end" on you? They are fidgeting and speaking non-stop nonsense and getting themselves more wound up by the minute. You *have* to get them to make eye contact with you and bring themselves back to the present moment before they can hear or process anything you are saying to them. These people will not even hear you speaking right away. Everything you say should be conveyed in the most soothing voice you have.

"Hey...hey...hey, look at me. Look at me. (Make solid eye contact with them) Hi. (You just made eye contact and you immediately meet it with a warm reassuring smile). Please calm down. Take a deep breath. Breathe (::in::out::) I've got you. I've got this. It's ok. Just breathe and calm down for a second. (One brief second of silence rockets them straight into panicking again.) Hold on, hold on! No, no, no. Just breathe. Calm down. Breathe. You have to stay calm so we can get through this together. I'm going to help you. Just stay calm. It's ok."

I use this with patients who are on the verge of a panic attack and also with my children when they are spiraling into a total meltdown. This is also a useful tactic with a person who has PTSD and has been triggered. They are mentally in a completely different place than you are and you have to guide them back into the present moment. You won't know you have their attention until you can make and hold eye contact with them.

Obviously this would not be appropriate in a retail or office setting, but in a healthcare setting you can hold or squeeze the person's hand while speaking to them, if they are calmed down enough to be ok with being touched. I've even rubbed patient's backs a little bit (slow back and forth or slow circles, you are trying to help calm their central nervous system) while I explain what we're going to do next. I might pat them on the leg or the shoulder. Giving a point of physical touch will help them get out of their head and back into their body, so to speak, so that they can connect to you and what you are trying to tell them. This is the same reason I advised you to squeeze your own hand or arm when you are wound up. It is calming to your nervous system and signals your stress chemicals to clear up and go away.

In this scenario, the person has lost control of their ability to calm themselves down and you are helping to facilitate it for them. Get them to focus on breathing, slowing down, focusing their thoughts. Reassuring them "I've got you. I've got this. It's ok," is the equivalent to telling yourself, "I'm not actually in danger here. Everything is fine." Cut off any attempts they make to start ramping back up again. This will put you right back to square one. Do not proceed forward with any information or instructions until you feel sure that the person is in a calm mental state so they can receive your information.

In this case, whether with adults or children, if you have had to help bring them down from a total panic or fit, keep your words and instructions short and simple, and give it to them in pieces so they have time to process what you've said. My little one is very prone to panicking when he gets upset. Once I've gone through the process above, and he is no longer so upset that he can't function, I will let him know what I need him to do next, which is always a series of instructions designed to help him calm down further. I'll say:

"Ok bud. You're doing great. Thank you for calming down. What I need for you to do now..is go upstairs..and go to your room..and lay down on your bed for a few minutes..ok? You are not in trouble..I just want you to take a few more minutes to relax..ok? Awesome. I'm coming right behind you. I'll be there in 5 minutes..ok? Great. Go ahead. I'll be right there."

I *do* ask him "ok?" a lot when I'm giving these instructions because I need to know that he hears me and understands what I'm asking him to do. When someone is panicking, their fight or flight response is in overdrive and their ability to receive and process information is barely working. By speaking more slowly, and in pieces, I'm giving his mind that extra processing time it needs. By checking in and asking him to confirm that he understands what I want him to do, I avoid further confusion (which can kickstart the panic again) on his part. If he's not able to confirm that he hears and understands (by nodding his head or saying "ok" back to me), then I can repeat the small part he didn't catch.

HOW TO AVOID BEING A KAREN (MY APOLOGIES TO ALL KARENS)

I'm going to let you in on a huge bit of advice from my fifteen years of working with the public in areas of retail, collections, and healthcare. There is one simple shift to your approach that will open so many doors for you when dealing with any sort of customer service issue. More people than you can count will go from, "there's nothing I can do" to, "let me see what I can do for you." It's not 100% guaranteed, but it's the next best thing. Are you ready? Really ready? Ok here's the secret: tell the person you are stressed and you don't know what to do. It's the truth, isn't it?

I'm not saying to do this as a first option. The first option is to find the person or call the number you think is the correct contact to help, and calmly explain the situation and what you want to happen. Are you looking for a refund? Reversal of an erroneous charge? Waiver for a deadline you missed? An itemized copy of your latest bill? Explain what you need and be polite and patient. Honest to goodness this will create so many peaceful and successful interactions all by itself. The person on the other end of the situation is a person getting an hourly wage to put up with a never ending amount of craziness from the public. If you are being polite and patient, you are automatically the favorite person they've spoken to all day.

Sometimes you catch someone who is in a bad mood, overwhelmed, or new and hasn't had enough training. Maybe they have way too much going on in their personal life to be effective, or are so busy following a protocol that they forgot that you are a real person who is also out here trying to do your best. Maybe they are generally a very cranky person who is rude to everyone. These are the ones most likely to give you grief right off the bat, so try to be extra polite and patient here and see if that does the trick.

BUT sometimes you are getting a "no" at every turn. Maybe you are making a request that you know should be honored because you've had the exact same problem before and the last person handled it without any difficulty. This is where you find yourself at a crossroads. Do you escalate the conversation or give up? What is the most successful approach here? My answer comes from being on both ends of this situation. The Just Scan the Coupon section will detail my thoughts on the perspective of the person behind the register/counter. For now, we are going to review what to do if you are the customer and becoming increasingly frustrated with a particular situation.

If you didn't know it already, calling someone an idiot rarely ever endears them to help you. I know there seems to be a lot of confusion around this concept, but if you are in doubt, just take my word for it. Raising your voice at someone automatically kicks in their fight or flight response. Since they are not allowed to run away from you, you're going to get the "fight" response. And to help clarify, loudly declaring that you need to speak to that person's manager isn't winning you a popularity contest.

Let me be VERY real with you on this one: if you are dragging a manager out of their office or from another section of the store where they are trying to get one of their 500 required tasks done for the day so you can cause a gigantic commotion and start making demands, you have now angered 1) the original person you were dealing with 2) all the coworkers of the original employee who are simply trying to live their lives and get to closing time without someone like you ruining their day 3) the manager who DOES NOT want to deal with another person yelling at them either 4) all the other customers in the area who want to have their needs met and don't appreciate you making the situation so uncomfortable for everyone and holding up the normal flow of things, and in today's age of social media 5) everyone on the internet who sees the video that someone posts in order to publicly shame you. I'll get off my soapbox now.

So, how should you handle a situation that isn't going your way? How do you encourage that person to help you instead of telling you there's nothing they can do? Be willing to be honest and a bit vulnerable with them. How about instead of saying, "You don't care about anyone. You're a jerk!", you could say, "this extra charge is really stressing me out right now because I only have enough money to cover this purchase, but no more. I have a bill coming out tomorrow and if we can't get this fixed, I'll be late and get hit with several charges. Is there anything at all you can do?" Believe it or not, this person might be overworked and underpaid, but they usually aren't heartless. And so many studies have come out proving that if you can give a person even the smallest reason why you need something, they are significantly more likely to help you with it.

What about asking someone to do something a bit extra because you don't know how to do it yourself? I certainly don't know everything and I'm sure you don't either. Most people can empathize with others not knowing how to do everything they know how to do. This is one that comes up a lot at the cell phone store for me. I am young and look like a well put together person. You would look at me and assume I know how to do things like connect to an iCloud or transfer data from my old phone to my new one, but I don't. Technology is something that my brain has an unreasonably difficult time wrapping itself around. And it's an area where I get overwhelmed to the point of tears easily, if I'm being honest.

So when I walk into the store and ask for help with a problem my phone is having, the person usually assumes that if they say, "oh, you just go into your (whatever) and change your (whatever) settings", that I will say, "ok great!", and just do it and walk back out the door. Asking them, "can you do it for me?", would typically get a raised eyebrow. 'Ok, lazy, why do you need me to do it?' I can practically hear the commentary in their heads.

I will respond to the instructions by asking, "would you mind helping to walk me through it? I get confused so easily and I don't want to have to come back and bother you about it again." They never have a problem with that. It doesn't usually take long after a minute or two of them looking over my shoulder and having to give a few, "No, that one. No, click on that one. Ok, you hit the wrong thing go back. Ok, it's that one", before they will offer, "do you want me to do it?", and I very gratefully hand my phone over and let them do whatever needs to be done. Just be honest: I don't know how to do this and I get confused and overwhelmed very easily.

Keep the volume of your voice a bit lower. Remember the fight or flight thing? Are you tired of hearing about that yet? If your needs are above and beyond what is typical, it could be stressing them out. Maybe it's getting close to closing time and they don't want to have to stay late. They might work on commission, and the extra time they are spending with you is taking an opportunity from them to help the next customer who wants to purchase something. You don't have to fall all over yourself apologizing, but do recognize that your extra needs might be inconvenient for them, so stay calm, patient, and thankful.

Be appreciative of them going out of their way to help you. Saying something like, "I really appreciate you taking the time to look this up. You have been so helpful to me. Thank you for doing this." can help make up for a lot.

Maybe you are on the phone with customer service and they are apologizing that it is taking so long to grant your request or look up the answer to your question. I will usually respond by saying, "No need to apologize to me. I am very grateful to you for taking the time to help me figure this out. It's been very stressful for me, and it means a lot that you are taking the time to help me get it resolved." Scout's honor, people are so underappreciated for the things they do. If you can acknowledge and express gratitude for their efforts, they will usually do everything they can think of to help you.

I'll give you a very personal example. Everyone has a horror story about trying to purchase their house, and we are no different. To cut to the chase, our mortgage company completely dropped the ball on our paperwork for the closing and things were not ready on their end on time. After using our unilateral extension to hold the contract for 8 days after the initial closing date, and 48 hours into this extension, I'm on the phone with the regional director of the company trying to desperately get this thing to the finish line. [I'm a teensy bit Type A and my real estate agent and I were using a team approach to badger the people who were doing their best to ghost us.]

This man was telling me that because they didn't have a piece of paper (that I had *specifically* asked if they would need the first day I called to start this process, and that I had told them would take 30 days to get and could not be rushed, and that they had confirmed with THREE separate people would not be needed, that at the last minute they decided they did need after all), that we would not be able to close on the house. At all. Bye bye dream house.

Nevermind that we had spent the previous few years preparing for this amazing step. Nevermind that we had already told the kids that the house was ours, that they had already picked out their bedrooms, and that they had been begging us to drive by the house nearly every day to look at it and imagine how great it was going to be to live there. Nevermind that the house we were renting was already 85% packed into moving boxes, our notice given to the landlord, and the moving company had been rescheduled for the next week because we were supposed to have moved in two days before. This man was telling me we weren't going to be able to close, and there was nothing that could be done about it without this one piece of paper. A piece of paper that I absolutely *could not* produce in the next four days.

His response to my stress was to say, "I really hate it for you. I wish we could have made it work out, but it looks like it's not going to happen. Sorry." ARE YOU FREAKING KIDDING ME?!?! You hate it for me? That's the best you can do?? Yes, I was the hysterical person that was like, "This is completely insane. You could fix this if you really wanted to, but you aren't even trying!" Their company had screwed up. Their processor had completely shelved my file and forgot to ever open it or work on it. I had been on top of them from day one, ringing every bell I could to let them know how concerned I was that things didn't seem to be getting done. I had sent in everything they had asked of me, even when they asked for the same thing multiple times, within 12 hours of every request, and they were going to let it all fall apart. I was devastated.

Me: "You aren't sorry! You don't seem to care at all that I'm about to lose my dream house. You couldn't possibly know what I've been through to get to this point or how much this means to my family."

Him: "Mrs. Crenshaw, I am sorry. Sometimes things don't work out. There's nothing I can do about it."

Me: "There IS something you can do about it. Your company completely botched this and you know it. I'm just another number on a sheet to you, but this is my entire life. My future. The house I'm going to raise my children in and you don't care at all."

Him: "Now, that's not true. I do care. I'm in this business because I care about helping people get into their homes."

Me: "Then why aren't you trying to help me get this figured out?"

Him: "I want to help you, but there's nothing I can do. Without this paper, it won't go through."

Me: "Do you really mean that?"

Him: "Mean what?"

Me: "Do you *really* want to help me or are you only saying that to shut me up and get me off the phone?"

Him (unfeeling): "I mean it. I want to help you."

Me (with pleading in my voice): "Do you really?..Do you *really* want to help me?"

Him (finally softening): "Yes, I really wish there was something I could do to help."

Me: "Then *help* me! If you really want to help me, and you really do mean that you are in this business to help people, then *help me*. I am totally powerless right now, and completely devastated. I have no control in this situation, and you have the power to fix this. I know you do. I don't know how, but there is something that can be done. There always is in a situation like this. Please. Help me."

Him: "...let me make a few phone calls. Give me an hour."

We found a way around it and closed two days later. It doesn't always work, but appealing to a person's humanity and reminding a person that they have power where you have none can sometimes be the key to unlocking the help you need.

HOW TO DEAL WITH A KAREN

There are times that it doesn't matter what you say or do, the person in front of you will refuse to be appeased. They don't *want* to calm down. They don't *want* the situation to be resolved. They want to be in charge. They want to prove their superiority and throw their weight around, and all the tactics in the world will not sway them from asking to speak to your manager. Pop culture has begun referring to these people as "Karens."

The stereotype here is that these people don't care about the rules because they are above the rules. They don't care that the coupon has expired. They are the customer and the customer is always right, so they should be able to use the coupon even if it is expired (thanks, Bed Bath & Beyond). They don't care if the company policy says that returns will not be accepted more than 180 days after your purchase. You should honor their return anyway, even if it's a year later, because they kept their receipt. You made a mistake when you rang up their purchase, so now you are a second class citizen who isn't competent enough to speak to them anymore, and even if you are capable of correcting the problem, they want the manager to do it to "make sure it's done right this time."

Mindset: This person has a problem; a really big problem. People who are kind, empathetic, and mature don't act this way. They can recognize that all people make mistakes, and they can accept when they have made a mistake that doesn't end in their favor (expired coupon or return policy). If I try to return something and I realize the item isn't eligible for return, I take ownership of the fact that it was my fault. I didn't read the fine print or return policy. I didn't act in time. I forgot about something I had meant to do and now it's too late. That is *my* fault, not the fault of the person behind the register or the company.

This person is acting entitled. They have made a mistake and are now expecting you to fix it. They generally have huge issues with feeling overpowered by their life circumstances or other people in their lives. They don't feel powerful or important deep down, so they overcompensate by acting "large and in charge" to everyone they meet. They may have even grown up in a house with overbearing (or absent) parents who never listened to them or took them seriously unless they were being very forceful and insistent. Like with complainers and gossipers, there is nothing you can say or do to change this behavior. Recognize it as a sign of a deeply wounded person and emotionally remove yourself from the situation.

You want to speak to my manager? Sure thing, lady. I was over having to deal with you 10 minutes ago. I would be overjoyed to call them over so you can be their problem now instead of mine. You want one better? How about I suggest we call the manager so we can head straight to "Go" and collect that $200.

Boundaries: The biggest boundary issue here is when the person starts to insult you or call you names. They can be as mad as they want, but they must refrain from name calling. That is totally over the line. Your voice should be even, calm, non-threatening but clear. You are not mad. They don't have the power to upset you, but you have a zero tolerance policy for this behavior.

"Ma'am. I understand that you are very frustrated right now, and I am doing my best to help, but I expect us to both be respectful here and refrain from name calling."

"Ok, I am trying to help resolve this situation, but it seems to be getting out of control. I think it would be best for me to bring in a third party to help make sure this gets taken care of properly and respectfully. Let me call in my manager."

JUST SCAN THE COUPON

Is there a way to avoid a situation like this getting out of hand? Yes...well sometimes. As I said before, you can't win them all. After a little while of working behind a register, I was able to find a few ways to see the escalation coming and cut it off at the pass. This is most often a situation that happens in a retail setting, but the idea of anticipating a problem and addressing it head on before it escalates can be applied in many ways. The thought process of a Karen is rooted in this idea that you *could* give them what they want, you are simply refusing to do it. They want to call your manager because they are convinced that the manager will do what you are refusing to do, or has the power to override the policy.

If you are a person working in a retail setting, this is my advice: just scan the coupon. You and I both know that the coupon won't scan. There is a code on the coupon that was entered into the main computer with an expiration day and time on it. Once the clock strikes midnight, or whatever time the coupon is set to expire, the computer will automatically reject the code. You and I both know that, but the aggravated person is convinced that *you* are the one being a stickler for the rules and simply refusing to scan a perfectly good coupon.

If someone would come up to me with an expired coupon, I would say, "I'm so sorry, but that coupon won't work anymore because it is expired." If I saw even the smallest hint that this person was upset and about to open their mouth to argue with me, I would follow up with, "but I don't mind scanning it to see if it will work. Do you want me to try?" They would always say yes. I would turn the computer screen to face them so that when the message came up that said "Invalid code. Coupon has expired," they could see it in black and white.

This has done two things: 1) It has conveyed to them that you were *willing to try*, which is the biggest thing they want. *You* did not get in the way of their discount. 2) It has taken the problem out of human hands. This is the computer's fault now. Most people can accept a computer that won't budge much more easily than a person who won't budge. As a bonus, it will almost always prevent them from asking for a manager, because you have now proven to them that the computer is shutting down this operation, which means the manager is unlikely to be able to do anything about it either.

It's the same thing with stacking coupons or coupons that don't apply to certain items. You know beyond a shadow of a doubt that it's not going to work, but they don't. There is an amount of doubt in their mind, and it bothers them. What if you are wrong? What if the coupon would have gone through if you had just tried it? What if they could have saved that money, but you prevented it because you were so convinced that you knew what you were doing? Is it going to kill you to scan it and show them the denial? No it won't. Just do it and let them feel like they at least had a shot.

The other big time this comes up is when a customer wants a refund, but it's not going to go their way. They want to return something after the return window has ended. They want to return a "final sale" item. They want to get their refund by a different method than how they paid, in a way that the store policy doesn't allow. Or they want the return to go on their card when they don't have a receipt to prove that they actually purchased the item.

In many cases, explaining *why* the policy is a certain way

will help a lot. Again, they are convinced that you are refusing to help them or that the company policy is arbitrary and has no sound reasoning behind it. Explaining the policy can go a long way toward helping them see the logic behind it and why their request is not as reasonable as they want it to be.

For instance, in the department store where I worked, once an item was listed as "final sale," the item number would be removed from the computer system. There was no way to return the item because it no longer existed in the computer inventory. Even with a tag and a receipt, the item would ring up as $0.00 because it no longer existed. There was no way to get around that. It was the same with the receipt number. Our policy had a 90 day return window. On day 91, the receipt number and all associated data would be deleted from the system. If you tried to put in the receipt information, nothing would show up.

There were real needs behind these policies. Without getting too detailed, it would only show up as a loss on the books for the company to return an item so far away from the purchase date. From an accounting perspective, the book has to be balanced and completed at some point. You can't leave the balance sheet open until the end of time and expect to have a strong handle on the company's finances. There has to be a cut off point at which a file can be confidently closed with no chance of it reopening. Thus the time limit on returns.

I can't give you a cash return when you don't have a receipt. Yes, you look like a very nice person. No, I'm not accusing you of stealing something. No, you don't look like a thief. BUT there has to be a record of the transaction in order for the company books to be balanced. Maybe you are the most honest person on the planet, and you simply forgot that you purchased this item from the department store on the opposite side of the mall that sells the same brand we do. This is a business, and the business has to have strong policies in place that are fair and consistent in order to remain profitable enough to keep the doors open.

If you have explained the policy, and the person is still insistent that there must be a way for them to get what they want exactly the way they want it, just "try" and do it that way so they can see that it won't work. Scan the receipt and show them the message that says, "No record of this transaction." Type everything in and show them that you can't choose the "cash" button as an option. Scan the tag and show that the registered price is now $0.00. If you've gone through all this and you can tell that the person is getting more angry or plans on camping out at your register all day until the Universe simply shifts to give them what they want, offer to call your manager.

Again, you are presenting yourself as the messenger, not the decision maker. You are doing everything you can to assist them, and that will help to smooth over their frustration. By offering to call the manager, you are conveying to them that you are trying to help. It will at least take away their argument that you don't care or that you are keeping the solution from them on purpose.

INAPPROPRIATE COMMENTS

What if the person is not only being rude, but inappropriate? How to you handle sexual harassment or sexual comments that make you uncomfortable? Although this is typically something women deal with the most, it is not only a women's issue. Men are also the targets of inappropriate comments by women of all ages. Many women do not see the problem with making lewd comments to fit and attractive men because there is an expectation that the man doesn't mind or likes the attention. Men can be just as uncomfortable as women because of these inappropriate comments, so please make sure you are not perpetuating or condoning this behavior if you witness it.

This is another situation where being confrontational will usually make the situation worse. If you come across as immediately aggravated, you have given the other person total control of the situation. Your attitude needs to be one of confused bewilderment, not anger. Having some random stranger cat call you and say, "hey girl you get me all hot and bothered" or whatever, needs to carry the same weight as someone walking up to you and saying, "did you know that a housefly hums in the key of F?" Um...ok...that's weird. Why did you say that to me? Not mad, just perplexed.

Or what about, "hey you're so hot it really makes me want to do things." (Yes, I'm being PG and non-specific. Surely you don't need me to be detailed here.) You should feel as though the person just said, "Did you know that most of the ice in Antarctica is made of penguin urine?" Ew. That's a very odd thing to say and makes me feel a little uncomfortable. I wish you had kept that to yourself.

You might be disappointed that I'm not going to give you a list of witty retorts here, but the best thing to do is usually to ignore them and pretend like they didn't say anything. You are ignoring them the same way you would ignore a child who screams, "YOU'RE MEAN!" and then runs away because you asked him not to knock over the can display in the middle of the grocery store. The person who is being inappropriate is acting like a child, so you ignore them like you would a child that you don't know who is acting like a fool in the middle of the store. Ok, that's uncomfortable, I'll just walk away now.

That's good and well if it's a stranger on the street. What if it's a person you have to continue to interact with? I have had this happen on multiple occasions with older male patients in home health. They think they are being funny, and I don't. This is absolutely a boundary issue and must be dealt with right away. However, given the nature of the situation, there is an added dynamic in which I must be sure to remain professional at all times. There is no option to be rude or temperamental in these situations. Maybe some examples would be best. These are things that have actually been said to me while working and how I handled them:

Them: "Next time you come back I'll make sure my wife isn't here so we can be alone."

Me: "I think everything worked out fine. We'll keep it exactly the same way for next time."

<or> "If she's not here, I'm not coming! You're a mess!" (said with lots of teasing, but still making my point.)

Maybe they are on the porch and we are going to go inside for the visit.

Me: "How about we go inside."

Them: "Where are we going? The bedroom?"

Me: "We're staying in the kitchen and the living room and that's it. Now you behave yourself."

Me: "Are you hurting anywhere?"

Them: "I'm hurtin' for you!" (wink)

Me: "Now, that's inappropriate and I don't appreciate it. Let's try again. Are you hurting anywhere?"

Them: "I'm hurtin' for you!" (wink)

Me: "Mr. so-and-so, I'm here to help you. I don't feel comfortable with you making that kind of comment to me. It's inappropriate. Now, will you please let me know if you are hurting anywhere?" **

Them: "I told you. I'm hurtin' for you!" (wink)

Me: [Dead stare at the patient with full Mom Look deployed. I let the silence tick by one second at a time for about 10-15 seconds, refusing to be the next one to speak.]

Them: ".....no, I'm not hurting anywhere."

Me: "Ok, good. Let's move on."

**Yes, I purposefully did not change the word I used in this situation. For me, the boundary I was setting was that I wasn't going to skirt around my word choice because of his inappropriate reaction. When someone is insisting on being inappropriate and you start trying to appease the situation by using a different word to avoid the innuendo, you are giving them control because they are causing you to filter your vocabulary to only using "safe" words. In this instance, I chose to stand my ground and insist that he change his behavior instead of me changing my vocabulary. This choice was also influenced by previous interactions I had had with this patient. Being inappropriate was a "mode" of his.

There is a test I have to do as a physical therapist that is meant to detect or rule out vertigo (among other things). It requires the person to lay flat on their back with their head lower than their body. It may also require the person to change positions while lying down. In a clinic, the therapy tables are perfect for this. In a person's home, the only real place to do this is on a bed. I am VERY careful about the way I word this to the male patients after having this conversation more times than I can count.

Me: "Ok, I'm going to do a test on you, but you need to lie down for me to do it. The best place to do that is going to be on the bed."

Them: "Are you going to get in the bed with me?" (wink)

Me: "I'm going to spin you around a few times and see if I can get you to throw up." (tee-hee)***

***The nature of this test is such that if the patient is "positive," they will likely have an overwhelming sensation of spinning that often makes them feel like they are going to throw up. That's why I choose that phrase specifically. The point is that I'm turning their sexual innuendo into something completely the opposite and "ruining the mood." There's really no coming back after the way I respond here. They are also a wee bit anxious after my comment, and more concerned about what we're going to do than saying inappropriate things.

With the examples above, there is a pattern. I'm not getting upset. I'm not acting offended. I am being very matter of fact. The phrases I use the most in these situations are:

"That is inappropriate."

"I don't appreciate you saying that."

"That makes me uncomfortable."

I *completely* ignore the actual comment. I don't respond to what they actually say. I don't respond with "Don't say things like that!" "I can't believe you just said that!" "I'm not getting in the bed with you!" "Don't embarrass me by saying stuff like that!" "No we're not going to the bedroom!" Women tend to react in a very flustered manner when people say things like this and it only makes it worse. You can't get red in the cheeks, stutter your words, or get high pitched and squeaky.

Don't be mad either. Saying things like, "You're not going to speak to me that way or I'm calling the office." "I'm not coming here anymore if you're going to act like that." "What would you do if someone spoke to your daughter that way?", is going to feel like Christmas morning to this person. They set the trap and you are walking right in. Now they're going to dig and dig until they can get you to fly all the way off the handle.

The approach here should be the same as your child saying, "if you don't let me do what I want, I'm never speaking to you again!" You're thinking, "ok, slick, good luck with that." This person says something they shouldn't and your thought is, "ok, hotrod, whatever. Move along." Simply point out that the behavior is inappropriate and you don't appreciate it. This goes back to what we covered with rude comments regarding how futile it is to argue whether something is true or not.

If you say, "You can't say things like that!" the person can respond, "Sure I can. I say things like that all the time."

If you say, "No, I'm not getting in the bed with you!" the person can say, "Why not? Aren't I good looking enough for you?"

If you say, "I'm not coming back if you are going to act like that." he can innocently ask, "Act like what? Can't a guy admire a pretty lady?"

You can't win. Ever. As I've said over and over: don't take the bait. It's very difficult to argue with the statement, "That's inappropriate and I don't appreciate it." The best they can retort is, "It's not inappropriate! I was joking." Reiterate your statement, "It *is* inappropriate and it makes me uncomfortable. I'm asking you to keep those comments to yourself. Now...(change the subject)." Don't give them room to argue or continue. You made a statement and you are moving right along to your next point.

They could try to push and ask, "why does that make you uncomfortable?" This is a trap and intended to start an argument and give them some wiggle room to start digging into you. Don't give them an inch.

Them: "Why does that make you uncomfortable?"

Your response is: "It just does. Are you trying to make me uncomfortable?"

Them: "No, of course not."

You:" Oh, good. Then let's move on. So..." (change the subject)

What if they say: "You're just being touchy/too sensitive."

You: "Maybe I am, but it's how I feel. So let's avoid those comments and move on to doing some exercises." (Obviously, that's what I would say if I'm there to do therapy. You're going to say what makes sense for you.)

I have unfortunately had a few instances where a person was insisting on being inappropriate at every turn. Every tactic in my arsenal was worn out and yet, he persisted. I knew that the person did not intend harm. I never felt like I was in danger, but I was starting to dread seeing his name on my list because I was tired of dodging the constant comments. I finally had to deal with it head on and have a pointed talk with him. He was outside when I drove up.

Him: "Should we go inside for therapy?"

Me: "Yes, I think that would be best."

Him: "We headed to the bedroom?"

Me: "Mr. So-and-so, we've got something we need to talk about."

Him: "Uh-oh. Am I in trouble?"

Me: "Yes, a little bit. Let's go inside and sit down." (We go inside)

Him: "Now you know I'm only teasing when I say things like that."

Me: "Yes, I do know you are only teasing and I don't think you mean any harm by it, but it's got to stop. It's very inappropriate and it makes me uncomfortable. I don't like having to dodge those kinds of comments all the time and I need you to tell me that it's going to stop. It's not fair for me to be put in a situation where I am so uncomfortable. If you can't promise me that you're done making those kinds of comments, we're going to have to discontinue your therapy services and see if you can get them from someone else."

Him (very embarrassed): "Oh sure. Oh sure. You know I don't mean anything by it. I'm sorry. I'm not trying to make anyone uncomfortable. It'll stop. I promise. You won't hear another bad comment out of me."

We kept him on our services for about two more months and never had the first unwanted comment after that. I'd like to point out a few things that I did here. I made sure to convey the message that I didn't think he was a bad person (because I didn't) and that I didn't think he meant any harm (because I didn't). Even though the comments made me uncomfortable, he was a good person who loved to tease everyone he came in contact with. He was a big joker, and I'm pretty sure this type of interaction was normalized in his family.

I was not condemning him as a person, I was condemning the inappropriate comments. I made sure to focus on my feelings and to draw a crystal clear boundary line around the situation by letting him know that we could not continue to see him if the behavior didn't change. The last thing I did was employ his sense of fairness ("It's not fair for me to be put in a situation where I am uncomfortable"), which very few people react negatively to.

The last several examples have covered inappropriate teasing. I do want to mention instances where the person is making you upset, but I want to tread lightly here. If the person who is being inappropriate feels dangerous to you in any way, don't keep it to yourself.

At a bar or restaurant: Let a trusted friend or family member know. Send a text message to someone and have them call you if you are by yourself. If you are at a bar, let the bartender know! I've had several friends who were bartenders. They loved a good reason to kick someone out or call the police if needed. Bartenders usually take sexual harassment very seriously and have no Chill when you alert them to a problem you are having with someone. If you need to walk back to your car and feel worried that someone might try to follow you, let the bartender know! They aren't going to be allowed to leave the bar, but they can usually get the attention of someone who could escort you out.

You could also find a nice looking couple and walk right up to the lady and let her know there is a guy bothering you and you want to get to your car. Can one or both of them walk you out or keep watch for you until you can get in your car? I am specifically telling you to address the lady for a reason. Ladies will stick together, and I for one am happy to lend out my personal bouncer (my husband) to another lady in need. However, if I'm on a date with my husband and you walk right up to him and ask him to escort you to your car, you have made a gigantic social faux pas that isn't going to go over well with me or any other woman I know. Address the lady. This whole book is about avoiding awkward situations, right? Trust me.

I'm spending the time here on these options because confronting the person in this scenario is potentially dangerous and I want you to act accordingly. Telling off some guy at a bar is not a great move for your safety, but there is safety in numbers. Use your head on this one and prioritize safety over sass.

At work: This is an HR issue and very much beyond the scope of this book. Wherever you work, there should be an employee handbook with clear rules and guidelines for behavior expectations at work. If something is going sideways and your work has an HR department, these are your superheros and should be your first phone call for advice. Their job is to know and facilitate any issues related to federal law. Call them, ask them for advice, get clarification from them, and report situations to them that you need help handling.

I will give you my thoughts on covering your rear when it comes to work situations: you must maintain a professional demeanor at work. You cannot create a "grey" situation around yourself where your boundaries are unclear and can be widely interpreted. You cannot be hugging people, throwing your arm around people, sitting on your friend's laps, squeezing your coworker's arm and giggling about how big his muscles are, and then throw out a complaint to HR about how someone said something that made you uncomfortable.

I don't mean for you to be stiff and boring at work. I DO mean to keep a bubble around your personal space at work (your body) and refrain from a lot of teasing comments that could be viewed as flirting. This goes for the men equally. Don't be a mister touchy feel-y flirty funny friend guy and then get surprised when someone goes to HR and says you made them uncomfortable. Work related parties? If you are not treating your work parties like an extension of your lunch hour, you are opening yourself up in a big bad way. Familiarity off the clock *does* translate on the clock. You can say I'm wrong, but you can't say I didn't warn you.

Don't go to that Christmas party and overindulge because it's an open bar, and think no one will remember every lap you sat on or that too-short skirt you wore or how you were hanging on that married coworker. Keep your professional life professional. It will go a long way toward protecting your reputation overall and supporting any true complaints you need to take to HR to be taken at face value with minimal doubt.

SEXIST COMMENTS

There are two kinds of sexist comments: 1) the ones that are actually sexist, meaning that the person believes what they are saying and 2) the ones that are only being said to tease you and make you mad.

I'll address the teasing ones first. Here's the thing: the only point to these comments is to get a rise out of you, so if you don't lose your cool, you win. Teasing back is the only way out. Learn to loosen up and roll with it. Not only will you win because you didn't get mad, you will get all the Cool Girl points for having a great sense of humor and making someone laugh. Ultimate win.

Them: "Woman, go make me a sandwich."

You: "You know good and well I don't know how to make a sandwich!" (If you are me)

<or> "Sure, no problem. Were you wanting that garnished with parsley or arsenic?"

<or> "No problem, Sugar. I'll get right on that as soon as you get done taking out the trash and changing the oil in my car. I do think I'm getting the better end of the deal though."

Them: "A woman's place is in the home, not working."

You: "Oh my gosh that sounds amazing! I've always wanted to vacuum my house with heels and a pearl necklace on. You know what would probably be a great idea is a GoFundMe account. Were you looking to make a donation?"

Them: "I don't trust a woman to drive me anywhere."

You: "So you're offering to be my chauffeur?? I knew I'd make it to the top one day. What a sweetheart you are. I'll go get my lap dog and a martini for the road."

Them: "Women can't drive."

You: "What can I say? I like to live life dangerously. Really gets the adrenaline going, you know?"

The very best way to roll with this is to keep pushing it further than the original comment. You are doing the opposite of arguing, you are agreeing and acting like what they said was genius. Everyone can appreciate someone with a great sense of humor who doesn't take herself too seriously. The wit is in how well you can make them laugh, not in shutting them up.

Sometimes you will get comments that are truly bred from ignorance and condescension. In these instances, I will often use the same type of wit detailed above. The difference is that I'm not trying to get the person to laugh, because they aren't going to think it's funny. They really believe that women are second class citizens and there isn't a thing in the world I'm going to be able to do to change their minds. Their beliefs stem from decades of influence that I'm not going to be able to undo in one conversation. However, I'll drop a cast iron pot on my foot before I'll allow someone to make me feel inferior because they are small minded.

The reason I continue to use the strategy of pushing things further instead of arguing, is that it points out how ridiculous their comment is. It also conveys that I am not intimidated by their beliefs and that I won't be put under their foot by their ideas. If they make me upset or cause me to clam up, they've won. I don't have to have the last word, but I will respond.

I had this conversation happen with a patient one time. I

was screening him to see if he might need the social worker to come out. He lived alone but had a son and daughter-in-law who checked on him regularly. I asked if he needed anyone to help him with community resources.

Him: "I need someone to make me some food. Are you going to make me any food?"

Me: "No, sir. I'm the physical therapist. I'm here to work on your strength and balance."

Him: "Well can't you cook me something while you're here?"

Me (trying to make light of it): "Oh, you wouldn't want me to make you anything. I can't cook at all!"

Him: "You can't cook?"

Me: "Nope. Half the time I try to boil water I end up burning the pot. Cooking isn't my thing."

Him: "What use is a woman to anybody if she can't cook? Your husband puts up with that? How does he get fed?"

Me (irritated but refusing to show it): "My husband is actually the cook in our family. He's an amazing cook. I'm a lucky woman!"

Him: "Well I wouldn't keep you around if you wouldn't cook for me."

Me: "So that's all you want out of a woman? Someone to cook for you?"

Him: "Yep. That's what she's doing here (points to his daughter-in-law). Somebody's got to get me something to eat around here so I don't starve to death."

Me (ready to zip up this topic): "Well, if all you want out of a woman is a cook, I hope that's all you get."

I gave a good-spirited laugh, winked at him, and raised my

eyebrows at his daughter-in-law. She thought it was hilarious, he grunted, I changed the topic and he dropped it. I considered that a win. He was trying to shame me and I wasn't going to let that happen. I also didn't prove to him another belief I'm sure he had that "women are too emotional." If I had allowed myself to get upset, he would have written it off as me being hysterical and I would have reinforced his belief.

Very rarely, I will have a patient who refuses to work with me because I am a woman. In this instance, I find it to be very odd. That's about all I can say about it. It isn't personal because this person doesn't know me. It is simply a deeply rooted belief that he isn't in capable hands with a woman giving him direct care in a PT capacity. The patient has the right to refuse services from anyone for any reason. My job is to meet the patient's needs to the best of my ability. My job is *not* to force myself on people. With these things in mind, the conversation usually goes like this:

Him: "You seem nice and all, but I'm not comfortable having a woman as my therapist."

Me: "Ok, can you help me understand why? Is there something you feel embarrassed about that I can help with? Are you afraid I might not be strong enough to help you if you lose your balance?"*

Him: "No, I just don't want a woman doing my therapy. It's nothing personal to you. I don't feel comfortable with it. Don't you have a man you can send out here?"

Me: "I'm really sorry, but I don't. I only have myself and a female PT assistant in this area. Would you be willing to give it a try and see what you think after a few visits?"

Him: "No. If there's not a man that can come out here then I don't want therapy."

Me: "Ok. I wish you would let us help because I think you could really benefit from PT, but you have the right to refuse any service for any reason. I will let the doctor know that we won't be able to do therapy with you, but if you change your mind, I'd be more than happy to come out here and work with you."

Him: "Well thank you. I appreciate it, but I'll stick with the nurse."

Me: "I understand. I hope you have a full recovery very soon. Please let the nurse know if you would like me to come back out here to see you. I wouldn't mind at all. Have a great day."

In this instance, I could choose to be offended. I could choose to try to argue that women are just as capable as men. I could try to explain how educated I am and the degrees and certifications I hold. I could spend a lot of time and energy attempting to convince him that he is wrong to believe that I am not capable, but it would be a waste. The best I can do is refrain from taking it personally and assure the patient that I only want the best for him, and that I respect his wishes. Communicating that I would be happy to come back if he changes his mind leaves the door open for him to get the help he needs in the future. There is no conflict to resolve, only best wishes. You can't help everyone, but you can choose to be kind over being right.

*The reason I asked about the strength issue is that I do have to get past this barrier with my patients sometimes, especially those who are very tall, very weak, and/or excessively overweight. I know I don't always look physically capable because even though I am tall for a woman (5'7"), I am not muscular and I am fairly thin. I totally get it, and I would be in the wrong to be offended by this concern. It is a legitimate worry for their safety and I never mind explaining myself to my patients. I will always take the time to detail how I plan to be safe and assure them that I would never put them in a position that I felt was unsafe or that I was worried I couldn't handle. My patients have to trust me before they can fully participate in therapy, and it's my job to build and retain that trust.

INAPPROPRIATE QUESTIONS/ COMMENTS

Sometimes the conflict you have to deal with is an instance when someone has said something wildly inappropriate or rude, but they say it in a "joking" way. It is very hard to respond to these comments in a way that keeps you in a positive light. You don't want to let the comment slide, you don't want to agree with this ugly thing someone has said, but you also don't want to get offended and argumentative because it will make you look overly sensitive.

Mindset: Many times these statements are made without thought. The person says something they think is funny without taking the time to examine how insensitive or rude it really is. Other times, it is absolutely intentional and the person is being passive aggressive by saying this comment "as a joke" because they know it will be hard for you to call them out on it. My feelings are that if someone has made a comment that was rude and insensitive and has made me uncomfortable, I am well within my right to call them out for it and make them uncomfortable in return, if that's what it takes to draw my boundary.

Boundary: It is not ok for people to make rude or demeaning comments at your expense. I will not allow myself to become the target of criticism or shame because someone else decides to open their mouth. As much as I always want to give people the benefit of the doubt and be kind, this is the exception to the rule for me. Maybe the person truly didn't mean to be rude, but they were rude and I'm not going to let it pass unchecked. I expect others to treat me with respect and kindness and to refrain from hurtful comments. If they don't, we have to discuss it. Yes, even if it's grandma and she's "just kidding."

Here are some common examples of awkward comments "AC" and some example responses you could give "R."

AC: "You must be eating well lately. I think you've put on weight since I saw you last!" (ANY version of this. 'Marriage seems to be treating you well. You're obviously not skipping any meals.' Etc.)

R: "You know, that's a pretty rude thing to say to a person. How would you feel if I announced to the whole room that you looked like you had gained weight?"

They might respond: "I was just kidding. Don't get offended so easily."

R: "Kidding or not, I don't appreciate that comment. How about we refrain from discussing my weight?"

AC: "Are you ok? You've lost a lot of weight recently. Are you sick? You just don't look healthy to me."

R: "You know, I've been putting in a lot of effort into losing weight lately. I'm glad it shows, but I don't appreciate you implying that I'm sick. I'm very happy with the way I look."

Maybe they push: "Well I think you've lost too much weight. I don't like it."

R: "I'm not doing it for you. I'm doing it for me. I hear that the way I look is not your preference, but it is mine. I appreciate your concern for my health, but I would prefer it if we didn't discuss my weight any more."

IF they keep on: "My doctor is monitoring me closely and he/she says I am very healthy. Let's leave this topic to be discussed between my doctor and me."

Here's one that is a GIGANTIC sore spot for me. My boys were born 12 months apart. Yes, it was quick. It's also 100% absolutely, positively, undeniably inappropriate for you to comment negatively about. I will call out absolutely anyone for the horribly inappropriate comments that can happen in this situation or with those who have more than two kids, heaven forbid. And yes, grandmothers seem to be the absolute worst offenders here. Grandmothers get NO free passes. I don't care how cute they are, how funny they think they are, or how upset they will get for being called out. It's unacceptable. Let's field a few variations:

AC: "Haven't you figured out how that happens yet?"

R: "I'm pretty sure it's unprotected sex. Is that how it happened for you?"

AC: "Don't you know that's what birth control is for?"

R: "You don't like kids?"

Them: "What? Of course I like kids."

R: "Then why are you so concerned about me having them? I was hoping for a big family. You can't have a big family without more kids."

Them: "No I didn't mean that. I was just teasing you."

R: "I know you want to make a joke, but I don't want the joke to be at my expense. It feels like you're trying to shame me and that makes me upset. I'm happy that I'm pregnant. I hope you are too." (If it's a family member)

Them: "You don't have to be so sensitive about it. Maybe it's your hormones."

R: "It's not my hormones. That was a very inappropriate thing to say. You just commented about my sex life. How would you feel if someone made such a personal comment about you?"

AC: "Still trying to lose the baby weight, huh?"

R: "Did you seriously just say that? That is such a rude thing to say to someone. I created another human with my body and you are going to make me feel ashamed about prioritizing taking care of my baby and resting over exercise and dieting?"

Don't get mad, but call the person out. Name out loud what they did and call it for what it is. It's rude. It's inappropriate. It's personal. You don't appreciate that comment. It makes you feel shamed, embarrassed, or uncomfortable. How would they feel if someone made a similarly rude comment about them? They will almost always retort by saying that you are being too sensitive. You must very calmly reiterate in a matter of fact tone: you are not being sensitive. *They* are being inappropriate. Don't let them shame you and then shame you again for standing up for yourself. They were in the wrong and you will not budge from that stance. Don't be shy at all about responding, "that was a rude thing to say" and letting that idea hang in the air.

Even if it is someone who you adore and would never want to be mean or rude to, you can still kindly, but firmly, explain that you didn't like what they said and you don't want anyone to make those kinds of comments to you. Surely if they care about you, they would concede and apologize. You can assure them that you know they didn't have bad intentions and that you love them. But keep your boundaries firm here. You can love someone and still point out when they have done something that hurts your feelings. People who truly care about you don't want to hurt you and will respect your feelings when you communicate them clearly and consistently.

INVASIVE QUESTIONS/ COMMENTS

We have already discussed a few times when invasive questions might come up, such as in the Big 3 section. Refer back to those pages to review invasive comments and questions around politics, money, and religion. There can be so many times when you might be faced with an unexpected question that feels too personal in nature to answer, and you might feel like a deer in headlights thinking, "how in the world am I supposed to respond to that?"

When people ask very personal questions, there is usually a reason behind them that has more to do with themselves than you. They are asking for what's "normal" for you so they can decide if what they are dealing with is normal by comparison. Although I can appreciate the reason behind the question, it does not make me obligated to answer the question. You are never obligated to answer a question just because it was asked. I know that can feel like a paradigm shift in some cases. We live in a society that is so invasive and without filters. Everyone airs their personal details on their favorite social media platform in real time these days. It can really blur the line between private and common information.

I find that the two best responses when people ask a question I don't feel comfortable answering is to either parry back, "why do you ask?" or to put on your big kid pants and be honest by replying, "I really don't feel comfortable answering that question. Could you explain what you're needing? Maybe I can help." In this way, I set my boundary from the onset, but I soften it by keeping myself open to being of assistance. It's not that I'm not willing to have a conversation with you, but let's see if we can approach it from a different angle.

Them: "How much money do you make at your job?"

Me: "Why do you ask? Are you looking to make a career move?"

Them: "Do you and your husband fight all the time?"

Me: "Oh no. Did something happen between you and ___?"

Them: "How often does (embarrassing topic or situation) happen to you?"

Me: "Well to be honest I don't really feel like sharing that information. Can you give me a little context here? What's going on?"

Them: "Do your kids ever (something a little too specific or personal)"

Me: "Why do you ask? Is everything ok?"

UNSOLICITED ADVICE

Speaking of children, all parents know the certain brain burning situation where a well meaning (we hope) friend, relative, or stranger attempts to give you advice about raising or disciplining your children when they do not have any children of their own and you have definitely *not* asked for their opinion. This one might make you want to shoot laser beams with your eyes, but let's look at some less violent alternatives.

In case the intro here didn't clue you in, it is beyond rude and always poor etiquette to give parenting advice when you haven't been asked for it. It is down right unacceptable to give parenting advice when you don't have children. Period. I don't care how long you have worked in a nursery or daycare. I don't care how many children you've ever cared for. I don't care if you are a teacher. I don't care if you have your PhD in child development or psychology or...name your credentials. I don't care if you take your nieces and nephews every weekend for the whole weekend. It. Does. Not. Matter.

Before I had children, I had worked in a childcare center, babysat, and done nanny work for over a decade. I had finished my undergraduate degree which had included a fat handful of psychology and human development classes. I had had a baby on my hip nonstop from 11 years old and had college level education to go along with it. You know how prepared I was to be a parent? Barely.

You can have your opinions. Keep them to yourself. At the risk of getting everyone upset who was loving this book until this point I'll go ahead and say it: if you are not an equal member of the team, you don't get to join the conversation. You can educate yourself and have an opinion, but when the conversation comes up, you are a silent member. This book is about avoiding awkward conversations and how to keep your foot out of your mouth. It is about keeping conversations and social interactions pleasant and positive. Not everything I say will be welcome, but I want to help, so the truth has to be said.

If you are a man, I would strongly advise against vocalizing opinions on women's issues. You are not a woman, so you aren't a member of that team. The same thing goes for race and immigration issues. This book will not discuss how to respond to inappropriate racial comments because I am white. I am not qualified to give advice on that topic and I feel it would be grossly inappropriate for me to attempt to do so.

I keep my opinions minimal when it comes to the way my husband interacts with other men. Men are much more frank and sometimes rough with each other than women are. Sometimes I'm baffled that one man doesn't seem offended when approached in a certain way by another man or given advice that is straight-up-no-chaser. However, I'm not a man so I don't have to understand it. I might ask my husband, "so he didn't get mad that you said it that way?" but if he says, "no," I take him at his word. Men are from Mars, Women are from Venus after all, right?

I think in general, it's best to avoid giving opinions that are not asked for. Even when someone does ask your opinion or advice, you would be wise to run through a quick self-check before answering. Does this person *actually* want my opinion, or do they want validation? Are they really only asking my opinion so they can share theirs? If I give them my opinion, are they likely to listen to it or are they more likely to get offended by it? Even if they don't get offended, are they likely to use my advice? Is it a waste of my time and energy to tell them what I really think?

The other pitfall of being asked your opinion is that you might accidentally say something that seriously offends the other person. You would do well to tread lightly through your answer and be very aware of the other person's body language and facial expressions as you speak. Are they appreciating what I'm saying or do they seem like they are getting upset?

When someone asks for your feedback, you should approach your response from the perspective of wanting to help them. You are not telling them what to do, and they are not obligated to take your advice. You are sharing your thoughts and experiences, but the outcome is up to them, not you. If you are starting to feel as though they are getting upset or irritated by your answer, back off. Your only aim should be in the spirit of helping. If your words do not seem to be helping, retreat.

In general, I would suggest you avoid phrases that make you sound like you feel in charge of the other person's actions.

"I think you should…"

"What you ought to do is…"

"You need to…"

"Oh wow, you better…"

Instead, choose wording that focuses on what has worked for *you* while acknowledging that what worked for you might not work for them.

"For me, what has worked has been…"

"When I've been through a similar situation…"

"When I was dealing with that, what helped me was…"

Even if you use these gentler approaches, what you say may still be unwelcome for a variety of reasons (many of which have nothing to do with you). You might get to the end of what you wanted to say, or you may get the feeling that it would be best to stop in the middle of a thought/suggestion and wrap up. Ways to "retreat" or soften your words so they feel like neutral suggestions, not commands include:

"...but those are just my thoughts. You might feel differently."

"...at least that's how I felt when I was going through my situation. Not everyone has that same experience."

"...I felt like doing it that way helped me, but I know you and I have different personalities. You might not be comfortable doing it that way."

"...but I'm not trying to tell you what to do. I'm just sharing what worked for me."

Even though you are now a master when it comes to knowing when and how to share advice, you may still find yourself on the wrong end of someone else's social faux pas. What should you do when someone is pushing their unsolicited opinion on you? There are a few options here. Which one feels the best will depend on several factors, including how well you know the person, how irritating or inappropriate you feel their opinion is, and how pushy they are being.

Mindset: It can be helpful to remember that usually someone who is giving you their opinion means well. It might come across as bossy, uninformed, inappropriate, or overwhelming, but if they are taking the time to give you their thoughts, they are attempting to be useful to you. It can help you gather your thoughts and remove the emotional response to their words if you can remind yourself "they mean well." In these instances, the *distract* and *passive* approaches below are usually most appropriate.

There are unfortunately many times when a person is giving advice to you out of a deep need to be regarded as important, respected, or in control. They are much too attached to the outcome of your situation and they have inappropriately mistaken your right to direct your own life from their own fears or insecurities. This can come from anyone, but most frequently will come from close friends and family members. It can be especially difficult to disentangle yourself from this advice because of the many different layers and aspects to these relationships. In most cases, you would do well to try the *passive* approach first, but be prepared to lay down and hold a boundary by using the *assertive* approach if needed.

Boundary: It is perfectly fine for someone to want to share their experiences with you and to attempt to help you when you are going through difficulty, but it is absolutely inappropriate for someone to feel that they have the right to make your decisions for you. (Again, this is not a relationship book. Take the suggestions here as intended and seek counseling or outside support to navigate dysfunctional personal relationships in your life.)

When a person becomes emotional, upset, angry, or aggressive after you express disagreement with their opinion about your situation, this is a gigantic red flag that they are crossing your boundaries. If they try to shame you, guilt you, or call you names for refusing to agree with their assessment of the situation, you should immediately create an emotional distance from them and reestablish the boundary between asking their opinion and being obligated to it.

This is a two way street, and it is one of the most difficult lessons for me to learn in this life. I have had a countless number of instances in my life where I thought I was going to come apart at the seams watching people who I cared deeply about make decisions that I felt sure were terrible ones. The heartbreaking truth here is that as much as I sometimes wish it weren't true, I have no right to tell that person what to do.

They are autonomous in their own right, and the only control I have is in how I will react to their decisions. If their decisions are hurtful to me or to others, I have the right to refuse to support them, to end the relationship between us, or to limit my interactions with them to the ones I feel I can handle while maintaining my own emotional well-being.

Keep this in mind when receiving the opinions of others. You don't have to take their advice, and they don't have to like your decisions. Sometimes you will simply be at an impasse. It's unfortunate, but you must choose to do what is best for you. When you are being presented with unwanted advice, your three main response options are to distract them, to be as passive as possible, or to assert yourself when necessary.

Distract: This option will work well for people who never stop talking, such as the monologers, complainers, or those who are really giving advice out of idle conversation. You brought something up and they are keeping up their end of the conversation more than they are emotionally invested in the outcome of whatever it is you have told them. Let them get to a natural lull in their commentary and then change the conversation like a slight-of-hand trick. Suddenly you are on a completely different subject without really missing a beat. This one is my favorite whenever possible simply because it is the least disruptive or potentially confrontational.

Remember, you don't always have to respond to people, give your opinion, or let others know when you disagree with them. Letting someone say what is on their mind and then turning the conversation to a new topic is a beautiful skill set. Need an example?

Them: "Well if it was me, I would give them a piece of my mind and let them know how awful they are."

You: "I know it. You know what the boys did last week at school? They had the cutest project that was sent home....look,

I've got a picture. How cute are they?!"

Passive: You might be dealing with someone who feels very strongly about the advice they are giving you, and attempting to change the subject without a proper response would be noticed and upsetting. However, this might be someone you don't know very well or rarely see, and you are mostly looking for a way to put a bow on the conversation and move on.

If you truly want to get to the other side of the conversation without a fuss, your best approach is to agree with what they are saying or make neutral comments that are along the lines of, "I'll think about it." Review the "Responding without Responding" section at the beginning of the book for further examples, but some great responses in this category would be:

"Hmm...that is something to think about."

"Ok, yes. I'll have to think more about that one. Good point."

"Well I hadn't considered that before. Thank you for bringing it up."

"I feel like I need to really take my time before I make a decision, but I appreciate you sharing your thoughts about it."

All of these responses are aimed at addressing the points about a person wanting to feel useful and trying to help. Maybe you didn't take their advice, but you took their intentions seriously and you acknowledged their wish to be useful. Good for you. You were respectful and you made them feel valued, and that is a beautiful connection to have with someone.

Direct and assertive: I would only use this as a last resort with someone who is pushing you to commit to a course of action. Maybe they are simultaneously giving you advice while trying to make phone calls or online purchases to go along with their plans for you. You must step in and set the record straight right away because it will be much harder to undo all of this once they start the ball rolling or say something to someone else that cannot be unsaid. Maybe they are trying to force you to verbally commit to something that you know they will hold against you if you "change your mind" later.

As much as I can't stand this sort of confrontation (if I'm being honest), it is better than the alternative, which is letting yourself get run over. You are probably dealing with someone who has a very strong and forceful personality, and you will have to step up your energy to match theirs if you want to hold your own. You must convince them that you are certain about your position and that they will not be able to sway you to change your mind. If they sense that you are wavering, they will run over you.

The first thing I try to do is buy myself more time. The approach is, 'it's not that I disagree with you, it's just that I haven't made up my mind yet.' This is better received than an outright argument because you haven't actually disagreed with them. You are insisting that you are not ready to make a decision and you need them to back off a bit and give you a bit of breathing room and some time to think.

"I appreciate your opinion, but I am not ready to commit to a decision right now. I need more time to consider my options."

"I know you want the best for me, but I need time to consider what I really want to do."

"I understand that doing it that way worked well for you, but I don't know yet how I feel about it. I want to take my time before I decide. I don't want to rush into anything and then regret it later."

"I find that making snap decisions doesn't always work out the way I had hoped. I have a rule for myself that I need to sleep on something for at least 2 nights (or whatever) to make sure I feel the same way about it in a few days as I do now."

Most people who are strongly opinionated are people who put a lot of time and effort into forming their opinions. They feel so strongly because they've taken a lot of time to consider different viewpoints and draw their own conclusion. Using this against them (and I know because I AM a strongly opinionated person who is a recovering pushy advisor), they will find it very difficult to argue with your need to "take your time" and "consider all the options" because they inherently feel that this is a very wise thing to do.

Maybe someone has taken it on themselves to follow up with you and has placed themselves on your personal board of advisors, and you are getting the distinct impression that you are not going to be able to avoid telling them you don't want their opinion or that you disagree with their assessment of what you should do. Try the following:

"I appreciate how much you want to help, but I need to decide how to deal with this on my own. I need some time and space to figure it out, but I will give you an update when I have one." (Take back control over who is contacting who.)

"I've considered a lot of different options, including the thoughts you gave me, and I have decided that the best course for me is…"

"I love you for caring about me so much and always wanting the best for me. You might not prefer the decision I made, but I am confident that it's going to result in the best outcome for what I need."

You can also appeal to their wish to be helpful, not a nuisance, by saying something like:

"I know you are just trying to help, but I honestly feel a little overwhelmed by how many people are asking for updates on the situation. I promise I'll let you know how it all works out, but I would actually appreciate it if we could not talk about it for a while."

If you are in the middle of making a decision, or have already made a decision, and someone is jumping all over you that you or your decision are "wrong," then we might need to play a little Hank Williams, Sr.'s "Mind Your Own Business." However, instead of blasting it over your speakers in their direction, you can try some of the following assertive phrases:

"I love you, but I have to do what is best for me/my family, and that's what I have done. I'm asking you to respect that and respect me by dropping it."

"I know how you feel about the situation, but I am done discussing it with you. This is my decision to make."

"If you are going to insist on pushing your opinion on me, I'm going to have to keep my distance for a while until you are feeling less emotional about it."

DISAGREEABLE/ RUDE COMMENTS

Hopefully the full-blown arguments between you and others will be minimal. Disagreeable comments, on the other hand, are all too common in daily life. They are present often and everywhere and can be such an annoyance to an otherwise enjoyable day. These comments are likely to be the ones that will catch you very off guard and cause you to freeze in the moment and then think of 10 comebacks you "should have said" when you are laying in bed later that night.

Depending on how rude the comment was, or how malicious the intent was behind the comment, you have some options ranging from completely ignoring the person, or Responding without Responding, to calling them out ("that was rude") to a snappy comeback.

Here I am not referring to something said as a joke, which was addressed previously, but a statement that someone has made that is blatant bad manners and inconsiderate. Here is where my sarcastic side is going to show itself in full force. I don't feel obligated to bow down to someone insulting me unprompted. I feel compelled to address it head on. The boundary here is making it unmistakably clear that you will not tolerate someone treating you poorly or attempting to make you feel bad when you have given them no cause.

AC: "Did you do something different with this recipe? It doesn't taste as good as it usually does."

R: "Well, feel free to not eat it if you don't like it."

(<or> completely ignore them and turn your attention to someone else and start speaking)

AC: "I don't like those pants you're wearing. I don't know why people like that style. I think it's weird."

R: "Well I'll make sure to leave you at home next time I go shopping."

<or> "That's a pretty rude thing to say. I obviously like these or I wouldn't be wearing them. How would you feel if I insulted the outfit you are wearing?"

AC: "Are you ok? You look terrible."

R: "You don't look like you're trying to win any beauty pageants yourself. But thanks for noticing."

<or> "Wow. That was a very hurtful thing to say. Who in the world wants to be told they look rough? What if I said you looked sick today? How would you feel?"

AC: "You need to lose weight."

R: "You need to work on your conversation skills. Geez, what a rude thing to say to someone!"

PASSIVE AGGRESSIVE BEHAVIORS

Many times people will do things that are rude, inconsiderate, or unfair, but they will do it in such a way that makes it very hard to address because they are being secretive about it. These actions can usually fit in the category of "passive aggressive" because they could easily be explained by the person as an "honest mistake" or a miscommunication. If you address them in the wrong way, you come out in a very poor light and find yourself backpedaling and apologizing.

Trying to address a passive aggressive action is like trying to nail jello to the wall. Incredibly frustrating and usually pointless. The *only* way to go about it is to call attention to the bad behavior and suggest a corrective action while refraining from making any assumptive comments about the person's intentions. The person will always give some sort of "oops, that's not what I meant to do" BS excuse, and as obvious as their actions might have been, you cannot *prove* what they meant or didn't mean to do. You address by calling out what they did as an "oops" and then giving clear instructions to them on how to fix it. You bypass the intention completely.

Family member who is always making comments about your weight buys you a piece of clothing as a gift but "forgot" what size you are and buys something several sizes too large or too small and then makes a comment about your weight.

R: "I appreciate you thinking of me, but the size of this is significantly off. If you want to buy clothing for me in the future, it would be best if you check with me first to confirm my size to avoid a lot of hassle with returns and exchanges."

Them: "Oh I can't ever seem to remember. You know I wouldn't do that on purpose."

R: "Well if it's too much trouble to confirm my size before purchasing, we should probably agree to avoid buying items of clothing. I know how much you love to give gifts. We can stick to non-clothing items so there doesn't have to be any question about it."

Them: "Oh, but buying clothing is my favorite thing. I'll do better next time."

R: "I only think that's going to work if you feel confident that you can remember to check with me about my size first. I regularly go through my clothes and donate unusable items to charity. I don't want your gifts to end up going straight to the donation center just because they don't fit." (Big smile)

See what I did there? No wiggle room. I refused to accuse them of getting the wrong size on purpose. I also refused to let them back out of it by simply promising to do better next time. I cornered them into agreeing to an action plan that would give the result I wanted, and then strongly hinted at the consequences of their actions if they continued to "forget" in the future, without threatening of course...because it was just an accident after all. If they forget again, the donation shop can have a brand new item for their sale rack, and someone else can have the blessing of a new piece at a sharp discount. Everyone wins.

Group dinners: I'm referring to a common set up where a group of people or couples are all going out to a restaurant and sharing a table. The suggestion of splitting the bill, splitting the food, or having one person cover the check for anyone can sound fun in theory, but can be a breeding ground for power plays and cheating behavior. I usually see more instances of people asking how to deal with the problems of this set up more than I see people praising it as something they enjoy. However, I know it can be seen as a fun way to do things, and I also recognize that it is far more common in some places than others.

I personally will decline the group-pay scenario to avoid these issues. Simply tell the server that your bill will be separate and announce to the group which items you are ordering that you are planning to share. Even if someone tries to protest and guilt you into doing what everyone else is doing, I would say that I prefer to do it that way to keep everything more simple and straightforward. "It's a personal preference." You don't have to over explain yourself, and if the person continues to push, recognize this as overstepping your boundaries. You address your decision with the wait staff. They are the ones who ultimately ring up the bill and disperse the checks. If you have given clear instructions to keep your bill separate, they will do it.

If you can't bring yourself to lobby for a separate check, you have to realize that you are agreeing to the conflict driven behaviors that may come with it. You might have someone who is taking more than their fair share of the food or paying less than their fair share of the bill. This is really low grade behavior on the other person's part, and you do have the option of calling them out on it; however, even the "nicest" way of calling them out can still make you look like the bad guy, a cheapskate, or petty. If you are going to agree to a community eating or paying plan, you are inherently agreeing to the BS that can come with it. The only graceful way to avoid this is to insist on your own check.

The only scenario you may still need to address is the person who always insists on paying. This is how I would go about addressing this problem:

"I appreciate how generous you are and how willing you

are to want to treat all of us, but I want these dinners to feel more equal. We're not here to take advantage of your generosity. We are here to enjoy your company. I insist that we either split the bill or rotate who pays."

CONFLICTS AT WORK

As I said before, true conflicts in the workplace need to be dealt with through the proper chain of command and/or HR. This section deals with the little words, phrases, and habits that create (or destroy) a pleasant working environment, and help you to maintain your professional brand. We're going to go over words and phrases that can help keep your communications as smooth and peaceful as possible.

In previous sections, we have addressed common issues that can come up at work, such as monologuers, complainers, gossipers, and avoiding or dealing with sexual misconduct. I want to spend some time reviewing other issues that are specific to the workplace that can have a large impact on your day.

The coworker who lies or is two-faced: Oh this is the worst! I always tread very lightly with coworkers when it comes to trust and information because you never know who you can take at face value, and who is simply really good with first impressions. As much as I hate to come across as negative or pessimistic, I've seen and experienced way too many instances of someone flipping from "on your side" to completely untrustworthy, and it only takes one comment, text, or email to create this switch.

People like this usually have huge self-esteem issues. They feel fundamentally flawed or unworthy, and they live in a state of feeling like "it's me or them." They cannot, at their core, be a team player because in their mind, only one person can come out on top, and it has to be them no matter what. Sometimes the person is out to get you from the beginning. They need to know all the juicy details, and they will try to charm you to pieces so that you will let your guard down. These people are easier to detect because you can often feel the bad intentions from the start. Something seems forced and fake, and you aren't sure if they are trying too hard, have social issues that come across in the wrong way, or actually have bad intentions, but your gut is screaming at you to be careful about what you say.

Others really do want to connect and make a friend, but in the end their self-esteem issues get the best of them. This will often come right after you have received some kudos, either a nice recognition during a team meeting, a raise, or a promotion. The fact that you are doing well will send them into a tailspin of comparison, and they will find themselves overwhelmed with the idea that if someone else is getting praised, their job must be on the line. They need to even the playing field quickly to make sure no one thinks less of them, so they will start to dish on you to anyone who will listen, to make sure no one believes you are perfect.

I draw a very firm boundary in my mind between my work and personal life. If I work with this person, it is a work relationship, and will be until one of us doesn't work there anymore. In some cases, I still consider it a professional relationship long after we don't work together. In healthcare, people circulate in the same places and you never know when you might become coworkers with that person again in the future. Don't let an overly friendly atmosphere in between jobs cloud the new one.

There is never a situation where this won't apply, whether it is with a boss who wants to take the "let's be friends" approach, someone who answers to you who really appreciates your leadership style and wants to buddy up, or someone looking for a Work Bestie who can save them from the perils of boredom and stress than can come from the daily grind. I am always very guarded about what I say and share with my coworkers. If you don't give them an insight into your less-than-positive opinions about others or the company, it can't come back to haunt you. Keep your personal and professional lives separate.

No matter how long you have worked with someone, how much you hang out after work hours, or how much you want to consider them a true friend, all it takes is one wrong word on your part and a bunch of screenshots, and your work life can tank. For this reason I have the following rules for myself:

1) Do not speak ill of one coworker to another, no matter what. Hopefully I don't need to elaborate further on that one.

2) Use texting, emails, and phone calls to your advantage and always think about how the method you are using could be used to help you (maybe you need a hard copy of this person's answer so you *want* it to be in email or text format) or hurt you (pick up the phone and call or walk over to their office to have conversations you feel would be better kept off the record).

3) Do not share your personal drama with your coworkers. You and your spouse had a fight last night? Keep it to yourself, or call your mama or best friend later. Coworkers don't need to know things about you that can be leveraged against you because you now seem distracted, too tired, like a drama seeker, or simply unprofessional.

4) Never trust anyone to always have your back. When the chips are down, people will look out for their own best interest over yours 99% of the time. I know this sounds so awful, but as I have said elsewhere: you can say I'm wrong, but you can't say I didn't warn you.

If you find yourself in the middle of a situation where someone unexpectedly turns on you, create immediate distance. If you weren't following the above rules, implement them right away and treat this as a huge lesson learned. Don't try to play their game because you will both get sucked down into it and neither of you will be able to come out of it looking good. Rise above and do the best you can toward damage control.

If you find yourself in the middle of a "he said, she said" situation, call it what it is and refuse to play. Be willing to say, "I know what's true for me, but this situation is speculative at this point. I can't prove my position and neither can they. So what are we going to do from here?" Holding on to your truth like a sinking ship will only put you on the bottom of the ocean. Let go of your need to prove that you are right and move straight to the next step. Take your lumps if you have to, but don't dwell on trying to prove yourself unless you really can produce hard evidence. Sometimes pushing your point too strongly can backfire and make you seem more guilty.

The coworker who doesn't know what they are doing or is always trying to get out of work: We've all had the experience of working with someone who makes us think *how in the world did you get hired to do this??* The person can't figure out how to sharpen a pencil or turn on their computer, or they pretend like they can't so no one will expect anything out of them, but they're on your team and you are stuck with them. It's maddening, and especially frustrating if you have to rely on them as part of your performance review or team outcomes.

Often you will feel that your only viable options are to do everything for them, to ignore them all together, or to complain about everything they do wrong to your supervisor. The downside of each of these "solutions" is that none of them fix the problem, and many times can actually put you in a bad light. You can come across as a control freak, someone who doesn't play well with others, or a tattletale.

The best solution that I have found in these scenarios is to *partner with* your supervisor about *your* expected performance. You can request to meet with your supervisor and explain (very carefully, professionally, and without blaming or complaining) that you are feeling concerned about meeting your job expectations and/or your next performance review. You would like the two of you to come up with a detailed plan that outlines your supervisor's expectations of you over the next month, quarter, etc.

Your supervisor is probably (hopefully) not so out of touch that they don't know that your coworker is a problem. Supervisors usually do a great job of keeping their opinions to themselves about those working under them, and they remove themselves entirely from the drama "on the floor." They DO know about it, however. They know every bit of it. They keep their door open for a reason, and they hear everything said as people walk down the halls on their way to the break room.

You are not surprising them by bringing up Joe who couldn't/won't put together a powerpoint to save his life. Your supervisor already has an opinion about Joe. Their opinion about you is going to be based on how you handle Joe. Are you a tattletale, a pushover, or assertive enough to come to them and request a game plan to help get around the difficulty presented by Joe?

Instead of, "He doesn't pull his weight and I'm stuck doing everything," you can say, "I feel concerned about the responsibility of this project being spread evenly among all of us on the team. I want to make sure there is a clear task list for each of us so that we know which aspect of the project is each person's responsibility. I want to know which parts I need to focus on to make sure I am pulling my fair share of the weight."

This is about clarifying your responsibilities, not you minding Joe's business. If for some reason your supervisor really didn't know Joe was causing such a problem, your supervisor will now be keeping a much closer eye on the situation and will see it unfold as it happens. They will be able to see for themselves how things are really getting done and there won't be a, "he said, she said" issue at the end where everyone is trying to pin the problems on Joe and the supervisor isn't buying it.

Side note: If you take it on yourself to initiate this type of conversation with your supervisor, be aware that they will now be watching you more closely as well. You did stir the pot by bringing this to their attention, and they will want to make sure that you are not simply starting drama or overinflating yourself. You will do well to stay on your "A-game" and keep your head down or this will backfire.

The coworker who is always hogging the commission: This person is so difficult to deal with because they have a good argument for why they are doing what they are doing. If the best salesperson wins, can you really blame them for being the best? It can be tricky to know how you feel about this person, because you are stuck between feeling that they are being unfair and feeling that the setup itself is unfair.

The real problem isn't with the person being great at their job or earning the most. The problem is when the person becomes underhanded or overbearing to get what they want. Many jobs have moved away from a commission based model for this very reason: it can often bring out the worst in people and drain team morale (not universally; this isn't a business class and I can't go down the road on every market sector here).

Many places will try to balance this by having some sort of written or unwritten rules about rotating or distributing things to make sure everyone has a shot at making their money. I've seen options where the person at the register and the person on the floor will rotate every hour. When working retail, and during the craziest times (like Black Friday), I've seen those working commission working the floor like crazy while one person rings the register and alternates going down a list of everyone's ID numbers so that the commission for that day is evenly spread, and the flow of ringing up customers is not bogged down by who was technically helping who.

Many times those who work in a commission based environment will try to cover each other's backs and do their best to stay honorable, but not everyone is a team player. There are those who don't feel that it really is fair for everyone to make an effort to keep things even. They want the chance to shine and prefer each man or woman fend for themselves. Others may want to be balanced in theory, but their bills are so pressing over their heads that they can't pass up an opportunity to ring up someone else's sale as their own.

If you are working with someone who you know isn't keeping everything on the level, you are going to have to be more mindful of every move they make. You may have to politely insist on ringing your own sales into the register ("Thanks for the offer, but I like to ring up everything myself because I'm keeping my own log of my sales." or "I appreciate it, but I like to take my sales all the way to the finish line myself. I helped this person so I want to be the one to ring them up. That way you can stay available for the next customer.")

You might be dealing with someone who keeps asking you for a "favor" (read: sending you to the back to grab stock so they can stay out front where the customers are) and treating you like their assistant. You will have to draw a boundary here, even though it may be very uncomfortable. You are not working for this person, you are working for commissions and you have to be visible in order to do that.

The best approach here is balancing dual needs: "It's not that I don't want to help you, but I haven't had a customer in a while and I need to stay out front to make sure I get a chance to make a connection with someone. However, I don't mind keeping an eye on your customer for you while you go to the back. I can let you know if they make any requests while you are gone."

The most underhanded (in my opinion) is the person who takes a sale out from under you while you are in the middle of helping someone. Perhaps you have gone to the back to grab an item for a customer, and this sweet-talker has walked your customer over to another section and begun waiting on them hand and foot. Cue the Jaws theme (ba-dum). This behavior needs to be called out for what it is, and quickly. It is nearly guaranteed that they will say they didn't realize you were helping the customer. You can respond, "The golden rule when working on commission is to ask the person if they are already being helped before you try to assist them."

Do *not* ask them if they asked the customer. They will say they will and you can't prove it either way. They will also most likely volunteer to assure you that they did ask the customer if they were being helped and the customer said "no." Then you can reply, "I hope you really did ask them, but I find it hard to believe they would have said 'no' considering I've brought them several items at this point. I will chalk this one incidence up to an honest miscommunication, but I hope I can trust it won't be a common occurrence."

You can't prove what happened this time, and you can't say it shouldn't *ever* happen again, because that's not reasonable either. However, you can make sure they know you are calling BS on them, that you will be watching them like a hawk, and that you are more than willing to call them out on it if they do something like that again. It will make them less likely to try to get away with it, at least where you are concerned.

As a very last resort, you might consider asking to be scheduled on a different shift from that person to protect your sanity and your blood pressure. You would have to weigh the pros and cons of that move in relation to your specific situation, so I will be minimal with my thoughts here. My only further suggestion if you felt the need to do this would be to phrase your reason along the lines of, "I'm feeling concerned about my ability to have the opportunity I'm looking for on this shift."

Your supervisor might well know there's been some tension and may ask some clarifying questions about your request. Try to keep it as objective and non-accusatory as possible. Avoid any form of, "He's cheating and stealing all the customers and I can't stand it anymore." You are not here for the drama, so don't be the drama.

The drama queen/king: Speaking of drama, what about that coworker who can't seem to live without it? Everything is a big deal. The world is always ending. Their life is always a wreck. They've got all the latest updates on anyone you can think of, at the office or anywhere in the world. This person is a landmine waiting to be stepped on. Before you know it, you can be swept up in their real life soap opera, and your reputation can quickly go downhill as a result.

People generally don't like drama, and drama doesn't make for good management or promotions. Even the dramatic people are quick to identify others as the drama. It's insane! As soon as you identify someone else as an over-the-top pot stirrer, make some distance. You can absolutely be friendly and nice to them, but avoid getting too close. This does not need to be your work bff.

A lot of what they will have to say will fall under the categories of "complainers" and "gossipers," so refer to those sections for review on handling those conversations. The unique aspect here is the general grandiose behavior and exaggeration of everything they relay. The way I handle these aspects is by balancing them with my own energy. Remember the 'Responding without Responding' section? This person is going to get a lot of mild, "Oh goodness." "Well that sure is something." "Wow." comments out of me.

I tend to respond this way when anyone gets too dramatic with their storytelling, even if that's not their usual style. I don't enjoy it personally because it seems theatrical and fake. It becomes more about being the center of attention by telling the story, rather than the content of the story itself. If my energy stays more mild and reserved, the other person will tend to mirror that energy by taking it down a few notches. This way of reacting on my part will also communicate to them and anyone else listening that I am not an equal participant in the drama. I am polite, I am congenial, but I am too professional to lose my sense of sensibility.

The drama can also come in the form of angry outbursts. This is a whole other ball of wax because the angry person is at minimum a nuisance and at worst a cause of much anxiety in the workplace. Since this person is a ticking time bomb, they are best left to themselves. I try to completely avoid these people. I'll give a mild smile and a quick, "Hi, how are you?", and then high-tail it in the other direction. That is the full extent of my interactions with them.

This kind of drama is destructive and unpredictable. I don't want to be around when the person goes off, I don't want to be associated with them as someone who condones their demeanor, and I definitely don't want to become their next target. Treat this person as you would a wasp nest. Stay quiet, don't make any sudden moves, and keep your distance unless completely unavoidable.

Call this approach what you will, but for me it's just good business. This person has layers upon layers of issues that they refuse to sort out; their anger comes from a bottomless well and there isn't a thing I can do or say to fix it. Their fuse might be really long with me if I am generally nice to them, but it does run out at some point, and I will never be exempt from their contempt.

Condescending coworkers: If there was ever a coworker who might make you do or say something that gets your own butt fired, it's going to be this one. It's hard to explain exactly why condescension is one of the most difficult things to tolerate, but I'll take a screamer over this person any day of the week. At least with the screamer, we're being honest and calling it what it is.

The condescension might be so awful because it's passive aggressive. It's the smug look, the paternal tone, and the implication that you are incompetent or inferior that makes you want to really wring their neck. If you've never considered meditation before, it could be a great tool to add to your toolbox because being able to immediately access your inner zen is the best way I know to survive this coworker.

What you need to keep in mind (and I do understand the tall order here) is that the only people who are condescending to others are those who feel massively inferior themselves. The two-faced coworker and the condescending coworker are only one step removed from each other. The two-faced coworker is living from a place of needing to tear others down just to feel like the playing field has been equalized. The condescending coworker is using an air of superiority to convince both you and themselves that they know more than they feel they do and that they are more important and influential than they think they are.

While the two-faced coworker is actively trying to tear you down by hurting your reputation, the condescending coworker is more focused on trying to raise themselves above everyone else. Same inner demons, same intended outcome, different approach. There is no point in trying to beat this person at their own game. You will have a very hard time ceasing or calling them out on their behavior. If you do attempt it, you will usually end up making yourself look bad, or worse: playing right into their hands.

As with so many things in this book, you win by refusing to react. The person already feels completely inadequate and inferior. You're not going to be able to say anything to "put them in their place" because they are already there, and their overcompensation is on overdrive. The only way to take the wind out of their sails is to show that they don't have power over your emotions. They can't make you feel upset, embarrassed, or less than.

Sometimes when I'm struggling with frustration because someone is speaking to me in this way, I try to remember what's really going on, connect to the truth, and remind myself, "it must be really awful to walk around feeling so inadequate all the time. I wonder what they've been through in their life that makes them feel the need to be this way?" It makes it so much easier to blow off the tone and move on. This person feels crippling levels of inadequacy. That sucks. If speaking to me in this ridiculous way is what gets them through the day, whatever. At least I don't suffer from those problems.

If there is a specific person who constantly pushes and pushes, and ignoring or reframing it isn't enough, you can attempt to address it. This behavior does fall under the category of passive aggression, so it is very difficult to address. The person can easily slip out of it by claiming that they don't know what you're talking about or that they didn't mean to sound that way. We're back to trying to nail jello to the wall, so get your hammers.

As with all types of passive aggression, you have to focus on very specific behaviors that are bothering you, why the behavior is a problem, and a specific action that needs to be different for next time. You absolutely cannot make a comment about what you perceive to be the person's intentions; you will only win by going along with their claimed intention. Have you ever heard of the improv game, "yes, and.."? The idea is that whatever the person before you says, you have to agree with it and take it a step further. This is opposed to, "yes, but…" where you are potentially arguing with the person or trying to reverse or negate their suggestion.

You cannot get into an argument here, you must corral the conversation in the direction you want, like a sheep dog! Always give lip service to their innocence, because they will insist on it. [They only had good intentions and you misunderstood what they were trying to say.] They will die on that hill, so don't make that the battle you pick. You can call them out as sounding condescending or rude, but you will have to refrain from engaging in the argument they will try to start as a result.

Scenario 1:

Them: "Oh here I did this for you because I know you have trouble with these kinds of reports."

You: "I know you were trying to be helpful, and I appreciate that, but I do like to do these reports in a very specific way. Next time, I need you to ask me before you take it on yourself to complete one of these reports on your own."

Them: "It's no trouble at all. I only want to make things easier on you. I know you stay so tired from having so much on your plate."

You: "As nice as that is for you to think of me, I want to make sure you heard what I just said. I need you to consult with me before you do this again. I have to sign off on these reports, and it makes it harder for me to know what's in them when you jump ahead like this."

Them: "Oh sure I get that, no problem."

You: "Great. To make sure we're understanding each other here, you are agreeing that you won't finish any more of these reports without consulting me first, right?"

And let me tell you that I have reached a point in my life where I will absolutely call someone out when they are trying to mis-direct a conversation or avoid agreeing to something.

If I have to, I will absolutely say, "Hold on. I'm trying to make a plan for 'X' and every time I bring up 'Y,' you change the subject. I need a 'yes' or 'no' from you. Is this what we are doing or not?" Maybe it's because I'm a mom now. Mama ain't got time for this run around.

Scenario 2:

Them: "I wanted to make sure you understood that because I know you get confused about things sometimes."

You: "That's a very rude thing to say to someone."

Them: "I wasn't trying to be rude!"

You -- stay silent and let them try to wiggle their way out of it. The less you say, the more they will chatter. 'I only meant...' 'I was only referring to that one time...' 'You misunderstood, I was just trying to say...'

These people are the masters of twisting things around. If you don't say anything, they have nothing to twist except their own words. You have nothing to say to a person who has nothing nice to say. You can end the conversation by walking off, shrugging your shoulders, or giving an uncomfortable "well...have a nice day." They will forevermore be hesitant to try to take a jab at you like that again, because you have exposed their greatest fear: that they are flawed. They won't be in a hurry to go there with you knowing that you will call them out so quickly and then leave them to flounder.

Scenario 3:

Them: "Did that last memo make sense to you? Because the email you sent this morning sounds like you didn't understand it."

You: "What was it specifically that you need me to clarify from the email I sent this morning?"

Them: "Well I was concerned about...."

You: "Ok, well what I wanted to convey about that was…"

Note that in the above exchange, I refused to answer the question of whether or not I understood the memo. That was the part of the original comment that was the problem: it implies that I didn't understand something. Spin this on its head. Apparently this person *misunderstood* something about my email, so focus the conversation on what *they* didn't understand.

With people who have this problem, they are trying to put on a show, and you are refusing to buy tickets. Tight smiles, raised eyebrows, ignoring entire sections of what they have to say (so you can skip to the only part that matters), and silence will be your best friend. I won't walk into the maze of your conversation. We're going to stay on the outside edge and tread lightly. Move along please.

The coworker who won't quit talking to you while you are supposed to be working: Oh dear that sweet person who can't help themselves but to stand at your desk or cubicle and chatter your ear off for an hour at a time. The productivity killer. This person is usually well meaning, and often someone that you do enjoy speaking to, but they are killing your numbers or causing you to have to work off the clock to make up for everything you didn't get done during the day.

As much as you might prefer to talk the day away with this person (or you may actually wish they would move on), you have to find a way to cut them off without hurting their feelings. If you have an office with extra chairs, removing the chairs or keeping them piled high with stacks of things will help. If the person makes themselves comfortable, it's exponentially harder to get them to walk away. Removing temptation or opportunity can make an immediate improvement.

We've all seen the funny signs people post on the back of their office chairs that say something like "for my own sake, please don't talk to me or I will chat with you all day and get nothing done." Don't be afraid to print one of those! If someone stops by, point to the sign and let them know "I can give you all of 5 minutes before I'm going to have to cut you off for both of our sakes. I've got several projects that I have to focus on right now, and I've got to be more disciplined about working on them."

You can covertly set a quick three to five minute timer on your phone and put the phone face down on your desk when the person walks up. When the timer goes off, use that as your excuse to get back to work. "Oh, that's my reminder to start on that paper." This is the perfect place to introduce you to a southern phrase that has ended many a never-ending conversation. Repeat after me: "Let me let you go." or it's twin sister, "I'm going to have to let you go."

See the beauty of this one? I'm letting you go, but half the time you are the one who is going to walk away. It's the wonderfully sweet alternative to the never appropriate, "I need you to go," but with the exact same end effect. It's not you, it's me. It's my deadline, my task, my schedule that is causing the time constraint, but the punchline is that we have to stop chatting with each other so I can take care of the other thing.

The tattletale: You would think there would be certain advantages to growing up, such as never having to deal with tattletales again, but you would be wrong. Somehow this incredibly juvenile trait will go with a person to infinity and beyond if they never deal with the underlying problem. As with many of these difficult cases, the tattletale is coming from a place of inferiority. They go to extremes to make sure they are doing everything as perfectly as humanly possible for the satisfaction of calling you out when you don't.

These people often came from authoritarian or absentee homes growing up. Their own level of perfection in childhood may have been bred from a need to avoid extremely high levels of criticism. Alternately, the act of "telling" on someone else was about the only time they could get any attention. It is dysfunctional behavior bred from a dysfunctional inner world. Unfortunately, it is definitely your problem because this person is hypervigilant about taking note of and reporting every small variation in your performance.

The outcome may feel very similar to the person who is two-faced, but it stems from a different problem. The person who is two faced will usually be satisfied with feeling that you aren't doing as well as they are in one way or the other, or at least that you are not doing better than they are. Their interest in you waxes and wanes with their own perception of how the two of you are doing relative to each other. The two-faced person can easily become distracted by another person or situation and may lose interest in you all together.

The person who is a tattletale is hypervigilant about all people at all times. They are driven from a deep need for control and order, and this does not wax or wane. It is in full force all the time, and you will not be able to get them to lose interest in you. With these people, you simply must do your best to check and double check everything you do that they are involved in, knowing that they will find and report every small discrepancy. I wish I had better news, but I don't.

I would mostly avoid this person. They are always on the lookout for anything they deem to be incorrect, and you have few ways of knowing what they may feel they can use against you. Be polite and keep your head down. All of this would similarly apply to the person who feels the need to copy the whole world on every email they send. It is a dysfunctional need to be right, to have control and order, and to show their superiority through hypervigilance. These people are difficult to work with, but trying to address the problem will bring down a lot of unwanted heat on you, with next to no chance of getting them to stop this unwanted behavior.

The suck up: You know who I mean. They can appear out of nowhere and they are completely oblivious to how uncomfortable they are making everyone (even and especially the person they are focused on impressing). It is bizarre and cringe-worthy behavior, but it is harmless. Try to let this one roll off your back. The deep-seated need for approval is front and center here. Try to have compassion for this symptom that signals a deep inner hurt, and move on. This person isn't hurting you or anyone else.

If you are the target of their endeavors, I would focus my efforts on ignoring anything they do or say that is over the top, while trying to help redirect their focus to what you need them to do (their job). You don't want to reinforce the over the top behavior by mistakenly thinking that giving them a lot of praise will help. You mostly have to walk the line of staying just on the positive side of neutral. You are not hurting their feelings by being mean, or even exactly neutral (as they will perceive indifference as rejection). You want them to know you do not reject them, but you are trying to help balance their exuberance by keeping your responses more mild. Positive without being overly personal.

Instead of, "Wow, that's wonderful! Thank you so much!" you can balance it with, "Thank you. I appreciate how hard you worked on that." Just take it down a few gears.

Difficult supervisors: Unfortunately, not all supervisors have been hand trained by Tony Robbins to be the most amazing motivators, supporters, and thought leaders in their industry. Some supervisors are scattered and can't remember what they've told you to do, others are phoning it in all day every day and are as effective as the chair they sit in, and some out there are angry and overpowering.

You might have a supervisor whose lack of inspirational leadership doesn't really bother you, it all kind of works itself out. There is a groove in the office that keeps the train rolling, even if it's missing some wheels, and everyone is pretty satisfied with it. Sometimes your boss is a total hothead, but he never comes out of his office except during the monthly meeting, so as long as you avoid him it's not too big of a deal. Maybe he yells, but there's never any real aftermath to it. Although you're not a huge fan of this approach, you know it's not personal, so you usually roll your eyes when it happens and continue on with your day.

The time when there is a real problem is when the poor or bad communication is causing trouble for you specifically. Maybe your supervisor can't remember from one day to the next what she's asked you to do, and then gets frustrated that you are working on something "that you shouldn't be." Maybe she knows exactly what she's doing, and she's letting the blame roll downhill onto your shoulders by asking one thing of you on Monday and something else on Tuesday.

Get it all in writing. She wants you to work on project A? No problem. Can you send that to me in an email so I can file it appropriately on my task list? Oh today she wants you to drop project A and focus on project C? Sure thing, boss. Can you zip that over to my calendar and copy so-and-so on it? Blame it on yourself. You are working on getting yourself better organized. You feel like you've been forgetting things lately and you want everything in hard copies. You are trying to streamline your many points of contact into one main method of communication so your task list isn't so scattered: you're worried things could start falling through the cracks. You are working with a career coach and they have asked you to start creating a consistent approach to your workflow to minimize errors and stress. You have been worrying that you are forgetting things.

Create a paper trail that you can refer back to when you are questioned about why you are hopping all over the place and not getting anything finished. You can provide these hard copies to this person who is creating havoc if they try to come at you with an "I never said that." You can also provide this info to the person above them or in a different department who wants to make heads and tales of why none of these projects are getting across the finish line. No matter what, cover your butt so that you have a leg to stand on if things get crazy.

Vocab at work: Hopefully by now you know the power of words and the huge impact that can be made from changing a word or a phrase into something that will be better received. The workplace might be the most shining example of this. One terse exchange or email can create a cascade of negativity that can feel never ending. Due to the increased stress created by the work environment, it can be easiest to offend others in this setting. On the other side, knowing how to present your ideas and concerns in a professional manner can make you stand out head and shoulders above the rest. Sometimes you only need one good example of a time when you "really handled that well" to earn the respect of everyone on your team. Here are some basic pitfall phrases and how to better present them:

"I already told you" vs "as we discussed in the meeting earlier this week..."

"That's not what I said, I said.." vs "in the email I sent on Monday..."

"They lied about..." vs "There seems to have been a miscommunication..."

"He didn't do what he said he would..." vs "It seems that he hasn't had a chance to..."

"This person has been lying about..." vs "I'm concerned about a communication issue regarding..."

"I don't have time to..." vs "I need us to go over my current task list so that you can help me prioritize which items you want me to focus on right now."

That last one brings up a common concern. What if you are being asked to work on a project, but you are already swamped? Don't pitch a fit about it and don't try to turn yourself into a human time machine that can do the work of multiple people. Reframe the situation as one of priorities.

"I've got too much on my plate! I can't possibly add one more thing!" Can become:

"I want to use my time wisely by working on the top priority projects first. Here is my current task list....which of these items do you want me to focus on now and which ones can be pushed to a later date?

Maybe someone insists that it all must be completed right away and nothing can be pushed until later. You can respond:

"Ok. Thank you for letting me know that all of these issues have equal priority. I want to make sure that all of them can be completed by the deadline, but I am also confident that I will not be able to complete all of them well and by this deadline by myself. Who else can be assigned to this task to make sure it is completed in a timely manner?"

You are only one person and there are only so many hours in the day. You owe the company an honest day's work and to do the job you were hired to do to the best of your (reasonable) ability, but you don't owe them your soul. We live in a society that is at war with itself right now, hung between the extremes of trying to retire by 30 and working 24/7 right up until the day you die from exhaustion.

The age of cell phones, internet, and social media have not only blurred, but completely erased the idea of "clocking out" at work. It is no longer possible to leave the office. Even if you are physically out of the building, laptops, ipads, tablets, cell phones, and zoom calls can follow you anywhere. The expectation has become such that if you have access to the internet or your cell phone, you can be working. While this can, at times, be a lifesaver, it is more often than not a soul killer. We must now learn the art of reestablishing the boundary between what is reasonable and what is not. Don't kill yourself trying to do the work of multiple people. If you need help, *ask for it.*

One last thought about keeping silent and pushing yourself to the point of exhaustion: it actually hurts everyone. If you keep your mouth closed and refuse to alert anyone that you are overwhelmed, everyone suffers. You suffer because you are becoming more and more burned out by the day and eventually you will break and likely quit the job. Now the company has suffered losing a great employee.

If you pretend like the workload is doable, there is no reason for the company to believe otherwise. You have now set this incredibly high bar as "standard" for yourself and others. This means that you will continue to be expected to perform at this rate until the end of time (you suffer). It also means that anyone else in your role will be expected to perform at this same rate (they suffer). If you can do it, everyone should be able to! Being miserably overwhelmed does not make you a hero, it only makes you miserable.

If you bring up your concerns to the company and they continue to insist that you should be able to work at 150% capacity 100% of the time, you need to walk away. Don't let your life be crushed by a job. There is so much joy and support to be had in the world. This company may have been the center of your daily life for a very long time, but it isn't actually what matters in the end. Joy, love, connection, friends, family; these are the things that make life worth living. If your job is robbing these things from you, then the company culture is dysfunctional. You can't fix the company, but you can go find another one to work for.

Maybe your current position has reached the end of its course. It's time to part ways, either on your terms or not.

Should you pour gasoline on that bridge, flick a lit match, and watch with sweet satisfaction as the bridge burns to the ground in a fire-fueled glory? I mean you could...but probably not a great idea.

I have had a handful of jobs in my life that have all ended for different reasons. I was leaving for college (lots of jobs ended due to moving), progressing from retail to a "real job" after graduation, had a great new opportunity on the horizon that was going to be a huge upgrade for me, or things had reached the end of their place on my journey. Sometimes I was very hesitant to go, and sometimes I couldn't wait to start on the next opportunity.

Leaving a job is the trickiest part. You are so ready to move on that you may feel reckless, especially if you are leaving because you've had enough of the job and there are already hard feelings. As tempting as it can be (believe me, I've been there) to want to tell everyone what you really think of them, list everything that anyone has done that you felt was wrong, and leave in a blaze of glory, it's not a good idea.

On a practical level, you never know where the path will lead, and you may need to reach back out to people months or years down the road for some kind of assistance. You might possibly need some information, a reference, or even your old job back. Flipping everyone off and giving a shout of "see ya never, suckers!" as you squeal out of the parking lot will definitely leave an impression, but might also come back to haunt you later.

Even if you are sure beyond a shadow of a doubt that you'll never be darkening the doors of that place ever again, people circulate in certain fields of work. You might never go back to that company, but someone you've worked with there might become a coworker later in life. You don't want the awkward memory of that final exchange following you around.

Maybe you are switching fields or locations all together

and feel sure that there is no way setting off a stink bomb in the office right as you are leaving could ever come back to bite you...I would still advise you to take the high road. If you are a person reading this book and you have made it this far, you know my thoughts on mindset, boundaries, and emotionally detaching yourself from difficult situations that you can't control. You want the last impression you leave to be of someone who is cool, calm, collected, and professional. There may be hurt feelings, but you're going to rise above it.

Yes, as much as you might be dying to leave and counting down the minutes until your final time stamp out the door, the whole office is also shifting around you leaving. They are also preparing for the change, and it can make them also feel emboldened or cavalier with their words and actions. Especially petty people may make your last days even harder than they already were, provoking those choice words to come to the front of your mind. As I have said over and over, if the other person is unable to get a rise out of you, you win.

All of their kicking and flailing, finger pointing, nasty comments, and sugar sweet emails dripping with poison will fall around you like snow if you can come back into the center of the storm and breathe. You gave your notice, you did your job, you wrapped up your last day and said your good-byes. Walk out with your head high and a smile on your face. They didn't win, you did; and now you are on to a bigger and better adventure!

PART 3

Don't forget your FREE companion workbook!

https://courses.yourconversationexpert.com/workbook

ILLNESS, CAREGIVER BURDEN, AND DEATH

Oh my sweet friend, we have made it to the final section of the book. What a roller coaster ride it has been! I'm so glad you have stayed with me this far. I am really excited to explore these topics with you. This section is very near and dear to my heart because I deal with these difficulties every day. It feels a little odd to say that this is my area of expertise, but it is something that I feel very passionately about.

I often say that physical therapy is 50% physical and 50% therapy. A lot of what a physical therapist asks you to do is not technically complicated (unless you are doing sports rehab!), but the mental strength needed to participate can sometimes be overwhelming. When a person has been through a traumatic accident, emergent medical issue, or has suffered a difficulty that may alter how they live their lives forever, there is a lot of anxiety or depression that can form.

Working in home health, my patients are often the oldest and most medically fragile group of people. They have suffered a lot in their lives, including loss of loved ones, loss of independence and mobility, loss of memory, etc. When someone of this age has to rely on others heavily to get through a situation (either temporarily or permanently), those closest to them also have to shift their lives.

Many times a person has arrived at the point in life where their children have all grown and flown the nest. Then they are suddenly faced with the need to care for a parent who lives in a different home, sometimes far away, and coordinate all kinds of medical care, doctor's appointments, and medications. They have to figure out how to manage all of that while continuing to work, because they are ten to fifteen years away from retirement.

Other patients of ours might be younger but undergoing extremely difficult life circumstances, such as cancer, MS or a stroke. These patients may have young children they need to care for, but barely have the strength to take care of themselves. Their main caregiver might be a spouse who is having to choose between staying at home to care for them and working to keep the lights on.

I want to make sure and review all of this because, in my opinion, it is a vital part of feeling like a well-spoken person who doesn't become daunted by conversation. This could be you, a friend, a family member, or a stranger you come across during your day. If you have some context to draw from when it comes to these hard topics, you will be able to connect with someone in a way that is meaningful instead of smacking your forehead every time you think about what you said the last time something like this was brought up.

ILLNESS

I'd like to tell you a story that I'm sure my husband will be thrilled for me to share. When we had been married for around a year, I became sick. Nothing terrible, but a pretty crummy flu that made me really miserable for about a week or so. Most people agree that women tend to lean towards "nurturing" while men tend to be "fixers," and this can create some difficulties when communicating with the opposite sex. My husband and I are no different.

All I wanted to do was sleep and rest, but after a few days of it, my hubby was getting anxious for me to get back to normal. He kept suggesting that we should go places. I guess he thought that acting like nothing was wrong would make it all go away. Maybe he was really bored and was tired of tip-toeing around the house. Regardless, he kept asking me if I wanted to go to the grocery store with him (no), or to a restaurant to eat a good meal that would make me feel better (no), or to ride around in the car for a bit to get some fresh air (no).

Being so newly married, I was desperate to avoid hurting his feelings or starting a fight, but I was so tired and achy I could barely stay upright, and I was becoming more upset with every new suggestion. I finally burst into tears which completely shocked him. He ran over to me, bewildered, and asked, "what's wrong??" and through tears I sobbed, "I just want my mom!" Ok, he said, we could go up to see her that weekend (we were living about an hour away at the time). "No! I want her right now!" Still confused he asked, "Why? What's wrong? What do you need?" and I managed to choke out, "When I'm sick she never asks me to go anywhere or do anything. She just hugs me and snuggles with me and tells me she's sorry I don't feel good, and that's all I want right now!" (Cue the floodgates to open).

Ok, I was being a little bit hysterical. I'll blame it on the fever, but it was also made worse by my anxiety around the fact that I didn't know how to communicate what I truly needed at that moment. My husband, being a military man, gave me a loving but pointed Look that said, 'Alright, I get it. Pull yourself together,' opened his arms up wide and gave me a really big long hug. He said, "I love you. I'm sorry you don't feel good," and then helped me back to bed. We've been married almost 14 years now and even to this day, when I get sick the first thing he says is, "I'm sorry you don't feel good."

I share this story to make a point. Often when we are faced with a person who is suffering, it makes us uncomfortable. Either we don't know what to say, and we want to get out from under the conversation as quickly as possible, or we genuinely feel upset for this person and wish we could do something to make their situation better. Our well-meaning, but misguided, efforts become focused on trying to "fix" the problem. We end up saying things that we know aren't helpful because we don't know what else to say. We try to assure them that everything will be fine at the sacrifice of acknowledging their current reality.

What do you do when you touch something that is burning hot? You pull away from it immediately. What do you do when you step on something that is painfully sharp? You get off of it as quickly as possible. Humans are hardwired to pull away from discomfort. We have many reflexive reactions that will pull us away from noxious stimuli before our brains have even registered the event.

This tendency spills over into our conversations with others. When we encounter a topic that makes us uncomfortable, we try to get off of the subject as quickly as we can. The problem with this is that we know, deep down, that the other person is suffering, and we know that making light of it only increases their suffering and feelings of isolation. When we express hard emotions and are met with an unfeeling comment, we receive the message that our true feelings are not welcome.

As a herd species (and humans are), we will do what we can to change our behavior to be more palatable for the other person, even if that means pretending that everything is ok when it isn't. At the very least, we will stop discussing it or change the topic to make the other person more comfortable. No matter which of these options we choose, we feel deeply alone because we are now suffering in silence.

As the person who is bearing witness to another person's suffering, I would ask you to commit to staying present and leaning in. Be willing to go there. Be willing to hear the sad news, the hard times, the heartbreak and to resist running away from it. This person is going through something very real and very difficult. What lifts their spirits is to feel heard and supported, and you do that by listening and validating their feelings. Let's review some common phrases people will use (awkward comments, "AC") to respond to bad news and my suggestion for a better replacement "R."

AC: "Don't worry, it will all work out."

R: "I'm so sorry you are going through this right now."

AC: "I'm sure you'll feel better soon."

R: "It's so hard when you don't have any energy. Are you getting enough rest?"

AC: "Don't be so upset. It'll be fine."

R: "I hate that you are so upset. Is there something I can do to help?"

AC: "Yes, but that was a long time ago." (Implying that you should be "over it.")

R: "Sometimes it feels like it was just yesterday, doesn't it?"

AC: "They are in a better place now."

R: "I know you must miss them so much."

AC: "You're making a really big deal out of this. Calm down."

R: "This has obviously been very upsetting to you. Can I give you a hug?" (There I go hugging people again!)

AC: "I hope I never have to go through that."

R: "I can't imagine how hard this is for you. I wish there was something I could say that would make it better. I'm here to listen to anything you want to share."

These suggestions are universal for all illnesses. It could be temporary such as the flu, surgery, or injury; or chronic such as stroke, heart attack, or other medical condition that has left long-lasting effects. I want to touch on another aspect of injury or illness that can be present more often that you might imagine, and that is the dreaded "what if." It is best to focus on the present moment, even if that moment is difficult, rather than trying to redirect someone's focus to an uncertain future.

If you are speaking to someone who feels a large amount of anxiety around regaining their prior level of function, resist the urge to assure them that everything will be ok. This could be an athlete who is incredibly concerned about getting back onto the field or court, a laborer who is deeply worried about regaining their physical ability to return to work, an artist or musician who just had hand surgery and is about to come apart at the seams with anxiety about getting their dexterity back. It could be anyone for any reason, but they are very concerned that their life may never be "normal" again if they don't recover fully.

Trying to assure this person that everything will be ok is rarely helpful. This person knows exactly what is needed to succeed, and they know how far they are from that level at the present moment. By telling them that everything will be fine, you are shining a light on the difference between what they know and what you know. You would comfort them a lot more by helping to redirect their focus on what can presently be done to help their situation, and reminding them that no one knows what the future holds, so try to cross that bridge when they come to it, and not before.

I go over this a lot with my patients who have had strokes. I will call their fear out (naming your fear takes away a lot of its power). I usually see them within 1-4 weeks of their stroke. I will tell them "I know your mind is all over the place right now. I know you are very worried about how much of this is permanent, how much movement you are going to regain, or what will happen if something doesn't come back (they usually nod vigorously here). Please, please try to not obsess about it. I know that's hard to do, but we are months and months away from knowing how much you will or won't recover from this. [I go into tons more detail about stroke recovery here.] Right now what we need to do is focus on resting, getting good nutrition, and participating in therapy. I need you to really prioritize your home exercise program, and work hard with therapy when we are here. I don't have a crystal ball. I can't see the future and neither can you. As hard as it is, focus on today and what we need to do right now to get you one step closer to normal."

I *never* tell them they will get back to normal, because I don't know that. I will tell them the things I am seeing that are really encouraging to me. I will tell them what typical recovery looks like. I assure them we are going to do everything we can to get them as strong as possible. I give them action steps they can do to feel more in control of their situation (rest, nutrition, exercise). Saying, "don't worry, you'll be fine", is an unhelpful thing to say. They don't feel any truth in it because there isn't any truth in it. I don't know for sure that they will get well and they know it.

Alternatively, when I see them getting frustrated and I feel the anxiety rising, I don't focus on pep talks and action steps. I stop everything, have them take a rest break, and open up a dialogue about how they are feeling. "You seem really overwhelmed right now. Talk to me. What's got you worried?" "I can tell this is really frustrating you. It's *so* infuriating when our bodies don't do what we tell them to do. I can't imagine how overwhelming all of this is for you. What do you need? Do you want us to keep working on this or do you want us to switch to something else and give this a rest for a while?"

When a person is spiraling about the future, help them come back to the present moment. They feel out of control, so this is a good opportunity to let them know you are here to help. See if you can help make a game plan for them. What can we work on right now that will help you get closer to your goal?

When a person is overwhelmed about the present moment, stop everything and acknowledge their feelings. Validate how they are feeling ("This is really difficult." "I would be overwhelmed too right now. I don't blame you for being upset." "You seem really frustrated. Is there anything I can do to help?") or admit that you don't know how to help. It is *perfectly* acceptable to say things like "I want to make you feel better, but I don't know how." "I wish I knew what to say to make this better for you." "I don't know how to help, but I want to." No one expects you to fix all their problems or know the perfect words to say. They want to know that you care and that you want to help. That's it. They want to feel supported.

You know me at this point. A big go-to of mine when I have no words that seem to fit is simply to ask "Can I give you a hug right now?" Hugs are healing, and I'm not just saying that. Physical touch, physical connection, a squeeze to activate the peripheral nervous system; hugs are truly magic. I don't mean a quick one either, I mean a real true actual hug. When people are upset and overwhelmed, they hold so much tension in their muscles. When you give someone a real hug, you will feel their bodies relax and let go of some of that tension.

When I was in undergrad, every semester during finals there was a group of kids on campus who went around with signs that said "Free Hugs." It was honestly the best thing and I took them up on it nearly every time. Just hug people more, ok? But don't be a creep. I feel like that should be implied, but in case you are that one person who needed me to clarify...

CANCER

We need to talk about cancer. It's a really heavy topic and one that can make many people supremely uncomfortable. The more uncomfortable you are with it, the more cringy your comments will probably be, so let's get really clear about some do's and don'ts.

Very few diagnoses can have the life-altering and devastating effect of hearing that you or a loved one has cancer. This diagnosis comes with immediate life and death questions, and our culture (in the western world) is about as uncomfortable with the concept of death as humanly possible (more on this subject specifically in a little bit). Cancer is scary and overwhelming. So much changes immediately after cancer is suspected or confirmed in a person. They are suddenly thrust into a whirlwind of scans, medications, and doctor's appointments.

Not only is the person's whole world turned upside-down in an instant with treatments and monitoring, but this change can go on for an extremely long time. A person can be immediately met with 12 to 24 month treatment plans, and these are not quarterly or monthly appointments. Many times these plans consist of 3-5 treatments a week for a year or longer in order to maximize the chance of survival. It's also possible that a person can go through all of that and still succumb to the disease.

Cancer is horrible. Full stop. I doubt there is a single person reading this book who can say they have never known anyone with cancer. Why then is it so difficult for people to have a conversation about cancer if it is so common? Because it is so very scary. We need to have some real talk right now. If we don't, we have no hope of improving our ability to handle this topic. When a person tells you they have cancer, it stops you in your tracks. You immediately feel as though you are staring at a dead person walking and, whether you realize it or not, this confrontation brings you face to face with your own mortality.

It goes a little something like this: 1. Omg you're going to die. 2. How old are you and how old am I? 3. How did you find out and is there a possibility I could have cancer and not know it if you had cancer and you didn't know it? 4. What were your symptoms and would I feel worried if I had those symptoms or would I ignore them? Do I know when to go to the doctor? What if I have symptoms I ignore and I wait too long? 5. Did they catch it fast enough and what happens now? You're going to go through so much, what if I had to go through all that? What if I had to suddenly stop working? 6. Wait, how are you going to pay for all that treatment? What would I do if I had to pay for all that treatment? Do I have any policies that would help pay for that? 7. Who's going to take you to your treatments? Who would take me to my treatments? 8. Are you ok? Of course you're not ok. You could die from this. How would I feel if I found out I had cancer and I might die from it? 9. Oh my god I'm not ready to die.

Because people tend to internally spin out of control when they hear about someone having cancer, they will often say things that sound really random, out of touch, or overly positive in an attempt to shut the conversation down because they can't handle it. They will also engage in a lot of redirecting by changing the topic entirely or changing the focus of the conversation from the person in front of them to someone else they know or heard about (cringe) who had cancer.

I'm going to be very honest about this behavior: it's the worst. Let me guess the ending to your story. The person you know (or heard about) either lived or died, right? You are either 1) attempting to tell a story about a person who *did not* die from cancer in order to assure this person that they might also *not die* from cancer, or 2) you are trying to find a commonality between this person and another random person both having cancer so that they won't feel alone. However, you forgot to prescreen this story, because the person in your story didn't make it, and that's a terrible story to tell someone who is facing the same struggle.

Either way, your story is irrelevant to this person because his or her fate is unknown. Someone else living or dying from cancer has no correlation to the person in front of you living or dying. Someone else living through it will rarely give them hope, because they are worried about their own life and family, and their story may or may not turn out as well. I hope I don't need to elaborate any further on why you should never tell a person a story about someone who "didn't make it." What is your point exactly? How in the entire world is that helpful? They are already going down that dark hole every day. They don't need you to push them into it.

What you are really doing when you tell these stories is changing the subject. Oh sure, you are still technically talking about cancer, but you are no longer talking about <u>the person standing right in front of you</u>. This person in front of you has worries, needs, fears, and a sickness that could kill them and you can't stand to think about any of it, so you change the subject to someone else. You remove the emotions and your connection to your own fears along with it. You can't stand the overwhelming thoughts and emotions you are having, so you box it up with a bow and pass it to the left.

I definitely get it. It's really hard to face this stuff. It's draining and upsetting to allow yourself to really go there and be real with yourself about what that person is going through, but this person's cancer is not about you. Maybe this is only a hell of a fight this person is going to go through. They're going to live another 50 years and tell everyone that they know that they are a champion and kicked cancer's ass. Maybe this is how their story ends. You don't know and neither do they, and you have to square with that.

Being in the part of healthcare that I am, there are times that I know that the person has been handed a death sentence. It's really hard because it's not a matter of "if," but a matter of "how long until." We'll get more into that a little later, but this is my point: stop trying to wriggle away from the conversation. This person doesn't have the luxury of not thinking about it or pretending that it's not a big deal. This is every minute of their life right now, and they need all the love and support they can get.

The very best thing you can do is to meet that person where they are at that moment. You have no control over their cancer or any part of the process. They will be on a constant roller coaster ride of emotions. They will go from determined, to overwhelmed, to depressed, to peaceful, to regretful in the span of less than a minute sometimes. They will have good days and bad days. They will have days that they are sure everything will be fine and days they may be ready to give up.

Be there. Witness their emotions and let them know you are there for the ride. This goes equally for a person you know and love and will be there through the whole process with, or someone you run across in public who ends up emotionally dumping all their feelings on you because you happened to say "hi, how are you?" right as they were reaching a breaking point.

Remember me crying to my husband at 20 years old, "I want my mom to hug me and tell me she's sorry I don't feel good!" This person doesn't need you to cure their cancer or tell them some amazing story that will cheer them up indefinitely or give them an inspirational speech. They need someone to hear them, to listen, and to acknowledge that what they are going through is really hard.

People want to be seen and heard. They want to know that they are not crazy and that the emotions they feel are normal and justified. They want to know that other people want to see them do well and that others care about their outcomes. They want to feel connected to other people and energetically supported.

The other day I had to go to my local urgent care. There was a new young mom who walked in with a baby car seat that was covered with a pretty pink coverlet. As soon as she signed in at the desk the baby started crying. It was one of those tiny newborn baby cries that make your heart melt (ok, it does mine because I love babies!) and lets you know without seeing her that this one is fresh out of the oven. (I was actually a little excited when she sat down across from me.)

As a mom myself, I also know that when your baby starts screeching in the middle of a crowded room full of sick people, you start to panic. The fear is very real that someone is going to jump in your face and scream at you to get your baby to be quiet, and you start to become very overwhelmed when the crying persists.

We are 18 solid months into the Covid pandemic right now and everyone in the building was wearing a mask. I knew the mom was trying very hard not to take her baby out of the car seat for obvious reasons, but rocking the seat and shushing wasn't going to do it. I also felt a huge rush of compassion for this poor young mom, thinking about all the stress and worry she had been through from the first day she learned she was pregnant with a "covid baby."

How many doctor's visits did she have to go to alone? How many headlines scared her half to death about the safety of her baby? Was she panicked at the idea of having her baby at the hospital when it was potentially full of so many sick people? Did she get to have a baby shower or did she miss out on that?

My heart hurt thinking about all she had been through in the last year and how overwhelmed she must be around the clock right now.

She finally gave up and pulled the baby out so she could hold her, and the crying was still on full blast. She pulled out this thin burp cloth and my first thought was 'surely she's not going to try to swaddle her in that. It's not big enough!' and then I realized that she was very clumsily trying to hold the baby with one hand while unfolding the burp cloth with the other so she could nurse in the middle of this waiting room. Oh my heart. I nursed both my boys and I know the struggle. Her hand was shaking as she kept dropping the blanket into her lap.

Covid or not, I jumped up and said, "here Mama, I've got you", and took the blanket, unfolded it, and held it up for her so she could get the baby latched in privacy. She took the blanket when she was ready and I sat back down. She got on the phone and called her pediatrician. The call relayed that the baby had been throwing up and she knew she had been in twice about this already, but could they possibly fit her in right away so she could be checked one more time? BLESS that office for saying yes, because when she hung up she started packing everything to change plans.

She must have checked the car seat fifteen times, making so many micro adjustments to get it just right, and her hands were visibly shaking the whole time. I really wanted to give her a big hug, but of course that would not be appropriate at all given the pandemic, so I settled for catching her eye and saying with as much love as I could, "I want you to know that you are doing a great job. What you are going through right now is really hard, but I promise it gets better. You will get through this and you are doing really well right now. Just hang on."

She almost started crying and so did I. Whatever support she had, it wasn't enough. She was so overwhelmed and I wish there was more I could have done, but at least I could let her know she was seen and maybe give her a little bit of hope.

You are seen. What you are doing is hard. You are doing a great job. Keep going. Let me know how I can help. I've been where you have been and I can promise you it gets easier. Just keep going. Just hang on. You will get to the other side of this. There is no book tip or swaddling technique or paci recommendation in the world that is going to do the same amount of good as conveying love and support. I can't fix all of this new mom's problems. I really can't fix any of them, but I can provide a moment of connection in her day that might help her to feel a little bit of hope or a little bit of peace that she's not alone.

I tell you this whole story to try to reframe the conversation around cancer. You can't fight cancer for this person. You can't take their treatments. You can't take away their nausea or pain or debilitating fatigue, but you can let them know they are not alone and that you acknowledge that what they are going through is hard. That's all you need to do. No fancy inspirational speeches required. If you are at a loss, try some of the following:

"This is so overwhelming. Are you ok? What can I do for you?"

"I'm so sorry you are going through this. This is so hard."

"I wish there was something I could do to make this easier on you."

"I don't know what to say, but I'm here for you and I want to help."

"I'm so proud of you for fighting this day after day. What you are doing is so hard and you are doing a great job."

"That is so much for someone to go through."

"Don't worry about me. I'm here for you. What do you feel

up to doing today?" (in the case they are apologizing for not feeling well or being up to the plans you had)

Do your best to meet someone where they are. If they are happy, be happy. If they don't want to talk about it that day, don't! If they are upset, validate it. 'This is total crap and completely unfair for you to have to deal with. EFF CANCER!' If they are depressed, sit with them. 'This is overwhelming. I would be overwhelmed too. You are not alone.' Don't look at them with sad "you're dying" eyes. That feels patronizing and is definitely unwelcome.

When they are feeling positive, celebrate it. Yes! We've got this! When they dip a few days later, don't hold them to the positivity they had a few days before. 'Oh come on, remember how you were feeling at the beginning of the week? You've got this! It's going to be fine!' Nope. That was then and this is now, and tomorrow will be another day. You are not the train conductor, you have bought a ticket next to them in the train car. You go where the train goes.

A few quick "don'ts":

1) Don't ask them about all their symptoms. You don't need to know how much the person is throwing up or whatever else you might be curious about. You can ask "are you tolerating your treatments well or are they wearing you out?" but leave the details at the door unless they want to bring them up.

2) Don't ask them if they are going to die, how long they "have" or anything related to that question. Right now, they are fighting cancer. Let's focus on that. You could ask "have you had any recent follow ups from the doctor? Did you get a good report?" if you know the person well and this feels appropriate.

3) Don't ask them if they're going to lose all their hair. Maybe they will, or maybe they won't. They are fighting cancer. Let's focus on that. Hair grows back. It is either the least of their worries or one more thing to be stressed about that does

no good to dwell on.

4) Don't have a whole conversation about your friend whose hair grew back and did crazy things, having "cancer hair" or anything related. Swallow this story. Again, they have bigger issues to worry about and your friend whose hair turned from blonde and straight to brown and curly is only stressing them out more. So now I'm not even going to look like myself anymore? What will my hair look like? Will I like it? What will my spouse and kids think? Don't do that to them. If they bring it up? "Well, whatever happens will be a new adventure. We'll just have to wait and see."

5) If they end up wearing scarves or wigs, don't make a big deal about it. You giving a huge dramatic sonnet is only drawing unwanted attention. Tell them they look nice the same way you would complement a new dress or pair of shoes. "That's a beautiful scarf. I like how you've styled it." "How fun that you found a scarf that perfectly matches that outfit!" Refrain from any comments about a wig. THEY look nice, not the wig. The end. If they say they feel self conscious about it? "I think it looks great. It's very natural."

6) Do not tell them that there is a plan for them. I know it's tempting to want to find the good amidst the bad by saying that there is a reason for their suffering or that they won't be given more than they can handle, but this is very isolating. You are effectively telling them that they shouldn't be upset, that they must now search for an illusive "meaning" for their suffering and the suffering of those they care the most about who are helplessly watching on the sidelines, or that they must find a superhuman ability to fight this evil because they should be able to handle it, right? Saying these cliches falls under the same category as changing the subject by relating a story about someone else. You are avoiding the real issue of the *real* pain and suffering this person is going through by dazzling them with words about higher meanings. At this point, you

know how to do better than that, so do better.

I want to make a picky distinction between saying, "this is hard" vs "I know this is hard." Unless you have also fought cancer, it would be easy for the person to prickle at the words "I know.." because you don't. When you are going through something with that level of gravity, you are very aware of whether people actually **know** how hard it is, so be careful and aware of how you phrase this.

In order to cover the entire scope of this conversation, we need to go over the awful reality of someone facing the knowledge that they will die and their time is limited. This could apply to several different illnesses and circumstances, such as a fatal heart condition, worsening respiratory failure, hospice, ALS, etc. Death is a part of life. Some of us are taken by surprise, and others are given the opportunity to settle the thought in their own minds first. Resist the urge to project your own fears about death on this other person who is having to come to terms with a very real end date to their time on earth. Be willing to connect to them and to sit with those hard emotions.

Them: "I'm going to die soon."

You: "I know. I'm so sorry."

Them: "I don't want to die. I'm not ready."

You: "I don't think any of us are ever ready... You are a very loved person, and that is something to celebrate and smile about."

Them: "I want to know that my spouse/kids will be ok."

You: "They will be. They will be so sad and they will miss you very much, but they have each other and good support systems to help them. They might be sad for a long time, but they will find a way to keep moving forward."

Them: "I'm so tired."

You: "You've been through so much. You have fought so hard, but your body is very, very tired. It's ok."

Don't tell them there is still hope when they are transitioning into this final phase. Don't badger them into "trying harder" or guilt them into feeling like they have done something wrong by getting worse instead of better. Try to extend peace and understanding towards them. Honor the full circle of life by acknowledging it when it arrives. Listen to what they have to say without interrupting.

They may be able to come to terms with it before anyone else does. They may be in a ton of pain or dealing with chronic illness that is very difficult to bear. They may be at peace and ready to move on to the next life and to greet all those who they have lost along the course of their lives. They might tell you, "I'm ready." To that you can reply, "It gives me peace to know that you feel peace. I love you. I'm here for you."

DEATH

Death is a guaranteed and inescapable part of life. Most of us have been raised in cultures that are very uncomfortable talking about death. It can make it very difficult to know what to say when issues surrounding death are suddenly brought into the conversation. Working in healthcare, and especially in home health, having conversations surrounding the topic of death is much more common than I would have ever expected.

I am grateful for the chance to become better able to have conversations on this topic in a way that provides connection with someone else. Often in our discomfort around discussing death, we inadvertently make comments that create distance between us and the person experiencing the issue. We are uncomfortable with the topic and therefore make comments that show our discomfort, which can create feelings of shame and isolation in the person who most needs comfort and connection.

I believe firmly that when a person can step into this topic and approach it with the intention to show love to the person with whom they are speaking, it can create immense feelings of peace and love in both parties. As women, we are most in tune with our natural energies when we are stepping into the role of a nurturer. We can embody our inner goddess energy by opening ourselves up and facilitating the love, comfort, and compassion that people so desperately need when they are hurting. If you can look at this topic in this way, you can appreciate one of the highest callings of your feminine energy, and use that to bless those with whom you have the privilege of discussing this difficult subject.

If you are a man, you are most naturally in tune with the masculine energy of protection. You can step into your highest self by surrounding a person with an energetic wall of safety around them, so that they feel more able to show their vulnerability without feeling like the whole world will fall apart around them if they do. You can provide a safe space for them to share their worries and fears, and assure them that you are strong enough to take it all without breaking under the weight of it.

This does not require you to have the perfect thing to say. It is not about you bestowing wisdom on someone. It is not about you trying to take away their pain by diminishing it or replacing it with "happy thoughts." The true essence of elegance in this scenario is to provide that person with the platform they need to express whatever feelings they are having in the moment, and to acknowledge those feelings with respect and warmth. You are not there to teach, preach, or do a song and dance in the hope that this person will somehow forget about death. In giving this person the safety and space to say what is on their heart and mind, you are truly at one with your highest energy, and therefore doing the highest good. That is the mark of a truly elegant person.

This subject is so wide and deep, and there are so many different ways that you might converse with someone on this topic, that I have broken it down into three sections. We will address them as past, present, and future. This will make more sense as we continue.

Overall, the most important thing to keep in mind when having a conversation about the death of a loved one is to tune in very strongly to the cues that person is giving about how much they do or don't want to talk about it and how much grief they are still experiencing from the loss. Some people are very private and find the conversation itself to be uncomfortable for them. They don't want to talk about it or answer any questions, and they will make light of it a lot of times in an effort to move on and avoid the discussion entirely.

Someone expressing their sympathy can actually make them feel very uncomfortable. This can be the case for someone who has not processed their grief and doesn't want to be faced with it. It can also be the result of a person having had a hard life and feeling that they don't have the luxury of expressing or feeling difficult emotions. There is also the strong possibility that this person feels very uncomfortable about the topic of death and is unable to converse about it, even when it concerns them.

If the person is giving you the impression that they don't want to talk about it, absolutely do not press them. Try to find a balance between hurrying off the topic yourself and gracefully moving on to another subject because you are following the lead of the other person that it concerns.

There are times when someone might give you the impression that they don't want to talk about their grief because they don't know how, or they don't feel like they can express anything about it without crying, and they definitely don't want to cry in front of you. In these instances, I try to move the conversation on to happy thoughts of the deceased person by asking questions about what that person was like, what their interests were, etc. More below.

DEATH - PAST

In this section, I want to focus on the topic of deaths that have happened in the past. Although there is no specific timeline to define when a death would transition from a present issue to a past issue, the best cue for you to take is how strongly that person is still grieving. Anything within the last 12 months is going to feel so fresh that I will put it in the "present" category.

For me, this conversation occurs frequently when speaking to my patients. I have found ways to sidestep some of these awkward conversations by learning to ask better questions when I'm interacting with people. Please see the section on demographics for further explanation. One thing to keep in mind when speaking to someone about the death of a loved one that happened in the past is that although the level of grief subdues overtime, the depth of the loss often remains.

The person may be able to speak about it without crying now, or they might never be able to. Please don't assume that because a death happened decades ago that it isn't still a very painful topic for that person. I would say that the strongest grief that carries on throughout a person's life is often the loss of a child. There is something unimaginable and horrifying about losing a child. It goes against the natural order of things, and it is every parent's worst nightmare. It does tend to be much harder on the mother than the father, but not always.

Let's go through some things not to do. A huge etiquette rule is to not ask specific questions about how the person died. You are not trying to conduct an interview to fill out this person's death certificate. Please don't react to a comment about someone dying by asking how they died, where they died, how old they were when they died, what kind of cancer it was, or how long after they found out that they were sick did they die?

Asking these questions comes across as nosy at best, and forces that person to relive the experience of that person dying in a level of detail that is not helpful. Please resist the urge to start playing twenty questions when someone tells you of the loss of a loved one. Asking these types of questions gives that person no room to direct the conversation as to what they do and don't want to say about their loved one.

Don't try to make it better. There is nothing that you are going to say that will fill the hole that has been left by this loss. There are no words that can come out of your mouth that are going to make it suddenly okay that that person lost a child, spouse, or parent. It just isn't, and the harder you try to cheer someone up, the worse you're making it. Let me be very clear about that; the only way to the other side of this conversation is to go through it with grace and love, not around it. Skirting a conversation, ignoring the pain that that person has experienced, diminishing their level of grief, or in any other way trying to pretend that the loss "wasn't that bad" or that "they should be over it by now" is making it worse. Please don't be that person.

The biggest example I can think of here is the unbelievable cringe worthy "at least." This may be something you have never considered before, but hear me out. There is something about the phrase "at least" that makes your entire comment sound dismissive. It's a "lesser of two evils" kind of comparison that I have never felt any sort of comfort from and I'm sure very few people have.

One of my grandfathers died from cancer when I was in high school. It was the first personal loss I had ever experienced and it was a devastating experience to me from the beginning. My grandfather was one of my favorite people in the entire world. Everybody loved him; he was the life of the party. My grandfather was an amazing person and the news that he had cancer, like it is in all cases, was devastating.

It felt like the world was ending, and it felt like my world was totally out of control. One of the most upsetting parts to me was that he had undergone treatment and had been given graduation robes and a certificate, and all his scans said that he was cancer free and everything was fine. Within six months of that, he had passed. The cancer wasn't actually gone and it felt like I had been lied to in the worst possible way.

I can't tell you how many people came up to me and tried to comfort me with a phrase starting with "at least." The two biggest phrases I heard during time of his visitation were "at least he didn't suffer long." and "at least he's not suffering anymore." I was barely holding myself together, with very little willpower to maintain my composure. I can't tell you how close I was to absolutely screaming every time someone said something to me that started with "at least."

Here's why: "At least" is something you say when you're relieved by something. You tell someone that someone else had a car wreck and they respond with "at least no one died." or "at least no one was seriously injured." You get a diagnosis that has a medicine that will cure it and when you tell someone of the ailment they respond "at least it wasn't something more serious." Please don't try to comfort me by telling me that I should be relieved that my loved one has died. Please. Don't.

I make a very conscious effort to never use the phrase "at least" when I am speaking to someone who has experienced a loss. What I will say instead is a phrase in two parts. I will say, "I'm glad that __" but "__." For example: "I am glad that he is not hurting anymore, but that doesn't make up for the fact that he is not here." "I'm glad that she didn't suffer long, but mostly I wish that she was still here." " I'm glad that he didn't experience a lot of pain when he was sick, but in a perfect world he never would have been sick at all." Yes, it is good to try to find the positive, but there is no positive sentiment in the world that will outweigh the pain caused by death.

The phrase "at least" it's so ingrained in the commentary around death, that even the loved one will use it when describing how they're dealing with the loss, but I hold steady that there is no amount of positive sentiment that is good enough. If someone tells me with regard to their own loss something like "at least he's not hurting anymore" I nearly always respond back with my "but" statement. Maybe they will say, "at least he's not suffering anymore." and I will respond, "yes, but I know you must miss him terribly."

I think it is much better to help vocalize the depth of that person's loss. They've had so many people try to comfort them by masking how deep the grief is that they have started to regurgitate the same to anyone who asks. You don't know how many times I have had someone start to choke up when I return their "at least" statement with the statement that gives them permission to actually vocalize their loss or grief.

A small note on, "I'm sorry for your loss." I understand that this is the most commonly uttered phrase when someone says that they have experienced a loss. This is exactly why I have a problem with using this phrase verbatim. It feels robotic and unfeeling. There are a hundred ways to express yourself other than this exact phrase word for word. Make a half of an effort to change it up even just a little bit. The two easiest variations would be, "I am so sorry to hear that. What an awful loss." or, " That is such a terrible loss. I am so sorry to hear it."

While we're at it, let's also address the phrase, "I am thinking of you during this difficult time." Again, can you put a half a second's worth of effort into saying something that feels even slightly more original? What about, "I am sending love to you and your family." or " I am so sorry to hear this. I am thinking about all of you and sending wishes/prayers for comfort and peace." Let's strike the word "condolences" and the phrase "at this difficult time" from your vocabulary forever, shall we? They are overly formal and seem insincere and unfeeling.

Any time words come flying out of your mouth without any effort toward making a connection with the person you are saying them to, you might as well not say anything. The person feels no love, no comfort from that. As people who are striving to be the most well spoken and the highest versions of ourselves, let's all agree to do better. Ok? Ok, great.

When dealing with the topic of death in a way that is empathetic and graceful, I generally try to flow the conversation in this order:

1. Sympathetic response. First and foremost, acknowledge the loss before trying to move forward. This part of the conversation might be brief if the person has made peace with the loss and is no longer actively grieving, or the person may need the conversation to linger a bit here. They may need some comfort and a listening ear. This is the part that so often gets skipped, or acknowledged so robotically, that you may as well have not said anything. Don't linger in sympathy if it is not needed, but do not let your discomfort cause you to rush past someone else's needs.

2. Learn a bit about the person who has passed. I don't mean you have to write or read their biography, but it is healthy to transition the conversation to the person's life if possible. You can ask what sort of work they did or how they enjoyed spending their time. It usually makes the person you are speaking to feel uplifted to remember the positive and keep the person's memory alive by sharing a few things with you. One or two questions is enough.

3. Draw a concluding statement from the information you received. This comment is all about the person you are speaking to, and you are taking their lead here. Would they be best served by a comment about their loved one? A comment about their level of involvement in care in the last stages of their loved ones life? Do they need comfort from the end of a long and drawn out difficult relationship?

4. Gracefully move to the next topic. Once you feel that the loss has been properly acknowledged and the person you are speaking to has had a chance to tell you what's on their mind, you can confidently move on to the next subject. No need to dwell forever on the difficult.

Alright, let's get down to brass tacks. There are so many combinations of loss. I'm going to try to cover as many as possible with a couple of examples in each scenario of things that you can say in an effort to remain elegant, graceful, and connected to that person. Big breath in! Here we go:

Loss of an Older Parent: An adult who has lost their parent to age and/or mild to moderate health related causes. The adult might be in their 40s, 50s, or 60s and the parent lived to be in their 70s, 80s, or 90s. This is the most expected grief that a person encounters. We all realize from a very early age that the natural order of things is that our parents will pass before we will. The hope is that they will live to an older age with a full life in as much health as can be expected. Most people are able to come to terms with this loss a bit more easily than in any other scenario listed because consciously or not, they have been preparing for this to happen since they were in their teen years or even earlier.

In this case, I usually say something generalized to give the other person a chance to respond and help me know what the best thing to say would be. Please remember that we are referring to past deaths in this section. These comments are not necessarily appropriate for someone who is on the verge of losing a parent or who is in the early stages of grief following the loss of their parent.

"Oh I'm so sorry, I bet you miss them."

"Did you get to spend a lot of time with them?"

Red flag: unless the person has already indicated a level of closeness with this parent or expresses a lot of grief when speaking about it, do not ask the question "were you close with them?" You might accidentally be opening a can of worms of 40 years of repressed anger that are all going to come out on you at once. You always have to be careful how you phrase questions.

"What kind of work did they do?"

If the person expresses a continued amount of grief at the loss and you want to say something comforting, vocalize this observation with a comment such as, "It seems like you miss them a lot. What a blessing to have had such great parents." or "It sounds like __ was such a special person. They certainly were one of a kind."

Maybe they end up telling you a lot of awesome things that their parent did for them or other people. Acknowledge that and celebrate it with a comment like, "What a wonderful person. They had such a positive impact on so many people. That's amazing. I bet you are so proud of them."

On the other hand, maybe the person's parent was a source of stress and frustration for them. Maybe they tell you that their parent was hateful or difficult and they don't have a lot of positive things to say about them. Don't try to judge or change that person's lived experience. Acknowledge their difficulty. Usually people who had difficult or absent parents feel a lot of anger or loss at the childhood or support they never had. However, don't make the mistake of trying to comfort that person by bad mouthing the parent either. Do you know the old saying "I can make fun of my family, but nobody else can?" Don't take the risk of saying something that will offend them.

The best response is one that is supportive but neutral. We are all human and we are all flawed. Some of us are better able to overcome those flaws, and some of us aren't. I usually make a comment somewhere in the neighborhood of, "I'm so sorry to hear that. Sometimes people aren't able to be who they want to be for others." or "It's so hard to go through life without getting the kind of support you need." or "It sounds like that was a really difficult relationship for you. I'm so sorry to hear that." or "It sounds like they had a lot of struggles that they were dealing with and really couldn't be there for you like you needed. That's so hard."

The situation might be a little bit more extreme where the person had a problem with addiction or was neglectful, or abusive. If that is the information the person brings forward, I do tend to take a stronger sympathetic stance leaning towards disapproval of the way that the parent handled the situation. I am still not bad mouthing the parent, but I want the person with whom I am speaking to feel validated and accepted.

My comments in this instance might be closer to, "that behavior is never excusable. I'm so sorry that you went through that." If the person seems very upset by these memories, I might say something like, "That is so much for one person to go through. I hope you have the support you need to work through all of that so that you can make peace with everything."

Loss of a younger parent: There is an added element of tragedy here. We all know on some level that we will suffer the loss of our parents, but we expect it to happen when we are at a minimum, middle aged. When we suffer the loss of a parent at an age we didn't expect, when the parent doesn't seem to have lived a full life, there is an added feeling of loss for the time that could have/should have been. They never met my children. They weren't able to be there on my wedding day. They didn't get to see me reach important milestones in my life that I know they would have been so happy to celebrate with me, (such as a college degree or a huge career accomplishment).

Those celebrations are sprinkled with a touch of sadness because we feel the loss more strongly at those times. The loss itself comes with the increased burden of knowing everything they will miss from that moment forward; things that the majority of parents are able to witness for their children. The younger you are when the loss happens, the more overwhelming it can feel. Children and teens who lose a parent are also missing one of two people who are most vital in developing their foundational years. This can lead to many difficult emotions that may require extended counseling or other support services in order to fully process and overcome.

Some words specific to this loss:

"They were so young."

"No one expects to lose a parent that soon."

"They would have been so happy for you/proud of you." (especially appropriate during milestone events)

"They were so proud of you/loved you so much." (especially helpful when said by mutual friends or loved ones.

When my mother's father passed away several years ago, someone he had worked with for a long time came up to me at the visitation to express his condolences. I had never met this person, and I had never visited Papa's office at the bank (where he had worked until retirement). My grandfather was a generally quiet person when I was around, and I had always thought of him as a man of few words.

This person told me he knew who I was because he

recognized me from the pictures my grandfather kept in his office. For whatever reason, I had never given a thought to what my Papa's office had looked like or whether there had been family pictures around, but this news brought a smile to my face. He then further surprised me by saying, "He was so proud of you. He talked about you all the time." I'm getting emotional just writing that. Of course I knew my grandfather was proud of me, but I had never imagined him as the type of person who would brag about me to the people he worked with, because it was a different side of him than what I knew.

Keeping that in mind, I always make an effort to convey that type of information to others when I can. A coworker tragically died last year and it was unbelievably heartbreaking. He had one son who was in college on a baseball scholarship and if you met my coworker, you would know about his son right away. When I went to the visitation, I made sure to approach his son, whom I had never met, and tell him that he was the light of his father's life; that all his dad ever spoke about to anyone was him. Not much could console someone in the middle of that kind of unexpected loss, but I hope that in some small way that might have given him some comfort. We can know in our hearts that someone loved us, but there is another level of comfort in hearing it from someone else.

Loss of an older spouse: As with the loss of our parents, we inherently know that when we get married, the chances are very high that one of us will pass before the other (as opposed to a terrible accident of some kind where we pass at the same time). In some ways this also falls under the category of an expected loss, especially if you are both older and your spouse had been in poor health, but it doesn't mean that the loss is any less painful or that you are ever ready for it.

It is absolutely beautiful to see a couple reach old age together and celebrate incredible milestones such as 50 or 60 year anniversaries. I hope with all of my heart that I will be blessed to count myself among that group one day. However, there is another implication inside this amazing love story, and that is the fact that the person who is left behind almost can't remember a time in their life that their spouse was not there. This is a half a century or more, and these two souls have become so entwined that it feels incomprehensible to exist without your other half next to you.

I have many patients who begin to sleep in guest bedrooms because they can't stand to sleep in their own bed without their spouse beside them. I have male patients especially who begin to waste away because they can't stand to eat something other than their wife's cooking. Nothing else tastes right to them. Many times the spouse who passed away had been unable to fully take care of themselves for years, and the spouse who remains has been so engulfed in their caregiver role for so long that they aren't sure what to do with themselves anymore. They can feel like their purpose is gone.

Some people will be able to make peace with this loss more easily than others, just as is the case with any loss, but it doesn't mean that they don't continue to miss that person, no matter how long it has been since their passing. It could be 10 or 15 years later, but it is always appropriate to say:

"I'm sure you still miss them."

"I bet some days it feels like forever ago, and other days it feels like it just happened."

Most people don't want to dwell on the sadness here, but will be very glad for the chance to tell you a story about their late husband or wife. Many of my patients were married to men who served during WWII, and will have pictures of them in uniform in the house. I love to hear stories about how they met, if they were together while he was serving or after, and any fun stories about their younger years. I will frequently ask questions such as:

"How old were you when the two of you met/started dating?"

"What sort of work did he do when he got out of the military?"

"How long were you two married?" (do NOT ask how old the person was when they died. If they share, you can say "oh that's so young" if it was less than their early 70's because honestly, it was.)

"Did you two always live around here?"

"Was it love at first sight?"

"What sort of places did you enjoy visiting/traveling to for vacation?"

I love to tease the women by saying things like, "So you snagged an older military man? Good for you!" or commenting, "Look how handsome he was in that uniform! Look at that mustache!" I might ask to see a picture of their wedding. I *love* looking at older wedding pictures and I get so excited to see older style dresses and decorations. I might exclaim, "Look how young you both were! You looked so beautiful. Look how proud he is!" It's so much fun to share these memories with someone else. If my patient is a man who has lost his wife, I will comment fondly at how beautiful his wife was and how sweet she looked. Yes, there can be a mixture of sadness, but I have yet to find a person who doesn't light up when sharing these wonderful memories.

Loss of a younger spouse: This particular tragedy is so heartbreaking. It is the loss of an entire lifetime that was supposed to be built with this other person. It is almost always a sudden traumatic loss with no warning, with the exception of cancer or possibly one or two other fatal diseases that take some time but still feel like the loss is coming at lightning speed.

Regardless of the method of loss, it is usually accompanied by a deep well of anxiety and overwhelm. This wasn't supposed to happen. This isn't fair. This doesn't seem real. I can't trust anything. I can't count on anything. Everyone I love can disappear instantly and there's nothing I can do to stop it. The world is unsafe, I am unsafe, and everyone I care about is in danger.

Many people who are thrust into this situation can have lingering difficulties with anxiety and hypervigilance for years or even the rest of their lives. If someone they care about gets the flu, it can immediately send them spiraling into a worst case scenario. They can become overbearing, hypercritical, or emotionally shut down. If I don't care then I can't get hurt, they hope. If I can control every detail of this scenario, it is less likely to get to a point where I no longer have control.

Try your best to be understanding of these difficulties and where they originate. Many people will be left as single parents, simultaneously trying to manage their own grief with the grief/loss of their children, while also juggling the desire to help their children carry on as "normally" as possible to hopefully minimize their trauma. It's a horrible crossroads to live in. They feel pulled in opposite directions, wanting to feel the love and connection of a partner and wanting to create a typical balance of a two parent household for their children, while being horrified at the idea of "replacing" the love they lost and what others will think of them if they dare to venture for love again.

This person may ride the waves of grief for years. Try not to push them in any direction. Don't encourage them to move on. Don't tell them that their loved one would have wanted them to move on. I'm only being honest; if I ever lost my husband, I feel sure he would rise from the grave to punch any guy in the head who looked at me twice. He might want me to be happy, but you would never convince me he would be happy for me to be with someone else. The person who has suffered this loss knows their spouse better than anyone. They may have to contend with the monumental task of squaring with the fact that finding love again might not be what their loved one would have "wanted."

Instead, let them know that you love and support them. Let them know that you care about them and wish for their happiness. At the end of the day, that's what you really want, right? You want them to find peace and happiness, and that may come in many forms. Don't try to frame it in regard to their spouse. It's really adding another layer of guilt and pressure to the situation. So now you're telling me that my loved one who I'm grieving is possibly *upset with me* because I haven't moved on? What kind of mind-bending craziness is that? You could instead phrase it:

"He/she loved you so fiercely. They wouldn't want you to suffer endlessly. They would want you to find peace."

I feel confident that this sentiment would be true. Finding peace and moving on are two different things. Exact words matter and make a difference.

Loss of an older child: Many of my patients are in their 70s to 90s. One of the most difficult trade-offs of living this long is the increased chance of losing more close loved ones than most, including the loss of children. I have had patients who have lost older children who were in their 40s, 50s, or 60s, sometimes the loss is more recent or far removed. It might be tempting to want to write off this loss as less upsetting because their child was middle aged or retired. Maybe the child had been dealing with chronic health issues for decades that had finally caused their death.

Do not attempt to convince yourself or anyone else that this could possibly be true. No parent should ever have to bury their own child. It is a fear you have to swallow from the very beginning of their life, and it never goes away. This loss should be regarded as equally devastating as losing a child of any other age. The losses are different, and they hurt in different ways, but they should not be compared as easier or worse.

In all cases when speaking to someone who has lost a child, I speak to the tragedy out loud.

"That is an overwhelming loss."

"Losing a child is a parent's worst nightmare."

"I know there is nothing I can say to make this any better. I am so sorry."

Another word on comparing loss: at times in this situation, a person may feel a mixture of terrible grief and guilt that they "at least" had so much time with their child. This is usually a direct result of someone else speaking those words to them, (and this person has internalized the message) and now feels unable to fully express their grief. Grief is grief, and should not be compared. Every once in a while I will have someone make a comment to this effect, that they should be grateful for the time they had. Although it is good to make peace with things that cannot be changed, I usually respond:

"I am definitely glad that you were able to have so many wonderful years with your daughter/son, but there is no amount of time that feels like enough when you have lost a child. The loss is nearly unbearable. I am so incredibly sorry that you have gone through this."

Loss of a young adult child: I knew a girl one time who had a twin brother who had died around the age of 22. She shared that her mother had told her that although it always hurt to speak about her brother, it nearly killed her when people wouldn't bring him up. She would rather feel her broken heart while knowing he was remembered, than feel like she was dying because people were acting as though he had never existed. I have always remembered this and made a point to resist the urge to skirt the conversation about someone's lost child.

Humans do this crazy ostrich thing where we convince ourselves that if we don't say the words out loud, no one will know the hard thing we are all avoiding bringing up. As yet another reminder, don't play 20 questions here. Skip the when, where, what, why interrogation. Tell me about your son. What did he like to do? She went to college? What was her major? He left behind two children? I bet he loved being a dad. I bet she was such a good mom. He accomplished what in his career? I bet you were so proud. Did he live around here? Did you get to see her often? I know you wish you had gone to visit more, but I'm sure they knew how much you loved them and I bet they know now how much you miss them.

He used to sneak out of the house all the time? What a rascal! Boys are such messes. She had boys falling over her left and right? Of course she did, look how pretty she was! Everyone loved her? I bet they did. She had such a sweet smile. He was very respected in his field? Sounds like you raised a good one. Ask questions, give this person the chance to enjoy these amazing memories and share them with you. Celebrate the beautiful life of this wonderful person who is gone way too soon. You aren't reminding them of something they have forgotten. They feel the loss every day, but sharing their stories can bring them a little closer to feeling that person's presence again.

Loss of a young child: To be honest, I can barely deal with this one. Especially considering that my boys both fit into this category, even hearing about another parent losing a young child will have me instantly sobbing. Thanks, social media. In this category we are referring to past loss, so let me focus on that here. As with many previous areas, I tend to stick with, "I can't even imagine the overwhelming amount of grief you must feel." or "That is every parent's worst nightmare. I am heartbroken to hear that you went through something so awful."

There is so much sadness around the idea that you were never able to see this child grow up. You never found out what they were going to be or who they were going to marry. Their life ended before it had even begun. With a child the loss is either instant through an accident, or a long and drawn out battle with cancer, and it is always traumatic for the parents. Of course my patients lost young children for other reasons such as unknown sickness or diseases that had no cure at the time. Even a child lost more than 50 years ago will bring tears to a mother's eyes, so be kind and compassionate. Never assume that they don't still grieve the loss.

DEATH - PRESENT

We have reviewed many things at this point that are equally relevant to any situation. In this section, I want to focus on a few points related to the death of a loved one that someone is currently experiencing, meaning the funeral and initial grieving process.

I come across this quite a bit in home health. Many times my patient is on restorative services with us, but they have a spouse on hospice who passes away during the time they are on our services. Maybe it's our patient who took a sudden downward turn before we helped transition them to hospice, and their family member is calling us directly to let us know that they passed away in the night. I have also been with a patient doing therapy when they have received a call about a friend or family member passing.

In all of these instances, the news is sudden and many times catches you off guard. You can often find yourself stumbling at this news with a jumble of words, totally at a loss for how to respond appropriately. We will go over a few scenarios and how to handle them.

Person who was on hospice or otherwise terminal passes, and a family member is letting you know about the news. The pain is very real, and the person might not have been ready, but they knew it was coming. They are overall grieved but not surprised.

"Oh, I am so sorry to hear it. This is so hard. Please let me know when the arrangements have been made so that I can come to the visitation/funeral."

If you are unable to attend the services for whatever reason:

"Oh, I am so sorry to hear it. This is so hard. I'll be thinking about you all day and for the next few days as you go through all of this. I know it will be tough. Thank you for letting me know."

Maybe there is another family member you want to especially send a message to:

"Please tell ___ I'm thinking about them and sending lots of love."

Person has had a sudden accident or medical emergency and has died unexpectedly. You and the person telling you the news are both completely unprepared and shocked. This is the one and only time I'm going to give you a blank check to ask questions and be honest with your shock and upset. The person who is calling you is likely in shock themselves and trying to process what has just happened. They might not know which way is up and are also in the process of gathering information. If you are acting too calmly or accepting of this news, it will come across as unfeeling and cold. Feel free to ask:

"What happened? When? Are you sure? Where are they now? Have you been able to go to the hospital yet? Are you ok? What do you need from me right now? Do you want me to come to where you are, or check on you in a few hours after you've had a chance to figure things out?"

If you are not as close to this person you could exchange the last half about coming to help the person to more of a "please let me know what you find out. I'm so sorry this has happened. Let me know if there is anything you need. I will be happy to help."

Sudden or expected, it is always appreciated for you to follow up with a message (not always a call; they might not be ready or able to have a conversation about it for a while) a day or a few days later that says something like, "I want you to know I'm thinking of you. I'm here if you need to talk." You could also add, "Please let me know if you need anything because I'm happy to help in any way I can."

The person might take days or weeks to respond, or never respond at all, but they likely will see the message at some point and feel grateful for the support. Don't take it personally if they don't respond. Hopefully they are getting tons of these types of messages and taking ample time to rest. They might not have the energy or emotional bandwidth to respond, but that doesn't mean they don't appreciate it.

I need to take a moment to address something very important. If this person has lost their spouse and they have young children (this seems to come up most frequently when young children are involved), DO NOT UNDER ANY CIRCUMSTANCES make the asinine comment that, "at least you have (the child) to remember them by." This person has a spouse and a child, and they have just lost one of them forever. They don't need help remembering their spouse, and they certainly do not feel comfort in the idea of being a single parent. I **understand** that you are doing that thing again where you want to zip past the hard emotions and jump to a positive thought, but this isn't it, kid.

This person has suddenly been tasked with the overwhelming charge of raising this young child without their partner, while also being responsible for helping to make sure the child is able to remember or know about their other parent. This person is now trying to figure out how to be both mom and dad, without their partner in crime around to tell them if they are doing it right or not. This person is simultaneously only functioning because of their need to care for their child/children and barely able to function because of the overwhelming task in front of them.

Don't try to make this better. Don't think you are going to say some magical thing that is going to take away the pain. This type of comment is not helpful, but instead isolating and infuriating. It relays you as someone who is completely out of touch, not someone who is sensitive and supportive.

Go back to the basics we have reviewed so much at this point. Focus on the true tragedy at hand, not on skipping the grieving process all together.

"This is such an overwhelming loss. I am heartbroken for you and the kids. I want to help. What can I do/what do you need?"

"I can't imagine how hard this is. I'm sure you are trying to figure out how to get through all of this without (your spouse) here. You are not alone. We are all here for you and the kids."

"I can only imagine how hard the next few weeks and months will be for you and the children. What can I do? What do you need? Can I bring food? What do the kids like to eat? Do you want me to come over and help with dishes and laundry? I'm here for you. Is it ok if I check on you in a few days? I want you to know you are not alone."

A person has lost someone who they were spending day and night caring for due to a terrible long term illness, whether a parent, spouse, or other family member. Resist the urge to blow off this loss as expected or a relief, even if the person was very sick and the caregiver had been taxed by the other person's needs. Don't try to pass over the pain and loss by skipping straight to "They're in a better place now" or "At least they're not hurting anymore" or heaven forbid you suggested that they would be relieved by no longer needing to care for their loved one. The person may be feeling a strong mix of emotions, but that is not for you to direct or sort out. Focus on the present moment, which is one of grief at this very fresh loss.

Someone has lost a child, expected or not: A very dear friend of mine lost her first child within hours after his birth. She told me once that when she had to bury him she wanted to crawl into the ground with him and lay next to him forever, and I will never forget her sharing that with me. There are no words that can ease that amount of grief. The only thing you can do is remind them that you care, sit with them, hug them if they want it, squeeze their hand. You can offer, "I don't know what to say to you because I know nothing I say can help, but I love you and I want to be with you. Is it ok if I sit next to you for a little while?" Sit and expect that they might not say a word, even if you sit there for hours, and that's ok.

In this instance, you can also offer to do anything for them you think might be helpful. They will likely be walking around in a fog for a while and unable to attend to basic tasks. Offer to pick up groceries or bring them a meal. Offer to do laundry or dishes. Offer to take care of the yardwork. Prayers are nice, but actions speak much louder than words. Don't try to chat with them. They won't have the energy to keep up their end of a conversation, but you could offer to sit a while so that they won't be alone.

Miscarriage: It is important to me to touch on this subject, as miscarriage effects such a large percentage of people. This is yet another instance where so many people try to skip right to the light at the end of the tunnel, completely bypassing the very real hurt, pain, and grief that is being experienced by the person who has suffered this loss. In many cases, there is an added layer of hurt because people can be so dismissive of this loss as "no big deal." Here is a list of things you should *never* say in response to learning that someone has lost a pregnancy:

"At least now you know you can get pregnant."

"The next one will work out."

"At least you weren't further along when you lost it."

"You can just try again."

"Maybe there was something wrong with it, and that's why you lost it."

"Did you __(lift something heavy, fall down, exercise too hard, etc: literally anything that is **blaming the mother** for why the pregnancy was lost. How insensitive can you get?)"

"So are you going to try again?"

"Was it (the pregnancy) an accident or did you plan it?" (The implication is that if you didn't plan it, you shouldn't be as upset because it somehow...counts less?)

"At least you already have two kids. Some people can't get pregnant at all."

Notice how many times "at least" came up on this list. No matter how early in the pregnancy the loss was, it was a loss. From the moment a woman finds out she is pregnant, she is having a baby. She starts looking up her due date, planning for a nursery and maternity leave, thinking of names, imagining her future with this new child in it. Her life was changed the moment the test said "pregnant." When that is all torn away from her, it is devastating.

Beyond the lost future and child she now mourns, her body is having to go through the process of returning to its pre-pregnancy state, which can be painful and exhausting. Please be kind and considerate of all of this. Just because you never saw a baby with your eyes does not mean it did not exist. The fact that she was the only one who ever experienced this child can be further isolating. Many women can suffer from feeling that it "wasn't real" or "didn't count" or feel guilty that they shouldn't be so upset if it was an early loss. Validate her by acknowledging this child as one who did exist, if only briefly, and that you mourn the loss with her, or mourn that she had a loss.

In case you need further explanation as to why the above phrases are so hurtful, let me bring to light that many of them are incorrect. Just because a woman can get pregnant one time does *not* necessarily mean she can get pregnant again. If she has suffered from infertility, she is keenly aware of this. Simply trying again does not guarantee success, and many people are privately going through very expensive infertility treatments in order to have a chance at conception. There could be a very real chance that they *can't* try again, because they can't afford another round of treatments. This might have been their last shot, and the grief feels especially hard to bear knowing this.

Even if a person has children already, it isn't fair to put the idea on them that they are not allowed to grieve (or are less justified in grieving) this loss. Each of their children are separate beings, and this loss is a loss in and of itself and should be treated that way. You wouldn't say to a person who lost a child "at least you've got another one." I meant heaven help you if you would because that is a ridiculously terrible thing to say. It's no different here.

How do you have a conversation about a funeral? It can be uncomfortable to know what to say when someone mentions that they have returned from a funeral for a close friend or loved one. What can you say in this situation? Surely it's not a great idea to say, "I hope it went well" or "I hope you had a nice time." Oh dear, no. Maybe they say they are going to a funeral later that day or the next day and some frozen part of your brain almost says, "have a nice time." Oh help us!

Here are some things I usually choose to say at these times:

"I hope that all of your family is able to come to the service and be together to support each other."

"I'm glad that so many people were able to come and say their goodbyes. (Your family member) was a well loved person and it shows."

"How was the service? I hope it gave you comfort and some peace/closure."

"Who spoke at the service? Did they do a good job?"

"I hope the weather holds out so that you are able to have the service he/she deserves."

"Please take it easy and don't push too hard today. Everyone is coming to support you. Let them take care of you."

"I bet (family member) would have been so pleased. It sounds like everything went beautifully."

If you go to the visitation or service, you can offer love with comments such as:

"They did a beautiful job with the casket/ flower arrangements. Everything looks so nice."

"They look so peaceful. This is a perfect outfit you picked for them. Everything looks just right."

"I love seeing all of the pictures you brought. So many wonderful memories."

"It seems like the funeral home is taking good care of you. That makes me happy."

"The service was perfect. It was a beautiful way to honor (family member).

DEATH - FUTURE

The last aspect I want to discuss on this topic has to do with the imminent loss of a close loved one. We have already reviewed this from the viewpoint of the one who is terminal, but what about the person who is going to be left here to deal with the loss? They are going through so many emotions and trying to come to grips with the fact that their lives are on the verge of changing in a way that will forever leave a hole in their heart.

Most of us are familiar with the 5 stages of grief: 1) denial/shock 2) bargaining 3) depression 4) anger 5) acceptance. These stages are not linear, meaning that you simply move through them in order from start to finish. They are cyclical, meaning that you can move back and forth among the stages as new waves of grief come over you. The person who knows that the loss is coming will naturally start to cycle through these stages leading up to their loved one's death, and then repeat and go through new waves and cycles once death has occurred.

Don't try to force them to "come to grip with reality" if they are in denial or shock. Don't try to argue with them when they are bargaining. Don't chastise them for their depression ("there's no point in getting this upset. It doesn't change anything"). Don't admonish them for their anger. Don't assume that their acceptance is permanent. Show compassion and understanding, and give them space to feel and express their emotions.

Responding to the 5 stages:

Shock: "You are right. It doesn't feel real."

Denial: "Nothing is done until it's done. Only time will tell us for sure."

Bargaining: "I know. I wish it worked that way. This is all so overwhelming and unfair."

Depression: "It's perfectly normal and understandable to be so sad, but make sure you are only visiting that place, not setting up a permanent residence. There are so many people here who love you and want to help you."

Anger: "You're right. It's not fair. Yes, this is complete BS. No, they don't deserve to have this happen." If the anger starts to become focused on the healthcare workers who "couldn't save them," do help to balance their thoughts. It is not healthy or helpful for someone to go down the road of blaming a person for being unable to defy death. I am not referring to true negligence or malpractice, but if the person has been well cared for, or if the recent surgery was a last ditch effort at buying time, gently remind the person that it is their loved one's time and no one has the power to stop death.

Many people who have been serving as the main caregiver for this loved one will start to question themselves. They will start to doubt their knowledge, skills, and effort. Have they done enough? Have they missed something? Should they call the doctor to report something that might be helpful? Should they push them harder to do their therapy? Should they insist on that trial medication someone mentioned to them? Would they survive if they could make that specialist take them a week sooner? Should they insist that their loved one get out of bed more often?

Again, this is the time to help gently give some perspective. Their loved one is very sick or very old. They have a terrible diagnosis or prognosis and the doctor has told them they don't have long. The caregiver has given great care and has done the very best they could, and they should rest easy knowing how well cared for the loved one has been.

In home health, we will often be the ones who identify the need for a patient to transition to hospice, and will start those conversations as we feel they are appropriate. It is such a delicate and difficult thing to do because it can very easily feel that we are "giving up" on someone to them or their loved one. It is very important to me to review with the patient and/or family what the journey has been up to this point, and how the person can benefit from the wonderful services that hospice can provide.

Many times this conversation will come down to a therapy need. Hospice is a supportive service that is focused on comfort care. Home health is a restorative service that is focused on improvement of condition and function. It is common for someone to feel that if the person can "just get more therapy and walk again" that they will have a turn around and begin to heal. At these times, I will have a conversation about therapy expectations, specific desired outcomes, and the effort required to reach those outcomes. Sometimes the person continues to want to try. Other times this discussion highlights what is truly realistic and what is not.

I review this because sometimes the best way to give someone closure or comfort is to help them put aside the "what ifs" for the reality of what has already been tried and what is reasonable to continue to try. We tried this and it didn't help. We asked about that option, but they weren't eligible for that treatment. I know they said they wanted more therapy, but it is too much for their body. They simply cannot tolerate it.

When you can help the person go through the checklist in their mind of everything they could have/should have done, you will usually find that every box can be checked. You can go further than saying, "you have done all you could," although that is very acceptable. It can help them to truly *believe* they have done all they could when you take the time to walk through it with them. When they are satisfied that no stone has been left unturned, it can help to bring the peace of knowing that there really is nothing else that can be done. It is simply that person's time.

CAREGIVER BURDEN

The subject of caregiver burden is one that is incredibly personal for me. As a matter of fact, these last two sections are very personal for me, and they are interrelated. My grandfather suffered from early onset Alzheimer's disease that progressed over a 15 year period into eventual complete debilitation. The next section is an in-depth look at the unique challenges associated with dementia, so we will save that discussion until then.

My grandmother was the primary caregiver for my grandfather, with daily assistance from my aunt and uncle who thankfully lived in the same neighborhood. My Gran did an amazing job of taking care of my Papa. As a matter of fact, when his disease had progressed to the point that he could no longer recall her name or exactly who she was, he would look at me when I visited and say, "she takes great care of me."

What I learned through this process was how cripplingly overwhelming it can be for someone to be the primary caregiver for a person who is no longer able to care for themselves. As my Papa's disease became worse and worse, my Gran's world became smaller and smaller. They eventually stopped going to the church they had been founding members of and had attended for more than 45 years because my Papa had started "vocalizing" (common with this process. It's a loud repeated sound that the person makes compulsively and without awareness that they are doing it) in the middle of their very quiet church services. It became very embarrassing for her, along with the added difficulty of getting him to and from the church due to his increased weakness.

My grandfather did go through a "wandering" phase that required my Gran to install door alarms and other safety measures in the house so that he wouldn't get out and become lost or hurt. It was very difficult for her to get good rest, always keeping an ear out for him. Eventually she was unable to leave the house at all without someone coming by to sit with him because it had become unsafe to leave him alone. He might fall or try to get out of the house, or otherwise need help with something that couldn't wait. Going to the grocery store became one of her few activities out of the house, and it required group coordination between family to schedule even a quick trip down the road.

It was hard to witness how stressed she was by all of this. She was embarrassed when her generally *very* quiet husband started yelling, "whoa!!" out in public for no reason. My boys were so young that the yelling scared my older son because it was loud and sudden, so he became stand-offish with my Papa. This would make my Gran cry because Papa was scaring him. I assured her that it was ok and that he would be fine, but she hated it.

She was so grateful for all the help that my aunt, uncle, and cousin gave on a constant basis. She also felt guilty that she couldn't handle everything by herself (who in the world could?!), so she would rarely ask for extra help. This became a problem when she started having chest pains. She was at the store when the pains became so much that an ambulance had to be called to take her straight to the hospital. Later the story came out that she had been having these pains for a few weeks, but she hadn't told anyone because she didn't want to ask any extra favors.

The didn't want to ask anyone to come sit with my grandfather while she went to the doctor "in case it was nothing." She didn't want to be any more of a burden than she felt she already was, and she suffered a huge blow because of it. To summarize, she needed an emergency bypass surgery to take care of multiple blockages in her heart. She was hospitalized for weeks and we nearly lost her then. The damage to her heart was so much that she never fully recovered. She was forever after unable to walk very far at all without becoming severely short of breath and needing to take a sitting rest break.

This was of course hard for me, to see her having so much trouble doing simple things like walking into a restaurant. As a healthcare provider, it has heavily impacted the care I give. I am very aware of the people who are primarily responsible for the daily or regular care of the patients I am serving. I spend a lot of time educating them and others around them about the impact of being in this position.

I have lost track of how many hugs I have given (there I go again!) to spouses and children when they are on the verge of shaking themselves apart with stress. This is what I usually tell people who seem to be having a hard time understanding the enormity of the caregiving task: think of a newborn baby. That baby can't do a thing for itself, right? You have to feed it, clothe it, bathe it, and change it's diapers. It probably wakes you up at all hours of the night crying because it's hungry or wet, or doesn't know where it is and wants to be comforted.

Now imagine that the baby is 200 pounds. Same level of care needed. How much more difficult is it to now feed, clothe, bathe, and change that baby? Imagine you aren't in your 20's or 30's anymore, but you are now in your 60s or 70s and having to give that same level of care. You know what you can do with a newborn? Take it everywhere you need to go. It's not a huge imposition to take the baby to the grocery store, the doctor, or to visit a friend or family member, but what if the baby is 200 pounds? You can't simply pick that person up and go grocery shopping, but you can't leave them by themselves at home either.

It's too much. It's too much for one person to have to manage by themselves. I point out that in a nursing home, there is an entire staff that is literally taking shifts to handle this responsibility, and you are trying to do it all by yourself. You can't expect yourself to be able to do this alone. It's not reasonable for you or anyone else to think that you can do this without a lot of help. Ask for help! Let people know what you need.

If I could make any lasting impact on the world, it would be to shine a light on this overwhelming amount of suffering that is going on all around us, that most people are oblivious to. In Western culture, it is common for families to be separate and for privacy and independence to be highly valued. It is so easy to assume that mom and dad are fine. They raised me. They've been taking care of each other for decades. They'll let me know if they need something. My sister helps them, I'm sure they've got it all covered.

Let me tell you about your sister: she is overwhelmed. She is running herself ragged trying to schedule every doctor appointment, every medication change and pick up, every missing item at home that needs to be picked up at the store. She might also be working full time and helping to raise her own kids. She is exhausted, on the verge of tears around the clock, and pretty resentful that you are letting her shoulder this by herself.

Even if mom and sister are managing, they are tired! There is no amount of help that feels like enough, because the work is never done and they can never relax. How do you start a conversation about wanting to help those who need help? The first thing to keep in mind is that these primary caregivers are overwhelmed, or at the very least: exhausted. They are equally overwhelmed by the idea of asking for help.

They don't want to be an imposition. They would rather

melt through the floor than ask you to come sit with so-and-so for a few hours so they can go to the doctor or the store. And they would absolutely die before they dared to be so selfish as to ask you to come help so they could (gasp!) relax and do something for themselves. How dare they take time out of your busy schedule to do something as crazy, wasteful, and unnecessary as having lunch by themselves or getting a massage? Going to visit a friend? Out of the question!

I have come into a person's home for therapy and had their caregiver meet me at the door and ask in desperation, "Is it ok if I leave for a minute to grab something? I'm only going to the gas station down the road. I'll be right back. Is that ok? Will you be ok?" and be gone for less than 20 minutes only to return apologizing profusely for 'putting that on' me. Oh dear, we need to call in the cavalry here. This is not acceptable! Who else can help you with caring for your mom? We need to make some phone calls.

If there is someone in your life that you feel called to reach out to and help, consider the following:

"I have been thinking about everything you are responsible for, and it struck me how much that is for one person to do. I want to help."

I could almost guarantee that if this is your parent or the spouse of the person needing care, the person's response will be something like, "Oh no. It's fine. I've got it all handled. Don't worry about us!"

If this is a sibling they might be more honest, but skeptical. "Ok...what were you thinking?"

If this is a friend, they will feel another layer of guilt that you don't "have" to help because you aren't family, therefore you aren't obligated. They will likely say something like, "Oh gosh, that is so sweet of you! You don't have to do that. We're fine, really. Thank you for offering though!"

Forcing your services on another person will not be welcome. Don't announce, "I'm bringing you dinner every Tuesday." or "I'm going to start picking up so-and-so from ball practice for you." This can be equally overwhelming to this person because you seem to be taking over their very carefully crafted schedule, and what you are offering to help with might be the lowest concern on their list, not actually helpful at all, or completely unwanted.

If you honestly want to help, play the detective a little and find out where their pain point is. What is the thing they hate doing, the thing that is overwhelming to them, or the item that always gets pushed to the bottom of the priority list and they can never seem to get to? Ask questions like:

"What are some items on your to-do that you feel are the biggest pain for you to deal with on a regular basis?"

"Is there anything you have to do that you wish you didn't have to deal with?"

"Is there anything you consistently forget to do because you never feel like you have enough time?"

"When was the last time you were able to get out of the house and do something for yourself like go to lunch or get your nails done?"

You couldn't possibly imagine how amazing it would be for you to offer to come and sit with the family member needing care for a few hours. Often all they really need is someone who can be there in an emergency. Surely you can handle that!

In some cases, it's possible that the person is getting everything on the to-do list done, but they are lonely. They don't get to do anything social or fun anymore, and it's depressing. Most people would be happy to take you up on an offer to bring dinner over (don't invite yourself over to visit and expect this person to cook for you!), and visit. After dinner, make sure to clean up instead of letting them do it. While you are there, you might be able to pick their brains a little more about other ways you could help.

Some people are so worried that their worlds will fall apart the second they start relaxing that they can't let go of any tasks to another person. However, they will usually be able to enjoy a friend coming over to visit for a little while. The person may be so glad to know that someone cares, understands their current situation, and wants to help, that they will feel relief and support even if they continue to refuse your help. Don't ever offer help that you don't intend to give, but don't force it if the person isn't able to accept your offer. After all, you offered for the other person's benefit, not your own.

The person may be so full of guilt that they make comments such as, "it's not necessary" or "I don't *need* to get my nails done" or "I don't know what I would do with myself if I had a whole afternoon with nothing to do." I would suggest you offer these thoughts:

"No one *needs* to get their nails done, but it sure does feel nice! You deserve to pamper yourself."

"You don't have to do anything. That's the beauty of 'off' time. Sometimes the best thing you can do is take a nap, go for a walk, or window shop for a few hours to feel refreshed."

"Just because you technically can do it yourself doesn't mean you should have to all the time. That's what friends are for. I'd be happy to help take something off your to-do list."

"It's not reasonable for anyone to expect that you could do all of this all the time without any help. You aren't a robot. I know I couldn't do everything you do without help."

"If it was me, I would be completely overwhelmed trying to do all of this. Please let me help. I want to feel useful and you need more support than you probably even realize."

Help to recalibrate their expectations of themselves. Do you know the saying about a lobster not realizing it's being boiled to death if you only increase the temperature of the water one degree at a time? We tend to do that to ourselves. We add "just one more thing" to our task list until it is staggering, but because it was added one item at a time, we convince ourselves that it must be doable.

This person may need to be reminded of what is normal and reasonable. Admitting that you wouldn't be able to do it is not meant to inflate their ego, it is meant to help give them some perspective. They need to take some of the pressure off of themselves and accept the help that is being offered. They are not being lazy or incapable, they are being human. We *are* a herd species, and it takes a village. Humans were not designed to go through life without help. It is something I deeply admire about cultures that are so community based. It is an amazing example to me of how things "should be" when I am privileged enough to witness it. Be the change, ya'll.

DEMENTIA

When I think about difficult conversations, this particular diagnosis comes to mind. I personally watched my grandfather go through every stage of the terrible disease that is Alzheimer's dementia, and it is a common diagnosis that many of my patients have. This is not meant to be a graduate level review of this disease, but I do want to go over a few basics that will help to frame the difficulty for you.

The term dementia is used to describe a group of symptoms that affect a person's memory and/or reasoning to the extent that they are no longer safe or able to care for themselves and make sound decisions. Dementia symptoms can fall anywhere on a full spectrum from mild to severe enough to require 24 hour care. Dementia usually does not develop until older age which is why many people refer to it as "old timer's disease." Some people mistakenly believe that dementia is a natural and expected part of aging, but this is completely false.

Many people live into their 90s or older with perfectly sound minds. The simple fact that a person is getting older does not mean that their mind is "slipping," and just because an older person forgets something, it does not mean that they have dementia. It is common for the older human brain to have increased difficulty with short term memory.

Some families that I meet think that the fact that dad forgot anything means he has full blown dementia. Other families believe it is normal for mom to have forgotten nearly everything except her name simply because she is older. There are tests available that can help to differentiate what exactly is going on. Further discussion is getting beyond the scope of this book. If you are concerned about yourself or a loved one, please reach out to your primary care doctor and let them know your concerns. They can help you from there.

What I want to focus on is how to best interact with those who are having trouble with their memory, both normal memory difficulties, and those that are part of a disease process. It absolutely breaks my heart when I see family members who are so personally offended by their loved one's memory problem that they become impatient, ugly, or hurtful.

As easy as it is for a family member to believe that aging equals dementia, it can also be a belief held by the person who is aging. Every single thing they have trouble remembering can cause alarm because of the thought that they are losing their marbles. This can be very scary and potentially overwhelming. As we age, our processing time does naturally slow down, meaning we might need someone to speak more slowly or repeat themselves in order for all the information to sink in. Our ability to "hold" new information decreases, so it is easier to forget something you said earlier in the day or why we picked up the phone to call you.

We can have more trouble focusing on new tasks, such as how to use a smartphone, especially when the technology itself presents a learning challenge. Sometimes I marvel at all the changes my patients have been through in their lives. Many of them grew up in houses that didn't have electricity, plumbing, indoor toilets, phones, or televisions and now we expect them to figure out how to have a zoom call with their doctor over their iPhone! Can we give them a break already?! Have more patience with them when they can't remember how to respond to your text or check their voicemails.

Let me relay a few other factors that can affect memory, or the appearance of a memory issue, that have nothing to do with dementia. The ability for a person to achieve sharp focus is heavily affected by their amount and quality of sleep. Anyone who has pulled an all-nighter studying for a test only to walk around in a hazy fog the entire next day can attest to this. Older people often have difficulty getting enough quality rest, and this can contribute heavily to their ability to focus and remember things. Stress can also play into a person's memory and focus. There can be many reasons that an older person may feel stress, including worry about their memory! If the person is hyper aware of every tiny detail they can't remember, and then feeling worried about their memory slipping, it can become a self fulfilling prophecy.

On a practical level, there might be another issue involved, and that is whether a person is having trouble hearing. How easy is it for you to remember something you never heard in the first place? Probably pretty difficult. Hearing problems affect a large portion of older adults, and how they feel about their trouble hearing can have an impact on many situations.

The person could be in denial that they are having trouble, so they refuse to get any help. They could be embarrassed about having to ask people to repeat themselves or speak up, so they sit quietly and pretend like everything is fine, when they are only catching a fraction of what is being said to them. It is common for a person to say something that sounds "crazy" because they are answering the question that they heard, which was not the question that was asked. This is not a memory issue at all, but a communication problem that might be easily fixed with new or updated hearing aids.

The last point to bring to your attention has to do with their environment. Have you ever heard the phrase "use it or lose it"? Most of the time, people are referring to a physical skill when they use this phrase. This sentiment might bring to mind football skills, flexibility, or playing a musical instrument. However, this is a natural way that the human brain will respond to a lack of cognitive challenges as well. Maybe you were amazing at playing chess until you stayed out of the game for a while. You might be surprised to find how difficult it is to win when you pick it back up again.

Memory can be affected by a lack of mental stimulation. Many people who are older spend the majority of their time alone, and it might start to show itself through an apparent decline in memory. For this exact reason, many senior centers, assisted care facilities and skilled nursing facilities will prioritize social activities, and may include puzzles and quizzes in their regular newsletters. It's amazing what a difference this can make in quality of life and sharpness of mind.

I go through all of this to say, don't treat grandma like she's crazy or incapable of caring for herself because she said it was Monday when it was Wednesday, or because she confirms your invitation more than once. If she starts to worry because something like this has happened you can respond:

"We all forget things from time to time. Don't worry!"

"I don't mind confirming with you twice. I'm excited that you're going to be able to come to my event."

"It's easy to forget what day it is when you're retired and don't have to work 5 days a week. I hope to get there one day!"

Assuring the person that you are not upset or bothered, and that they shouldn't be either, is the best way to handle things. It's also the best option when you are communicating with someone who actually does have dementia. Once they start to panic that something is wrong, they can become very upset. Be compassionate to the problem and assure them that everything is ok.

A person with dementia has many difficulties that can be upsetting to those around them. The loss of memory is the most widely known issue, but there are other problems that can arise when a person has this disease. The family of dementias affect many parts of the brain. Just like apps on your phone (I almost said 'just like a switchboard' and then felt like I was really dating myself on that one), different parts of your brain do different things and handle different tasks.

There are parts of your brain that are responsible for hearing, sight, speech, muscles, memory, reasoning, personality, and many other things. A person who has had deterioration in the areas of memory, reasoning, and personality may become rude, forceful, impatient, stubborn, illogical, or unsafe. This can be especially difficult for a primary caregiver who is a family member. The frustration might be due to a feeling that "this isn't my dad" or can stem from difficult parts of their parent's personality that seem to be on overdrive.

The frustration can also come from the anxiety and overwhelm of caring for someone who has always been able to care for themselves until this point. A child can feel guilt that they can't do everything their parent needs because they still have to work, and a spouse may feel frustrated that their partner who has always taken care of things (yardwork, cooking, paying the bills, etc), can't even take care of themselves anymore. Now the spouse is tasked with doing the things they've always done, with the added responsibilities of taking care of everything their spouse has always done AND physically taking care of their spouse.

I see a lot of frustration that also seems to stem from a general lack of understanding around what dementia is and what are reasonable expectations from their loved one. It is not reasonable to expect someone to remember something that their disease has erased from their mind. There is no amount of quizzing someone that will bring their memory back. Arguing with someone who has lost the ability to reason is a futile effort. Chastising someone for something they can't control is more cruel than helpful.

When a person has dementia, you must speak to and redirect them like you would a small child. I mean that in the most respectful way possible. You must have a reasonable expectation for what they can and can't do, and you must be able to recognize what will help to coax them in the direction you need and what will cause a complete meltdown. Let's go over some common frustrations that can come with dementia and how to respond to them:

Person is repeating themselves every few minutes. They can't help it. They don't know they are doing it, and fussing at them for it will only upset both them and you. You must realize that if they don't remember what they've said, they don't remember what you said either. In some ways this takes the pressure off of you to give a full answer every time. The second (or third, or fourth) time they ask a question or tell you a story, keep your answer shorter.

Repeat yourself in the same way they are repeating themselves, and don't feel guilty or upset about it. You can also answer their repeated question with a friendly, "You know, I'm not sure" to avoid going through your answer over and over. Distracting the person when they are on this loop can also help. Showing them a picture, a magazine, a bird outside the window, or a puzzle they can put together are all great options to help redirect their attention.

Avoid the exasperated, "I already told you that three times mom!" as best you can. Don't try to quiz them with an, "I answered that question five minutes ago dad. Don't you remember? What did I say?" Instead, repeat yourself with a quick version of the answer, tell them you don't know, or ignore the repeated question and distract them with something instead.

Person doesn't remember who you are. Don't take this personally, no matter how much you might want to.

Alzheimer's dementia affects short term memory before long term memory. It also continues to chip away at memory from most recent to farthest away. Generally, they will forget the people in the reverse order of when they first knew them. My grandfather forgot my husband and children before he forgot me. He forgot me before he forgot my mom. He remembered my Gran the longest. This is how the process works. It has nothing to do with loving one person more than someone else, and it did not hurt my feelings when he could remember my Aunt's name but not mine.

They might ask who you are. Tell them who you are without implying offense or hurt feelings.

Them: "I don't know you/I don't remember you," (person is suspicious or confused)

You: "That's ok. There are so many people coming in and out, it's hard to keep up with everyone! I'm so-and-so. I'm here for (whatever your reason is). How are you doing today?"

Them: (person feels stressed that they don't remember you) "I'm so sorry. I know I should remember who you are."

You: "Don't worry about me! I'm here to (visit, help out today, drop this off, see how you're doing, etc.). I've only been here once or twice anyway. It's so hard to remember new faces!"

Them: "I can't remember anything anymore. I think I'm having trouble with my memory."

You: "That's ok. We all forget things! I know I sure do."

Them: "Who are you?"

You: "It's me, Papa. It's Julie. I'm your granddaughter."

Them: "I don't remember you."

You: "That's ok. I'm glad to be here to visit with you and see how you're doing today."

Them: "Ok."

They will usually take you at your word, but telling them who you are will not "jog their memory," so don't expect that. Please don't plead with them, "You really don't remember me? Do you remember..." and think that bringing up the past will make something click. That part of their harddrive has been erased. If they sense that you are getting upset, they will often agree that they remember in order to calm you down, but they don't. It's not personal, it's the disease.

Person has no filter/is rude. To be honest, having a patient with dementia can often feel like a reality version of the show "Kids Say the Darndest Things." You never know what to expect them to say, and it can often be hilarious. Again, don't take what they say personally. Also, if this is your loved one and they have just said something incredibly rude to someone else, try not to get embarrassed. Healthcare workers especially are used to it and know exactly what is going on. We are not offended, I promise.

I once had a patient in a memory care unit tell me, "I hate your outfit. It's ugly." It was all I could do to keep a straight face. I thought it was hilarious, especially considering that we were in the dining area and she said it in front of a room full of people, including a handful of people who worked there and knew her well.

I simply responded, "Oh no! Well we can't win them all. I guess I won't wear this one again."

Doing therapy with someone, I am often asking people to do things they would rather not do. When they have no filter and they are done, they are done and I will know it right away. I have had multiple patients with advanced dementia declare to me, "I hate this. I don't want to do it anymore. I want you to go away."

Bless their hearts, they're just being honest. If it's not time for me to wrap up, I will see if I can reason with them or see if I can distract them.

I might say, "I know this isn't the most fun thing in the world, but it's good for you. I'm here to help you get stronger so you won't fall anymore."

Them: "I'm not falling."

Me: "Well...the nurses told me you have been falling."

Them: "They are liars. I've never fallen before."

Me (knowing full well they've fallen): "Ok, how about if we walk up to the nurse's station and ask them about it? We need to find out why it's on your chart if it's not true." Many times this will get them to stand up and do the walking they had refused to do earlier in the treatment. See how that works?

Person is refusing to do something you need them to do. This is the perfect place to address getting a person with dementia to agree to something they are refusing to do. As I've already said, this person has lost their ability to reason, and has also lost the part of their personality that feels obligated to be agreeable to others. Attempting to argue with them will be about as effective as insisting that a brick wall get up and move out of your way.

The key is to find a way to motivate them to want to do whatever it is. Use a little bit of trickery if you must. Which is worse? A white lie or a full blown argument? I had a patient once who was dead set on laying in her bed until kingdom come if she had to, but she wasn't going to get up and go into the living room for all the gold in the world. After several minutes of back and forth pleading from the daughter I finally asked, "Mrs. So-and-so, when was the last time you went to the bathroom? Would you like me to help you go to the bathroom?"

She sat right up and asked for her walker. After we were done in the restroom I pointed to the living room on our way past it and said, "Oh good, let's go in there so we can finish your therapy." She walked right in and sat down. Distract and redirect. Trick/motivate over arguing. They won't get into the car to go to their doctor's appointment? Will they get in to go to a restaurant for lunch? Don't worry, we're going to run in to see your doctor for a minute on our way to eat.

Person is inappropriate. Dementia can affect the part of a person's brain that is responsible for reasoning and keeping their "filter" in place. As a result of their disease, they can often make comments that are inappropriate for various reasons. They might be prone to make sexual comments, to tell dirty jokes, to cuss at people, or to walk around with no pants on. If this is something you encounter, remember that trying to help the person understand why this is inappropriate may be an approach with only mediocre results.

Don't exclaim to them that they should "know better" or that they "know that's inappropriate." They don't know it, and they will have a hard time processing your long and drawn out explanation as to why it's a problem. Keep your instructions clear and concise.

You: "That joke is not appropriate."

Them: "Sure it is!"

You: "No, that joke is offensive and you need to keep those jokes to yourself."

Them: "Oh whatever."

You: "Well whether you believe it or not, it's true. Will you agree to keep those jokes to yourself?"

You: "Dad, you can't say that to people. It's rude."

Them: "It is?"

You: "Yes, it is."

Them: "Oh, sorry."

You: "Mom, you aren't ready to leave yet. You aren't wearing any pants."

Them: "So?"

You: "Mom, that's not an appropriate way to leave the house. We have to put pants on you first so you will be properly dressed."

Them: "Oh, ok."

Keep it short, simple, and to the point. Don't get emotional about it or try to make them feel bad. They aren't trying to make your life harder on purpose. They don't know any better anymore.

Person is saying things that are incorrect. What about the person who is telling a story that is completely off the wall? They are telling you they served in a war, but they were never in the military. They tell you they had five children when they only had three. They tell you about a vacation they just went on, but they didn't.

I have more people who nearly jump off the deep end with stress listening to their loved one tell stories that aren't true. It's ok! They aren't saying something incorrect on purpose. The person's mind is very confused. They get lost in time, they get lost in their own head. What is it hurting for them to say something that isn't right? When I have a patient who has a documented diagnosis of dementia, I know that what they tell me might not be accurate. You know what I do? I look to the caregiver to give me an indication as to whether the information is right or wrong.

Me: "So you just came back from vacation?" (I look to the caregiver. Caregiver is shaking her head "no." Enough said. This person did not go on vacation. I change the subject.)

Me: "Tell me about your back. Your chart says you had a fall. How did that happen?"

Patient: "No, I didn't have a fall." (Daughter mouths to me "Yes, she did fall.")

Me: "You know what, your daughter says you did have a fall. Do you think you might have forgot about that?"

Patient: "Oh, maybe I forgot."

Me: "That's ok. We all forget things. (Turning to the daughter) Can you tell me how she fell?"

Daughter: "She was getting up to get something..."

Patient: "I was getting my knitting. I love to knit blankets for people." (Daughter shakes her head "no" and mouths to me "she doesn't knit." I ignore the comment about knitting and focus on the fall.)

Me: "Well when you fell, did you hurt anything?"

Patient: "Yes, I hurt my right hip."

Daughter: "Mom, it was your left hip."

Patient: "Oh, yes, that's right. It was my left hip."

Me: "Ok, do you have any bruises on your left hip? Can I take a look?"

Patient: "Yes, you can look, but be careful. I broke that hip a few years ago so it stays tender."

Daughter: "Mom, you've never broken your hip."

Patient (getting aggravated): "Yes I did! I broke it and I was in the hospital for a week!"

Daughter: "Mom, you were in the hospital when you had your knee surgery, but you never broke your hip."

Patient: "Yes I did! I broke my hip. I fell down my stairs and broke it!"

Daughter: "Ok, Mom. Whatever."

Me: "You know what? I've got all your medical records right here on your chart. Don't worry. I've got it all written down. I'll be careful with your hip. Is it hurting you right now?" (No record of a hip fracture on the chart. Patient never fractured her hip.)

Let me go through that conversation. When someone says something that isn't correct, you basically have three options: 1) Gently correct the comment, 2) Ignore the comment and change the subject, 3) Go along with the comment. The patient told me she had just been on vacation, but whether she did or not was irrelevant to my visit. I was there for a therapy evaluation, so I simply changed the subject. No need to point out that what she said wasn't true.

This level of confusion does let me know that the patient is definitely "a poor historian" which is a fancy medical phrase that means her memory is gone to the point that you can't believe much or any of what she recalls. You must seek confirmation of what she says from other sources, such as family members or medical charts. This knowledge will inform the rest of my evaluation, but there is no need to alarm or argue with the patient about a vacation.

The patient denied that she fell. This is important because it's the entire reason I'm there. It is a good idea to gently correct the patient to see if we can get her back on the same page as everyone else. Notice I said *gently.* Please don't snap at her and treat her like an idiot, "Of course you fell, mom, that's why she's here! You don't remember falling? You just spent a whole week in the hospital for it." For crying out loud, she didn't forget on purpose!

If they are adamant that they did not fall, I will concede, shift my approach, and say, "Ok, maybe the part about the fall was incorrect. I do still need to check your strength and balance though. Is that ok?", and we move on.

When I am correcting someone, I try to leave what I say open ended.

"I think this is what happened. Does that sound familiar?"

"Do you think you might have forgotten about it?"

"I was told this happened. Does that sound right?"

"I think that might have been what happened. That's what your doctor told me."

Their response dictates what I will do from there. If they are open to the corrected statement, I try to confirm it as best I can and reference a source they feel is reliable (spouse, child, doctor, etc.)

"Yes, I'm pretty sure that's what happened. That's what your daughter said."

If they are skeptical about what I said, but not necessarily arguing with me about it, I keep it more vague. I tell them I will confirm the information with someone they trust, which will help ease any discomfort they might be feeling.

"Well, I'm pretty sure that's what happened, but I'll check with your daughter. She'll know for sure."

"That's what the nurse told me when I came in. I'll check with her again before I leave."

"I'm pretty sure you did break your hip. That's what your doctor's note said, but I'll call and check with him again to be sure.

They might lapse on something big and then feel very embarrassed that they had said the wrong thing. They might have said they had five children and their son says, "Mom, there were only three of us." and she becomes very flustered and says, "I can't believe I said that. What in the world? What was I thinking? Why did I say that?" Be reassuring, and make a joke out of it if you can to keep the mood light. Move the conversation along if you can.

"That's ok! It was only a slip of the tongue. I bet some days it felt like five kids! How close in age are you boys?"

If you try to correct the information and they become upset, combative, or insistent about their story, let them be right! Who cares if it's right or wrong? As long as you know what is and isn't true, that's good enough. If you can't make heads or tails of the truth, contact someone who will know and get the correct answer from them. If they are absolutely insistent that something did happen that didn't, I will back off and take the blame for the misunderstanding.

"You know what? I think I misread your chart. Let me go back and fix that information. My mistake."

"Ok, no problem. I'll add that to your chart. I think the information that was sent from the hospital was incomplete. I'll contact your family doctor to get the rest of your medical history."

"You know, I completely forgot about that trip. I was thinking about Johnny's trip being cancelled last week. Sorry, dad."

Person doesn't remember someone has died. This situation is incredibly upsetting to many family members. They feel very anxious and torn about what to do when mom asks when dad is coming back from the store and he's been gone for 5 years. They complain that their son hasn't called lately and he passed away the year before. She asks if you've packed her bags yet to visit someone who isn't alive anymore. If something like this happens, pause for a second to see if they catch the mistake. Ignore the comment at first to see if they will forget as suddenly as it came on. If they are becoming upset and insistent? You. Lie. Repeat after me:

"He's on his way. He'll be back after a while."

"He's out with so-and-so. I think he won't be getting back until after you're in bed."

"No, there's no sense in waiting up. He'll be late and you need to lay down and get some rest."

"He went on a fishing trip with his buddies. He won't be able to call until he gets back."

"We'll pack your bags later. We're not leaving for a while. We've got time."

"We had to cancel that trip, mom. We're going to have to reschedule it."

Here is the thing: this person *doesn't know* that their loved one has died. They have no recollection of it, so if you "remind them" that this person has died, you are actually breaking the news to them for the first time. They will react as they did when this happened in the first place, and it will be just as upsetting. There is no good reason under the sun to put them through this and have them suffer the loss as a fresh wound.

To be clear, I am not referring to someone who is in the early stages and whose memory comes and goes. That person may need a gentle loving reminder "Mom, dad passed away last year. Don't you remember?" Their face may fall as they do recollect that truth, but they do still remember it.

Here is your litmus test: the first time you remind them and they become truly upset, as though this is the first time they are hearing it, that is the last time you go there. It isn't kind or necessary in any regard to put them through that sort of distress simply to make sure they have the facts right.

I had a family one time that I had to sit down and absolutely insist that they stop telling mama that her son had died 6 months prior. She kept asking how he was doing, why he hadn't visited, or mentioning that he needed to call her, and bless their hearts, they felt obligated to "tell mama the truth." They were so stressed because this was happening multiple times a day and every time they would tell her that he was gone, she would start sobbing and sobbing. It was tearing them all up.

They felt so much guilt at the idea of "lying" to her and I had to put a stop to it because it was breaking my heart too. I had to explain that it wasn't lying. It was them protecting their mom and showing her kindness by sparing her the pain and heartbreak of reliving that loss over and over again. What good did it do for her to be told the truth? What changed except her becoming overwhelmingly upset?

She asked me about him once when I was working with her. I smiled and said, "I think he just called you the other day. I'm sure he'll be calling again soon." and she smiled back and said "ok" and we went back to what we were doing. Once the family saw this, they finally understood. Please take it from me, for your sake and theirs, just gloss over it. Distract and redirect. It isn't lying, it's kindness. What a wonderful thing to not live with the daily suffering of knowing your son is gone forever. Let her have that peace in her heart.

Person is having hallucinations. There are certain types of dementia that can cause a person to have hallucinations. This can be confusing, and even scary for some people. This person is seeing people that don't exist..or do they? Is the house haunted? Is something wrong here? Rest assured, what is wrong is the terrible disease process that is causing a malfunction in the brain. The exact mechanism behind this phenomenon is still being researched, but it isn't necessary to know the exact cause in order to appreciate what is happening.

What is important to keep in mind is that this hallucination is just as real to the person experiencing it as your assurance of where you slept last night. Trying to argue with them is only going to serve to make them very upset because you are calling them a liar at best and crazy at worst. You might try to gently correct part of their story and see how they respond, but if they are insistent about what they know to be true, go with it.

I had a patient in a memory care unit tell me once that she had witnessed a black SUV drive up to "that door" (the emergency exit that was never used) that morning and throw a woman from the back of it into the hallway bound up with ropes. This patient was beside herself with upset and worry. "They've got her down in the basement. We've got to go check on her! This is horrible. How could anyone treat another person that way?!"

At first I tried to see if she would budge from her story. "Now, Mrs. So-and-so, I have a hard time believing they would do that to anyone! Are you sure you didn't misunderstand what you were seeing?"

She was adamant, 'I know what I saw and it's exactly as I said it was, and we need to go call the authorities.' Ok, now we roll with it. "Oh dear. That's awful. You're right, we can't have people being treated like that. I'm going to let the administrator know when we get done together. For now I think she's doing well. They've got her put into a new room. Let's you and me finish up our therapy while they work on getting her settled in. I'll go speak to someone about it in a few minutes." That calmed her down, satisfied her distress, and we were able to finish our session.

We've spoken so many times throughout this book about stepping back, understanding what is really going on with a person, and reacting to their needs instead of reacting to their words. I think this is a very fitting example to use to round out everything we have gone over so far. It's amazing how many things we can handle when we choose to flow through them instead of resisting them and holding onto the need to "be right."

FINAL THOUGHTS

We have covered such a wide variety of topics. We started with the basics of polite conversation, how to present yourself as a well-spoken person, and how to navigate some tricky topics that come up frequently when meeting new people or spending time in social settings. We learned how to handle conflict that might arise at the store, with strangers, in the workplace, or possibly with friends or family. We then shined a light in some of the darker corners of hard conversations we might face regarding illness and even death. What a ride!

This can be a lot to process and remember, but I want to encourage you. You have totally got this! Running themes throughout this book have been compassion, empathy, understanding, and elevation. The exact words and phrases I have given throughout might be easily forgotten in the moment, but if you can remember the ideas and feelings behind them, you will nail it every time.

My hope is that I can do more than simply give you a list of nice things to say and call it a day. I hope that this book will help to give you the tools you need to show love and compassion to those who need it most. It would make my heart full and happy to know that you feel more confident in your ability to help where help is needed, and to lift up others through your words and presence.

Being able to handle a difficult conversation and respond in a graceful and well-spoken way requires true understanding and a desire to leave a positive impact on those around you. What I wish above all is that you might come away from this book with an inspiration to show more love to those you come across, and the confidence to extend that love with the right words and actions.

With any circumstance you find yourself in, take a step back to assess the importance of insisting on "The Truth" over connecting with another person. My deep desire is to start a ripple that will be felt across the world and will result in the world becoming a better place to live.

Wow, I want to give every one of you a huge hug right now. We did it! Do you feel like we just went through something really great together? Because I do. I feel so honored to have shared these thoughts with you and grateful that you have taken the time to stick with me to the last page. I saw something once that said "write the book that is in your heart," and that is exactly what I have done.

I sincerely hope that something in this book will be a blessing to you. I would *love* to hear from you. Please share with me your thoughts about the book and the topics we covered. Let me know if there is something that I missed! I have a lot of exciting plans for the future and I would love for you to come with me on the journey.

To contact me or stay up to date on all the amazing things that are happening, please send an email to admin@yourconversationexpert.com or visit my website yourconversationexpert.com , and please follow me on YouTube for weekly videos and Instagram for more tips on these complex topics @yourconversationexpert. I'll see you there!

With so much love,

Julie

P.s. It would mean SO much to me if you would leave a review of this book on AMAZON so that others can benefit from your thoughts and feel confident that this book is worth their time. THANK YOU!

EPILOGUE

I hope that after reading this book, you feel amazingly confident going forward and speaking on any topic that may arise. However, even I can be caught off guard from time to time. I have days where I feel too cranky to rise above, and on those days I may not have the perfect response to everything said to me.

I want to encourage you to practice self love and forgiveness when those times happen (and they will). Just as you are doing your best to give grace to others and understand their shortcomings, be sure to shine some of that light toward yourself when needed.

There will be times when you desperately want to impress someone, but you stumble through everything you attempt to say despite your best efforts or preparation. Please believe that it is going to be ok. When this happens to me, I always take a deep breath and remind myself "what is meant to be, will be." It is the mantra of my life and I use it for new opportunities and new friends alike.

If I say something and think, "I can't believe I just said that. I sounded like an idiot!", one of two things will happen: the person will care or they won't.

If this person is meant to be a figure in my life, then the off-beat comment will not stand in the way. If the person wasn't meant to walk along through my journey, the most perfectly planned and executed response will not impress them. Trust that what is meant to be will happen, and rest easy in the knowledge that your ability to ruin a relationship with an awkward comment is very unlikely when your intention is well-meaning.

There may be memories from days long gone that still cause you to groan when you remember your words. We all know that we cannot change the past, and that dwelling on things we cannot change is pointless, but it's hard not to cringe at these memories from time to time.

To that I would repeat that what was meant to be, is. If the relationship has dissolved, it wasn't meant to play a permanent role in your life. It can be helpful to remember that some people enter our lives for a reason, a season, or a lifetime. That person must have been a "season" for you.

If you have wronged someone, it's never too late to apologize. If you made a comment in bad taste, you can ask for forgiveness. If the poor word choice was a minor offense, remind yourself that we are all growing and learning, and do your best to let it go with love. Sending you all of my best wishes!

PRAISE FOR AUTHOR

The author offers lots of practical ways to manage situations where people want to have conversations you'd rather not have. The advice is straightforward and easily applied. There are also sections dealing with how to handle situations with people who have advanced memory issues like dementia and things you can do or say and things you should not do and say that were very enlightening. I highly recommend this book if you want to learn to handle those awkward statements co-workers and family/ neighbors often make without hurting anyone's feelings or getting into a conversation that might lead to damaged relationships and hard feelings.

- 5 STARS - BURKBUILDS

Thoroughly enjoyed this book. The examples and advice given are practical and apply to everyday useful scenarios. Provides ways of dealing with uncomfortable situations while preserving dignity of all involved parties. As a disclaimer I have to say that I personally know Julie. She was a clinical intern of mine when she was in PT school and we have remained friends after that. When I heard she had written this book I was not at all surprised. Her rapport with patients and families as a PT intern was far above intern level. Beyond th at I remember and interaction with one of our physicians that resulted in him telling me how impressed he was with her communication skills. So, when I learned about this book I knew I had to check it out. I have learned so much from this, especially about how to react/interact in a way that helps out all parties at ease and resolve difficult situations. I highly recommend this book.

- 5 STARS - J BEACH

This gem is not yet another book lauding the power of please and thank you, or a take the high road reminder, but a real-life handbook for any awkward situation that you might encounter. Not only is she an accomplished writer, but she is a Doctor of Physical Therapy as well, working closely in intimate and delicate situations with many people during her career. Throughout our time together, Julie invites us in, cup of tea in hand, to chat, learn, grow, and FINALLY come to a place where we hunt for the awkward so we can practice our new skills! In this offering, Julie leads us through a lifelong progression of tense situations, cringe-worthy moments, and resolutions that create calmness rather than stress. She does this through a combination of elegantly erring on the side of decorum, and when necessary, finding a foothold for standing our ground with a smile and not losing our cool. Julie has previously (during college) worked in retail and collections, so her experience is vast. Throughout the book we find specific examples of actual conversations/comments and their responses which often times will give one or both people a way to back out/deescalate the situation without further embarrassment, or the mood of an event going sour. I enjoyed every part of this experience, from angry retail customers to handling inappropriate and uncomfortable comments. This book is a must have for everyone!

- 5 STARS - GENE C

Workplace & social intetactions can be difficult. This book talks to you like your smart best friend would do. Engaging narrative. Touchy topics. How to bow out gracefully. It's all here! Highly recommend!

Update: I had a delicate moment this weekend where an elderly lady at a store was embarrassed & didn't know what to do & her middle aged daughter was at a loss for how to handle. My mind went straight to this book!

- 5 STARS - CIGGYRN

If you find yourself shrinking away from anything that results in conversation with anyone outside of your comfort group, then this book is for you! Julie had a great way of injecting practical tips for just about every situation you can think of when it comes to navigating conversation. I found myself laughing at some of the examples because I have been there, and spent many a day after wondering "why am I like this?" I'm so grateful for her kind approach to conversational situations, and the validation this book gave me that there's nothing wrong with me, and I'm not alone! Thanks Julie!

- 5 STARS- TERA BARNES

Its 2022... options are everywhere and most are rude, people lost boundaries. I left social media and then came across this book! Answer to my prayers!!!

- 5 STARS- NATALIE JOHNSON

This book goes into new depths about hard topics, but in a light and refreshing way. Hard conversations are something that everyone avoids even if they don't admit it and this book really brings light to a taboo topic.

- 5 STARS - MEGPARHAM

I discovered this book when I met the author and we were discussing her work. I immediately purchased this book and read most of it in a single sitting -- I was hooked. Clearly the book is well researched, and it is certainly well written too. The author is quite empathic in her approach, adopting the tone of a coach who deeply "gets" how difficult these awkward conversations can feel and be. The book is full of immediately actionable advice, which is what I most loved about it. I hope more people discover it. Including teachers, who will love how professional yet personable the tone is. Five stars for sure.

- 5 STARS - ANONYMOUS

FREE COMPANION WORKBOOK

I hope you loved this book as much as I loved writing it, and that you have come away feeling empowered to implement everything you've learned.

If you would like to dive deeper, don't forget to download the companion workbook for further reflection and conversation planning.

Download the FREE companion workbook here:

https://courses.yourconversationexpert.com/workbook

ACKNOWLEDGEMENT

Writing this book has been a whirlwind adventure. I first and foremost want to express my gratitude for my wonderful husband who has always been my rock and the best partner a girl could ask for. Thank you, Love, for encouraging me instead of laughing when I said I wanted to write a book. Your support and belief rocketed me forward.

A huge thank you to JenniferAnn, who has become a fast and dear friend. Your enthusiasm, support, and willingness to roll up your sleeves and give hands-on help allowed me to keep marching forward confidently. You are immensely appreciated!

Thank you to the amazingly inspiring and encouraging content of Anna Bey and the A-List community. This book was created because of this community's constant search for self-improvement, and I feel honored to have been able to share my experiences and insights and have it received with such positive and encouraging feedback.

ABOUT THE AUTHOR

Julie Crenshaw

Julie Crenshaw is a Social Skills Coach and author. Throughout the last 15 years, she has cultivated a strong set of interpersonal skills as a result of working in major department stores, for a collections company, and as a physical therapist in the home health setting. She teaches on a wide variety of topics, from basic socializing and small talk skills, to dealing with conflict, to having conversations on difficult subjects such as illness and grief. As a doctor of physical therapy and a board certified specialist in geriatrics, subjects related to healthcare, patient rights, and caregiver burden are close to her heart.

Her mission is to empower others to feel confident in their ability to express themselves and their needs/desires more clearly, and to be able to handle difficult situations and conversations with ease. She believes that with a strong foundation of compassion, boundaries, and a healthy mindset, anyone can learn to gracefully connect with others, no matter the situation.

Made in the USA
Monee, IL
29 April 2023

32697331R00201